CLOTHING POVER

ABOUT THE AUTHOR

ANDREW BROOKS is a lecturer in development geography at King's College London. His research examines connections between spaces of production and places of consumption, and particularly the geographies of economic and social change in Africa. Fieldwork has taken him to India, Papua New Guinea and across Africa. Research in Africa has included extensive investigations of markets and politics in Malawi and Mozambique as well as Chinese investment in Zambia.

CLOTHING POVERTY

The hidden world of fast fashion
and second-hand clothes

ANDREW BROOKS

Zed Books | LONDON

Clothing Poverty: The Hidden World of Fast Fashion and Second-hand Clothes was first published in 2015 by
Zed Books Ltd, 7 Cynthia Street, London N1 9JF, UK

www.zedbooks.co.uk

Copyright © Andrew Brooks 2015

Designed and typeset in Monotype Bulmer
by illuminati, Grosmont
Index by John Barker
Cover designed by www.alice-marwick.co.uk

A catalogue record for this book is available from the British Library

ISBN 978-1-78360-068-7 hb
ISBN 978-1-78360-067-0 pb
ISBN 978-1-78360-070-0 pdf
ISBN 978-1-78360-069-4 epub
ISBN 978-1-78360-071-7 mobi

Contents

Acknowledgements

There was no single moment or event that led me to write an accessible book on globalization and the clothing trade. The idea developed as I studied, worked and researched in different places, from my small office in London to sprawling markets in southern Africa, until it had become something that I felt would not only be interesting and important to write, but also something I knew I had to do. Throughout time spent variously as a geography undergraduate and later a lecturer at King's College London, a volunteer in Papua New Guinea, an international development worker, a graduate student at Royal Holloway, a field researcher in Zambia and Mozambique and elsewhere around the world, there have always been friends, family and colleagues who have offered encouragement, support and guidance, for which I am very grateful. Kim Walker and others at Zed Books have also always been very helpful. Any errors are of course my sole responsibility.

For me, global poverty and inequality have always stood out as the defining issues of our time, yet it is frustrating how often work on these topics falls short of offering answers, a compelling argument or an engaging narrative. We have to work rigorously to understand how the world has changed and developed, yet in doing so try hard to make the analysis interesting and clear, as well as authoritative. My hope is that this book goes some way to bridging between the real experiences of the poor and the sometimes dry and introverted academic community, and tells a story of uneven development that is interesting for a broad audience by discussing the hidden world of clothing through diverse and colourful examples, while maintaining a critical perspective. The work that follows, therefore, is one that draws on my experiences and knowledge and tries to deliver a message and discussion that others may learn from. In the pursuit of this goal, special thanks must go to David Simon and Alex Loftus for their help and support, which inspired me to develop the project.

Introduction

Everyone knows that most Africans are poor. Life expectancy is low, education is basic, food is simple, and clothes are few. Curving around the south-east coast of the continent, Mozambique has a typically African economy. Many Mozambicans are dependent on subsistence agriculture or low-value exports such as cashew nuts, cotton and Indian Ocean shrimps. Beneath the shrimps and the warm waters are rich natural gas reserves, which could fuel development, but these resources are more likely to be stolen or squandered overseas, as recent economic growth has contributed to rising inequality rather than a reduction in poverty. Like much of Africa, Mozambique's national budget is dependent on support from overseas aid, and the liberalized economy is wide open to both exports and imports. The capital, Maputo, is an important regional port 30 miles from South Africa. Tree-lined avenues, a legacy of Portuguese colonialism, stretch out from the city centre towards poorer neighbourhoods. At the end of one of these avenues on the edge of the downtown is the sprawling and bustling Mercado do Xipamanine – Xipamanine market.

On any weekday morning the entrance to Xipamanine market is crowded; minivans clog the narrow approach road and hawkers circle, touting cheap Chinese manufactured goods such as plastic clothes pegs, polyester socks and pressed steel cutlery. Entering the market one passes through narrow alleys, between market stalls selling a mix of local food and international products: coconuts, mangoes, pineapples, fresh fish, suitcases, school stationary and stereos – pumping out the latest R&B beats from New York and Los Angeles. It is lively and vibrant, rich in all sorts of smells and muddy under foot. Moving further into the market you begin to encounter noisy traders negotiating the sale of cheap, low-quality, imported new clothing. There are soccer shirts with English Premier League logos or Mozambican flags, brightly coloured floral ladies' tops, and the novelty of Barack Obama-branded belt buckles. Beyond these new clothing vendors is the heart of the market, and here we find Mario's used-clothing stall.

Mario is in his early thirties; he migrated to Maputo from rural Inhambane province in search of work. He makes a living selling second-hand jeans imported from North America and Europe. Six days a week he comes to his simple wooden market stall and sets out his stock. The jeans are carefully arranged according to quality. Pristine pairs of Calvin Kleins and Levi's hang on display on improvised coat-hangers, while low-value torn and soiled denim is heaped on the ground on polythene sacks. Mario buys mixed consignments of used jeans shipped to Mozambique from rich countries. All of the jeans have their own unique and unknown stories; maybe they were outgrown by an American teenager, discarded by a fashion-conscious Canadian student, or worn out by a British construction worker. At one time the jeans have all been bought, owned and worn by someone in North America or Europe, and then recycled and ended up far away in an African marketplace. Some jeans show the marks of their previous lives; there are rips, scuffs and stains, and scraps of paper in the pockets. The dirtiest and most torn jeans won't be sold, and if Mario ends up with too many low-quality pairs he will lose money.

Traders in Xipamanine market are familiar with Western popular culture and work hard to identify clothes which will appeal to customers who are poor but nevertheless caught up in the currents of global fashion. Mario enjoys American hip hop and English football. He knows all the results and soccer gossip, and what tracks are in vogue with Mozambican teens. Although Mario recognizes Beyoncé songs, Manchester United players, and what styles of denim sell well, he does not know where the jeans come from or how they get to Maputo. Globally the used-clothing trade is a large and growing sector, but here in this cramped market business is usually slow during the long, stiflingly hot afternoons. Between sales Mario is preoccupied with more pressing matters than thinking about how second-hand jeans from the West end up on his stall. He faces the persistent dilemma of deciding whether to take a risk and spend more money on another package of used denim, save funds to pay for further education so he can try and find a formal job, or use the cash to provide for his young family. Like the other thousand or so second-hand traders in Xipamanine market, Mario has a precarious small business; while he is able to provide for his household, he still faces the constant demand for basic necessities at home. Ultimately he cannot escape poverty through selling second-hand clothes. For him this is his only means of making a living, and he does not dwell on the origins and impacts of the second-hand clothing trade.

Thousands of miles away in rich countries like the United States and Britain, few people ever think about what happens to their clothes after they have finished wearing them and given them away to a recycling company or charity. In many instances they will end up somewhere like Mario's stall in Mozambique. People often express disbelief when they hear that their unwanted clothes are sold in Africa, rather than freely distributed, and that companies profit through this business (as well as cheat, steal and smuggle). Billions of second-hand garments are traded globally ever year.[1] This book explores how second-hand clothing supply chains cut across continents, linking Americans, Canadians, Britons and other Europeans to Mozambique; spanning North and South America, connecting Europe with East and West Africa and stretching across Asia and around the Pacific. Used-clothing networks are different to other trade patterns as they reverse the flow of commodities; while new clothes are mainly manufactured in low-income countries and emerging economies like China, used clothing goes from the rich to the poor. Moreover they are intimate bonds of connectivity as they physically link consumers who wear new clothes in the global North (Australia, Europe, Japan and North America) to some of the poorest people in the global South (Africa, most of Asia, the Middle East and South America), who are dependent on buying and re-wearing the same garments.

The story of second-hand clothing is just one of the many sides to the hidden world of clothes that is exposed through this book. Using research from across the globe, colourful stories and hard data demonstrate how the clothing and textile sectors have played a major part in making different regions of the world affluent and impoverished. Starting with a biography of jeans, this investigation of the globalized economy first uncovers how one of the world's most common garments has grown to be so popular. It considers the origin and spread of jeans, and then maps out the production process from design to cotton growing, denim milling, manufacturing, advertising and retail. The lifespan of jeans provides an insight into the complex international journeys new clothing goods follow around the globe. A narrow biography of jeans provides one slice through the world economy, like cutting through a layered cake; some of the patterns of globalization are exposed, but it is equally important to understand the broader clothing sector as a whole. Therefore the following chapter provides more historical breadth and examines how today's global trade in clothing has been linked to the international spread of a free-market economy. Cotton, cloth and clothing production played an important role in driving forward global trade. Textile factories underpinned the Industrial Revolution and the development of capitalism. The expansion of this mode of production and economic globalization is explored. Recent trends, and the reasons behind the global shift in clothing production away from Europe and North America, are then introduced. Next, light is cast on the shadowy world of second-hand clothing, which has been less documented, despite used clothing being an important source of garments for hundreds of years. One example that is put to work here is an in-depth analysis of the collection, recycling and export of used clothing in the UK. Britain is one of the major exporters of second-hand clothing and the trade is long-standing and well established; yet it involves an uneasy cast of actors, including charities, immigrant traders, companies and even criminals.

Tracing the evolving roles of different countries in garment manufacturing and markets explains some of the divergent economic trajectories of various regions of the world; in particular some of the poorest and least-known places are discussed here. Field research from Mozambique, Zambia and elsewhere in Africa makes up the body of many of the core arguments. Africa has largely been neglected in writing on the clothing sector, yet the world's most impoverished continent has played an important role in the global history of garment production, especially in cotton growing. In the colonial period cotton was one of the major export crops, and through patterns of uneven exchange relationships of dependency between Africa and Europe emerged. After political independence, terms of trade hardly improved; here the long-term structural exploitation of African farm workers is investigated using evidence from Mali, Mozambique and Senegal. Africans are not just involved in the clothing trade as cotton growers, but like everyone are also consumers of clothes. Over a billion Africans are deeply impoverished, and clothing availability is an important livelihood issue as the poor lack access to affordable, good-quality, basic garments. Few clothes are made in Africa for local markets; understanding why there is so little manufacturing helps to explain how this part of the world remains so poor.

Today, China plays the dominant role in global clothing manufacture, while North America and Europe still generate the demand that structures the geographies of production and consumption, although the balance of market power is swinging east. Predominantly female workers in garment factories make clothes for export, generating profits that are driving Chinese gross domestic product (GDP) growth; the reasons behind large-scale labour exploitation are considered. As China rises it is leading the reconfiguration of the global economy, and part of this new shift is a growing embrace of Africa by China. In the clothing sector Chinese businesses have influenced production and markets, with mixed fortunes for Africans. Drawing on detailed research at a factory in Zambia, the workers' experiences of employment in a modern Chinese-managed clothing factory producing for global markets are documented, showing the opportunities and risks presented by China's new engagement in Africa. Following on from this, the impacts of mass imports of used clothes to Africa are investigated, which leads on to a chapter on Mozambique and a discussion of the livelihoods of traders like Mario.

Second-hand clothes are not just found in poor African countries; they are retailed around the world. Vintage fashion is a growing trend in the global North; case studies from some of the world's fashion hotspots – London, New York and Tokyo – show how the retro clothing and vintage sectors are linked to the new fashion industry. Other examples from middle- and low-income countries, including Bolivia, India, Papua New Guinea and the Philippines, provide further evidence of the flourishing of used-clothing markets and detail some of their diverse social and economic impacts in the global South. Next, some of the myths and realities surrounding the production and consumption of ethical fashion are investigated. New green and socially responsible garment sectors, which are intended to improve labour conditions and be more environmentally friendly, are being promoted by clothing brands. Ethical consumption and sustainable fashion are emerging trends; some of the contradictions and opportunities presented by alternative methods of manufacturing and retail are investigated, using different examples of fashion, from the mass-produced Toms shoes to the exclusive collections of Vivienne Westwood.

The business of making, selling and buying clothes affects everyone in the world. Apparel is a multibillion-dollar industry and one of the cornerstones of economic and cultural globalization. Western consumers have a huge amount of choice over what they wear, because poor people across the developing world grow cotton, dye materials and stitch fabric, and are paid low wages, which keep clothes cheap for those consumers to buy. These low wage levels cannot allow cotton farmers and factory workers to consume the garments they help make, and so a global division in consumption has emerged. People in the global North have grown used to the ever-changing supply of garment styles and the instantaneous and relatively effortless consumption of clothing. Rapid cycles of predominantly East Asian manufacturing and retail in the global North subsequently determine the onward sale of unwanted used clothing to Africa and elsewhere. The international used clothing trade is a countercurrent to the flow of new garments; it only makes sense when it is considered in concert with new clothing production and what has come to be known as *fast fashion*. To understand how and why hundreds of pairs of jeans end up on Mario's stall, first it is necessary to learn

exactly how the new fast-fashion clothing system of provision
has developed and explain why different countries have become
winners and losers in the global economy.

'Fast fashion' is a term coined by retailers to encapsulate how
trends move rapidly from the catwalk to the store. Manufacturing
is quick and cheap and consumers can easily take advantage of
affordable collections in shops like Gap, H&M and Zara, and get
involved in current fashion crazes. In order to appreciate how our
shopping for fast fashion makes us complicit in a system which is
denying people in the global South the chance to escape poverty,
we need to begin by thinking about where our clothing comes
from. Next we have to consider how, as the affluent minority in
the global North indulges in the rapid consumption of clothing,
the disposal of old garments has a knock-on effect and sets in
motion the international second-hand clothing trade. Flows of
used clothing reach the poorest of people in the Global South
and lock them into another relationship of dependency. The boom
in fast fashion and the little-known second-hand clothing trade it
has produced have shaped lives and determined patterns of dress
around the world. Divisions of labour in the clothing sector play
their part in keeping places of new clothing consumption rich and
areas of production and second-hand consumption poor. This
book looks beyond 'Made in China', or whatever label is found
in your clothes, and explores the hidden story of both where
clothes come from and where they end up. The relationships and
case studies drawn from around the world and across different
periods of human history illuminate and contextualize gross
injustices at the heart of contemporary globalization. To complete
this intervention the concluding chapter offers up some radical
alternatives to the current economic system which could challenge
the inequality embedded in global clothing systems of provision.

CHAPTER 1

A biography of jeans

Jeans are one of the most popular items of basic clothing. From their humble origins as the quintessential American workwear to their modern status as among the most ubiquitous articles of clothing, denim is worn every day around the world by women and men, young and old, rich and poor. Most people own a pair of jeans or at least one related article of denim. Jeans therefore provide a good universal case study that it is easy to relate to. However, a T-shirt, a sweater or a pair of socks could equally be scrutinized. This chapter maps new clothing production and explores where jeans are designed, where cotton is grown and denim is woven, and where jeans are stitched together and then marketed and retailed; it is a biography of jeans. Starting with design in San Francisco and cotton fields in India, travelling via factories in Bangladesh and Mexico, to retail in New York and London, this narrative illuminates how an everyday clothing item has a rich history and passes along a geographically diverse commodity chain.

The aim of this biography is to understand the 'systems of provision' which bring jeans to consumers. This means charting how jeans have become a default clothing choice for millions of people, and understanding where manufacturing takes place and who profits from – and who is exploited by – the global denim industry. A system-of-provision approach, first championed by economist Ben Fine, considers how the role of the consumer has emerged and is an inclusive way of examining the 'chain of activity that attaches consumption to the production that makes it possible'.[1] So, before we discuss the manufacturing process, it is important to examine the social history of jeans, to reveal how they have grown to be such a popular clothing choice. Complex relationships linking people around the world are involved in the final manufacture of a simple pair of jeans. A brief account of the different jobs and wage levels of farmers, factory workers and shop assistants is required, dividing the systems of provision into six main stages: origin, design, cotton growing, denim milling, manufacturing, advertising and retail. This biography will examine different labour processes from across the globe to provide a broad description of the trade patterns, rather than follow the same wads of raw cotton from farm gate to department-store rail. After the jeans' back stories, a section analyses the division of labour in new clothing commodity chains. There then follows a discussion of the theoretical approach employed in this book.

Jeans: a social history

The birthplace and early heritage of denim jeans are disputed. France and Italy as well as the United States lay partial claims to their origins. Sailors from Genoa (from which the name 'jeans' is supposed to derive) were said to have spread hard-wearing Italian cotton fabric; the name 'denim' can be literally translated as *de Nîmes*, 'of Nîmes', the Roman city in the south of France famous for its textiles. Where there is consensus is that the history of modern blue jeans began with the weaving of denim fabric and the use of indigo dye, a natural colour easily fixed to cotton. Blue jeans material is made from weaving cotton threads: the diagonal weft thread passes under two or more dyed warp threads. The characteristic blue jean colour and diagonal pattern are produced on account of the warp threads being coloured blue and the weft left white, which makes for a strong twill fabric and also gives the inside of jeans their lighter colour. In the 1870s Levi Strauss made the critical contribution of riveting the denim, which prevented tearing, and subsequently added five pockets and belt loops. These early models inspired the standard jean style, elements of which are seen in most contemporary designs. Levi Strauss's developments were so influential because they brought together a range of different useful component parts: copper rivets provided long-lasting toughness; rugged twill fabric gave robust protection; the blue denim colour was simple to reproduce, first using indigo and later synthetic dyes; blue also proved a neutral colour popular among buyers; and finally the five-pocket design was functional and later augmented by various combinations of belt loops, buttons and zippers to aid fit.[2]

The hard-wearing nature of jeans meant they soon became the trousers of choice for the American working man and were readily adopted by the iconic cowboy. Later, they provided part of the uniform of industrial workers during the Fordist phase of industrial development and mass manufacturing in the twentieth century, a mode of production that is discussed in Chapter 2. In the 1950s and 1960s jeans began to emerge not just as utilitarian workwear, but also as a casual and subversive mode of dress for women as well as men. Screen icons like Marlon Brando, James Dean and Marilyn Monroe adopted them as part of a costume which exuded characteristics such as youth, freedom and sex appeal. Hollywood colour films projected aspirational images of blue jeans, and young people in America as well as overseas imitated these dress styles. Denim gained both popularity and

notoriety in youth culture. However, jeans were not just passively
taken up by other cultures imitating America; they have grown
to have their own local meanings and significance. In the United
Kingdom they were associated with transgressive and rebellious
youth; in Eastern Europe they became politicized garments and
behind the iron curtain were identified as nonconformist dress;
whilst in Brazil the basic design has been adapted to reflect
local cultural dynamics. In Japan jeans have a complex social
history, which is discussed later. Towards the end of the twentieth
century jeans began to lose their subversive qualities in most
of Europe and the Americas and became something closer to a
default wardrobe item, no longer demarking a particular social
group and instead offering anonymity via their ubiquity. Jeans
have even moved from being an affectation of classlessness to
losing any genuine correspondence to class. In terms of everyday
ordinariness, wearing jeans has become a way to escape making
a decision, and putting them on is an act of conformity. We have
become conditioned to wear jeans as part of entrenched clothing
systems of provision. Buying and wearing jeans means participating in the market; and they are relentlessly marketed at every price
point from designer lines to bargain basement. The previously
rebellious connotations of denim have been reappropriated as part
of normal capitalist society. Jeans are the dress-down uniform
of presidents and prime ministers as well as the street outfits of
punks and protesters.[3]

Blue jeans have spread across the world and are worn in nearly
every country. In many places they are among the most common
item of dress. Although the USA is the largest market, with up to
half a billion pairs sold each year, sales in Asia, particularly China,
Japan and India, are also huge and expanding. Jeans have become
a default item of clothing because they can be easily manufactured
and meet both the practical and the cultural needs of modern
lives. Rather than thinking about their popularity as being either

led by customers' desires or an outcome of producer-stimulated demand, it is better to consider how jeans perform a function in the circuit of industrial capital. The spheres of production and consumption influence one another as the market for, and the use value of, jeans 'are shaped according to the modern relations of production and in turn intervene to modify those relations'.[4] *Use value* means the material worth of a thing in relation to the wants and needs of humans. Therefore the 'usefulness' of jeans is not incidental, but governed the initial role they played in the agricultural and industrial development of America. Hard-wearing denim trousers were practical, reliable and very useful. This use value was later reinforced by the global production infrastructure, which developed to mass-manufacture a robust and affordable garment that could be tailored to convey different cultural messages. Jeans are a product of industrial development and in turn have shaped how industry developed, leading to the emergence of jeans systems of provision.

Denim has a life and lives with the wearer. If wearers stretch to climb over fences the fibres will be pulled as they extend their legs; if they work bent over fitting carpets or scrubbing floors the knees will thin out and split; if they sit cross-legged the denim will stretch across and pull around the thighs. These daily movements will exercise the twill fabric and leave the imprint of the rhythms of each wearer's life. Old jeans can induce powerful feelings of warmth and reassurance. When someone wears their own familiar clothes they can rekindle memories of past events, soothe, and provide emotional as well as physical protection. Despite the lively nature of denim, the trousers themselves obviously do not have agency; any associations the owners might have are a result of the social relationships that the jeans embody, and this only has meaning in a given social context. When used jeans are transported somewhere new and taken up by a second owner they will form part of a new semiotic register, made up of a group of different signs and signifiers. This idea is important to understand in the context of the second-hand clothing trade and does not concern just our individual relationships with jeans, but also how they are perceived in a broader cultural context in a particular society. As anthropologist Daniel Millar has discussed, 'the first core semiotic marker was the association of jeans with the United States. But this is now seen as merely historical. People do not wear jeans in London today to appear more American even if that association is essential to understanding how jeans first became ubiquitous.'[5] America played a vital role in establishing denim systems of provision, but now jeans are globally entrenched as the most common form of trousers on sale. There is a world market which continues to operate semi-autonomously from processes in the United States. In parallel, at the level of individual garments, any perceived agency that a pair of jeans holds over a person will not exert that same affect when they are reworn by someone else. Just as their body will move in a different manner and stretch and work the threads in new ways, so will they also form new associations with the jeans, born of their own social interactions.

Designing denim

Levi Strauss designs jeans in San Francisco, drawing upon the heritage of the brand and the early connection with frontier livelihoods, like raising cattle in the Old West. The advantages of this location are not just historical; the proximity to an important contemporary core customer base – a hip youth market in a leading financial and cultural centre – allows designers to innovate and introduce fresh design details to the basic jean formula and target new consumers. For instance, Levi's recently launched a 'commuter' series after observing the popularity of jeans amongst cyclists in the Bay area and then promoted this design nationally and internationally, demonstrating the web of feedback between producing for an established market, and cultivating new patterns of consumption. After a new design has been decided upon, a product developer, also in San Francisco, picks up the ideas and works out the details. They make prototypes, fit the jeans to mannequins and models, check denim finishes, communicate the final design to manufacturers around the world, and liaise with merchandisers so the product will have its correct home within the Levi's brand.[6]

Elsewhere, Italian designer brands like Armani, Gucci and Prada have their headquarters in Milan, where the couture fashion sector can influence the designs of jeans. Milan also serves as a commercial hub connecting fashion houses to advertising agencies, distributors and the fashion press. Catwalk styles can be incorporated into denim designs and rapidly transmitted to overseas producers. Trend spotters and fashion bloggers are found on the high streets of London, New York and Paris identifying what is on-trend among key groups. Fashion scouts either purposefully or indirectly feed in to the creation of new and modified styles that will later be found in malls and on Main Street. These specialized professions also have an important role in determining how vintage clothes influence new trends and designs, which is discussed towards the end of the book. What all these activities in London, Paris, Milan, New York and San Francisco have in common is a location in the global North; this is skilled technical, metropolitan work, undertaken at trade fairs and in design studios and downtown loft workshops. All the labour processes associated with this type of work are relatively well paid, often graduate-level jobs, which stand in stark contrast to the low-skilled, poorly paid and sometimes dangerous production work in the global South. The design process is physically separated from the manufacturing enterprise in a way which would be totally unrecognizable to Mr

Levi Strauss, who in the 1870s produced jeans in San Francisco to clothe the Californian working man.

Despite the differences in design and the dispersion of manufacturing activities, the basic pattern of jeans is still fairly faithful to their early origins. A single design language is common to thousands of product lines drawn up around the world, and a whole lexicon of jean styles has emerged: baggy, boot-cut, boyfriend, carpenter, classic, cowboy, drainpipe, flared, hipster, low-rise, relaxed, skinny, straight. Each new subcategory has become established as a different genre of jeans with associated cultural values that wax and wane across social contexts. Details also matter in denim design; these include the type of stitching and the colours of thread, the use of a belt loop, the number and cut of pockets, the fly and stitching of the yoke. Jeans can be embellished with embroidery, glitter, rhinestones, bleaching and buckles. Some of the more minute details are only ever seen by the wearer, but a successful designer knows it is important to furnish jeans with the right stylistic notes to complement the familiar denim blueprint. Designs can allow you to be noticed or provide you with anonymity. Denim designers work to effect a balance between providing uniform and individual looks, which reflects societies own tensions between social liberty and conformity to prescribed patterns of behaviour. Aspects of design also live on to influence how jeans are valued in secondary marketplaces, like Mario's stall in Mozambique.

One of the distinctive properties of contemporary jeans is the way in which millions of pairs are deliberately distressed. Bleached-out, faded and torn denim is visible when one visits any branch of Gap, Macy's or Topshop. Denim is given effects to show a worn-in look, which is the output of particular types of labour activity, discussed below. This designer's trick establishes within jeans values of authenticity, which, depending on the social register, can relate back to earlier popular cultural history. Jeans can be made to look like the worn workwear of cowboys from the turn of the twentieth century or have the tears and fraying of mid-1970s' punk style. Vintage fashions influence design; yet the designer is also trying to build there a more personal association between the customer and the jeans. Designers play upon the 'lived-in' aesthetic, which can make denim more comforting and appealing. The clothes industry attempts to replicate the physical relationships our bodies forge with jeans, such as stretching, thinning and tearing them, to try to stimulate shoppers to buy them.

The role of the designer is important in forming the symbolic value of jeans. Whilst it is true that there is some correlation between relatively objective notions of quality and price, the association rapidly falls away as the retail price point climbs towards $100. Differentiation then becomes increasingly important. Designers in all price brackets play a vital role, increasing the social value of jeans, so that the retail price no longer represents the cost of the labour and materials involved in manufacturing. Consumers buy jeans unaware of the conditions of production, and the most fashionable jeans become a major source of desire. Buyers covet new trends or styles, and the yearning to consume becomes a form of control. In fact, control is central to social relations under capitalism. Principally, the inherently expansionist nature of the market means people have to be compelled to buy more and more goods. Both designers and advertisers play key roles in provoking people to purchase *authentic*, *fashionable* or *luxurious* jeans. Part of the design process in the global North is the stimulation of the market. Capitalism depends on forming and reinforcing aspirational images, and brands including Levi Strauss, Lee and Wrangler have achieved this by attaching themselves to the values of authentic, original and honest Americana. The designers play a key role in systems of provision by creating visual formulas that can be cultivated to emerge as part of sophisticated advertising and marketing strategies which cast a spell on the consumer.

Designers shape systems of provision for all jeans; this is most apparent with luxurious high-end fashionable jeans, but the same is true for the more mundane, affordable and less dramatic styles. Just as Diesel, Gucci and Victoria Beckham jeans are 'designer', so are those found in Primark, Walmart or Target. Each pair of trousers still has to be designed and the production process mapped out, even if this is a piecemeal replication of the basic five-pocket blue jean pattern.

Alongside aesthetics, culture is a diffuse yet powerful force that surrounds the production of distinctive values in different jeans and effects the acts of consuming and wearing denim. In Brazil there is a specific style of jeans which grew in popularity in the 2000s, where this distinctive domestic design born in the 'funk balls' of Rio da Janeiro became known locally as *calça da gang*, or more widely as 'Brazilian jeans'.[7] The design uses elastane within the weave to produce thinner denim with both horizontal and vertical stretch. Popular first among young women and associated with dance culture in the *favelas* of Rio where the design was appropriated and given meaning, these tight pants have developed local notoriety and given rise to some lurid analysis. They 'are often described as a "bra for the bumbum", that it is actually giving lift to the buttocks, although in practice it is more that it holds and reveals rather than lifts.' These designs spread from the *favelas* and were taken up by clothing firms catering for the middle classes; using the 'edgy' aspects of Brazilian culture and their relation to sensuality and sexuality, they went on to influence international fashion and designers based in California and Paris.[8]

Growing cotton

Wads of fluffy white cotton are the fruit of the shrubby, grey cotton plant. They are native to tropical countries, but cotton is grown around the world from Ukraine in the north to Australia in the south, in deep, well-drained soils with good nutrient content. The ideal climate is a constant temperature of 18–30 degrees Celsius (64–86 degrees Fahrenheit), sunshine, dry conditions and long periods (175 to 225 days) without frost. Sometimes known as 'white gold', cotton is a natural fibre mostly composed of cellulose; cotton strands are formed by twisting these smaller ribbon-like fibres together. After food crops, cotton is comfortably the world's most farmed plant. It is widely used in industry to make items such as bandages and bank notes, while the seed provides feed for cattle, can be pressed to make cooking oil, and used in cosmetics and soaps.

Farmers who grow cotton are faced with management decisions that include seed choices, crop rotations, irrigation strategies, and they increasingly have to consider the environmental impacts and sustainability of their work. Cotton growing covers around 2.4 per cent of global agricultural land, yet accounts for 24 per cent of insecticides and 11 per cent of pesticides.[9] Proportionally cotton uses a far greater degree of chemical input than most food crops because there is less concern over consumers' health (as they are not ingesting the product), but this can have disastrous impacts on agricultural environments and workers' well-being. A study from India showed the serious health consequences of indiscriminate use of pesticides by cotton growers: both the men who directly applied pesticides and the women who worked as helpers mixing chemicals and filling tanks showed signs ranging from mild to severe poisoning, which occurred after 83.6 per cent of interactions with pesticides. This includes extremely serious neurotoxic effects in 6 per cent of spraying sessions. No victims were able to seek medical care and marginal low-income farmers were more frequently exposed to severe poisoning than landlords.[10] In addition to the widespread use of pesticides, cotton is very dependent on water consumption, requiring an incredible 11,000 litres of water for every kilogram (or 1,320 US gallons per pound) of cotton grown, picked, produced, packed and shipped to make jeans. This 'virtual water' – the invisible agricultural and industrial consumption of water that goes into the production of goods – far exceeds the water requirements of food crops such as rice (3,400 litres per kilo) and wheat (1,300 litres).[11] Much cotton is grown in water-scarce environments; our thirst for new jeans and other cotton apparel is part of a broader pattern of trade which also involves the rapid consumption of other water-hungry goods such as coffee, beef and leather. Demand for these products is often driven by overconsumption in the global North, which threatens precious water resources, particularly in tropical and semi-arid environments. Environmental damage is occurring on a wide scale; for example, water extraction from the Amur Darya and Syr Darya rivers in Central Asia for cotton irrigation has led to the near-disappearance of the Aral Sea.[12]

Agricultural workers in the cotton sector have been treated in a disgraceful way for centuries. In the United States the history of cotton growing is inextricably linked to slavery, and in Africa is connected to colonial labour abuses (discussed in Chapter 4). What is clear, from both historical and contemporary perspectives, is that cotton has always been grown at great human cost. Among the particularly upsetting aspects of cotton farming are the many reports on the abuse of child labour in cotton-growing regions, including Egypt, India and Uzbekistan.[13] Labour exploitation is found throughout the global South. The international NGO Oxfam has detailed the tough life of a cotton grower in Peru:

> Lily Arteaga Cabrera, 47, also grows cotton in Pisco. She gets up at 5 in the morning to prepare food for the family and then goes to the cotton field at 8, where she stays until 6 in the evening. The cotton they grow earns them just enough to feed the family – but not very well. It is hard work but they are locked into a cycle of debt – they borrow to plant and then work eight months

caring for the crop until they harvest and earn enough to pay the debts: They rarely have any extra left over. Lily looks after the family money and has to budget carefully.[14]

This report was prompted by a change to the trade relationships between Peru and the USA, which posed a threat to the vulnerable livelihoods of cotton growers such as Lily Arteaga Cabrera. Research by Oxfam has highlighted how demand for cotton is keeping peasants, smallholders and agricultural workers in poverty across the global South and especially in the West African countries of Benin, Burkina Faso, Chad and Mali. Oxfam highlights how relationships of dependency with international cotton markets and trade regulations are structured against poor producers and have negative effects on farmers' livelihoods. The role of bilateral and multilateral trade agreements and cotton farming in Africa is discussed in greater depth in subsequent chapters. It is also important to note how Oxfam has been advocating for change, while also being embroiled in the second-hand clothing trade. This book later explores the impacts of second-hand clothing exports.

In general, cotton growing provides a poorly paid livelihood; furthermore, environmentally harmful approaches to agriculture are implemented throughout much of the global South. Unfortunately, the exposure of these travesties rarely translates into practical action. The barriers to a politics of radical social change, and how they relate to our addiction to fast fashion, are themes explored throughout this book. This is not to neglect the fact that some limited attempts have been made to address the pressing human and environmental costs of cotton agriculture in middle- and low-income countries, namely via accreditation schemes for clean, Green and fair-trade cotton. Turkey has been at the forefront of organic cotton agriculture, and jeans made from Fairtrade cotton are beginning to reach some department stores, like Marks & Spencer in the UK.

After China, the United States is the largest producer of cotton in the world, where much investment has gone into the development of high-yielding cotton varieties and efficient production techniques. The USA and other producers in the global North, such as Australia, grow cotton in less socially and environmentally exploitative ways. Cotton production is now mechanized and the environmental impacts are regulated, but this is only commercially viable as the sector is heavily subsidized in the global North.

Ginning, spinning and weaving

Harvested cotton is processed at a ginnery, usually in the same region as the cotton fields. Bales of cotton are then taken to a spinning plant to form thread, before being woven into denim. Ginning, spinning and weaving can occur side by side or be spread across continents. At the Mulungushi Cotton ginnery in Kabwe, Zambia, cotton used to supply a local factory, but is now processed for export to China, the world's largest importer of ginned cotton (this factory is discussed further in Chapter 5). After fluffing and drying, the cotton is opened to remove dirt and leaves, and then is processed by ginning to further remove fragments of stalk, seeds, soils and other waste from the fibres. Labour standards can be low in ginneries, as in the neighbouring cotton fields. Child labour has been employed in cotton ginneries in India, where workers are paid just over $2 a day for a 12-hour shift in dangerous conditions.[15]

Mapping out where the cotton fibres that make up a particular pair of jeans come from is very difficult; this is partially due to the type of cotton used in denim. Jeans do not generally require high-quality cotton. Short cotton fibres can be used, whereas long ribbons of fibre are needed to make fine and delicate garments such as dress shirts and underwear. In Zambia the low-quality

B-grade fibres are more likely to be used locally for hard-wearing twill fabrics such as denims, whereas A grades are exported to China.[16] At the spinning plant, tens of thousands of cotton fibres are spun and twisted together by centrifugal force to produce strands of yarn. It is not unusual to combine fibres from different areas to produce thread. Rachel Synder notes that 'a single foot of thread might contain fibres from farms in Texas, Azerbaijan, India, Turkey and Pakistan', and at 'a spinning plant in Italy bales of cotton from countries across Africa, America, Asia and the former Soviet Union can all be spun together'.[17] Labelling can also be inaccurate; for instance, Uzbekistan has an established reputation for producing high-quality cotton, which means that cotton from neighbouring states such as Azerbaijan is sometimes fraudulently labelled as Uzbek cotton to give it a higher value.

To make denim, the warp yarn is dyed in synthetic indigo dye and then woven with the weft thread into denim. The dyeing process involves strong chemical compounds. Even most organic cotton is dyed in this manner. Weaving combines different weights of fabric, and flexible yarns such as lycra or the elastane in Brazilian jeans can provide stretch. Industrial laundering techniques create different effects and looks; staples are used to gather fabric and allow graduated colouring and bleaching, just like tie-dyeing a T-shirt. Pumice stones are used to create stonewash. Glasspaper and brushing techniques create shine on fabrics. These activities are very water-intensive, which contributes to the high volumes of virtual water involved in the production of jeans. Laundering processes involve toxic combinations of chemicals, including formaldehyde, and appropriate safety equipment, such as boots, gloves, masks and eyewear are required to protect workers, though are often missing in developing-world factories. The effects of these chemicals goes beyond the workers and can harm local communities. Denim plants have a heavy ecological footprint; for example, in Lesotho a factory owned by the Taiwanese firm Nien

Hsing Fashion Group, which supplied Gap and Levi Strauss, was discharging deep blue wastewater polluted with chemicals, which contaminated the water table and a local river.[18]

Local environmental controls are often poorly enforced in the global South, but in manufacturing, spinning and weaving cotton factories are held to exacting international standards to produce denims with minimal faults. Tracing the origins of cotton is further complicated by standards such as those put forward by the American Society of Testing and Materials (ASTM), which leads to the production of uniform cotton threads:

> A brand in Japan can buy cotton from Mexico and Turkey and have it made into cloth in France and North Carolina and sewn into a garment in China and Bangladesh and sell it on store shelves in Tokyo and Madrid and have the constituency and quality be exactly the same for each garment in every country.[19]

At the Zambia China Mulungushi Textiles in Zambia, where the ginning, spinning and weaving processes, as well as the garment-making, were all carried out together, ex-employees reported that a consignment of jeans sent to the USA were returned due to the poor quality of cloth. Japan, in contrast, is known to be the home of the highest quality premium denims used in many top fashion brands. The expertise that has developed in Japan is linked to the country's social history and its access to American second-hand denim in the post-war era (discussed in Chapter 8).

The blending of different patterns of production and regimes of accumulation makes it difficult, if not impossible, to audit the multiple relationships between farmers, ginneries, spinners and fabric weavers that constitute the production of denim cloth. Throughout global jeans' systems of provision denim is usually produced in one factory and by one contractor and then sent onwards to garment factories where it is cut and sewn. Across the linked chain of transactions there is a co-dependence between

the designers, retailers, garment sewers and denim manufacturers. Designers and advertisers find inspiration from producers,
especially those who adapt and modify the traditional blue jean
appearance through processes such as textile laundering. Despite
these patterns of co-dependence it is normally either the designers at the beginning of the chain or the retailers in the global
North who monopolize the most valuable activities and extract
the greatest overall surplus, or profit, from labour, rather than
the firms and individuals in the middle of a system of provision.

Manufacturing jeans

Manufacturing jeans involves transforming woven denim into
final designs. Flat rolls of denim are transformed by the input of
labour and the addition of different design details. Subdivision
of labour is a hallmark of production systems in today's factories.
The trousers will pass through many hands as workers are allocated specific tasks; patterns are drawn and the two legs will
be cut by different operators; each seam is sewn by someone
dedicated to that job; one worker may rivet the right pocket, while
their partner takes care of the left. Sewing machines form long
lines across shed-like workspaces. Jeans pass from one employee
to another at a relentless rate, following well-rehearsed movements of the type popularized in the time-and-motion studies
of Frederick W. Taylor, which led to the scientific management
of factories in the early twentieth century. Once jeans have been
stitched up they might be cleaned and laundered to produce a
particular type of finish, such as fraying or bleaching, or workers
can grind, sand-blast and scrape jeans to produce lived-in looks.
Further down the line, labels are added and jeans are inspected.
Substandard garments are discarded for local retail or reuse, and
finished trousers are finally packaged before leaving the plant. A
detailed case study of labour standards in a clothing factory will

later discuss some of the horrific conditions found in garment industries.

Some recent broad trends and developments have affected jean manufacturing. Clothing production is no longer a major industry in Europe, and jeans manufacturing has long since expanded away from its origins in the United States. In Europe, even Italian fashion brands like Armani, Gucci and Prada have moved their manufacturing to Asia. Luxury brands have managed to sustain desirable values, which stem from their couture heritage still being controlled by designers, like those in Milan. The movement of clothing manufacturing out of Italy is related to the recent changes in the quotas and tariffs found in the global clothing industry (discussed in Chapter 2). Italy itself only became inundated with foreign jeans at the start of the twenty-first century; imports rose dramatically – by 260 per cent between 2000 and 2005 – as the market opened to Asian-produced fast fashion.[20] The undermining of Italy's clothing industry, along with other elements of its manufacturing base, is one of the reasons why the economy has suffered so badly in the recent financial crisis.

It is often argued that Americans who complain about the decline of national industry readily purchase foreign-made jeans at Sears, JCPenney and Walmart and therefore are themselves the cause of the problem. This argument is oversimple and gives the consumer too much autonomy and responsibility in decision-making. Consumers are like deer caught in the headlights when faced with jeans systems of provision and are led in their decision-making processes by designers, retailers and social pressure, rather than caring for an unknown labourer who produced the jeans, or feeling patriotic concern for national industrial strategy. American brands have relocated and it is unrealistic to expect shoppers to audit supply chains. Levi Strauss, although still headquartered in the USA, has gone through a process of de-verticalization, licensing the manufacturing to foreign firms. Much of the company's production is now carried out in Mexico. This buyer-driven, decentralized approach allows Levi's to move production to different factories around the world and take advantage of variation in labour prices and other associated manufacturing costs, rather than being tied to the comparatively high wages of the working classes in the United States. Meanwhile the highly profitable design and marketing processes are protected and retained by Levi's, in places such as San Francisco and New York. Manufacturing processes are not tied to the production of component parts and often take place in countries which do not grow cotton, weave denim or produce buttons, rivets and zippers. For instance, many of the component jeans parts are exported from China to Cambodia, another centre of manufacturing, where denim is cut and the finished articles assembled.

The term 'fast fashion' does not just encapsulate the rapid changes in trends and styles found in the global North and the pace of retail sales, but also the speed at which designs can be transmitted around the world and orders turned into garments. Digital pattern designs, subcontracting and flexible ordering are advanced production management approaches that the fast fashion industry utilizes to enhance profitability. Efficient use of labour is fundamentally important; workers are not always employed in sweatshop conditions. Sri Lanka has made improvements in working environments and prides itself on being socially and environmentally accountable whilst maintaining a competitive position in global supply chains.[21] Torreon in Mexico has good working conditions for jeans and many firms have clustered together to service the North American market, in an industrial area just four hours by road from Texas, producing denim trousers and jackets for brands including Calvin Klein, Old Navy, Sears and Target.[22] China is by far the world's largest producer of jeans. Most garment workers are female, although there is often a gender division in tasks. Work such as loading

and unloading materials and truck driving is more likely to
be performed by men, whereas the static production tasks are
primarily undertaken by young women in their late teens, twen-
ties and thirties. Work in garment factories is a classic example
of global patriarchy. Women pay the price for decisions made
by men, as factory ownership in clothing manufacturing as well
as senior management positions in international clothing firms
are overwhelmingly male.

Labour standards vary around the world and there are countless cases of worker abuse. Chapter 5 provides a detailed case
study based on testimonies from garment workers. Three brief
examples among thousands are: migrant workers from South
Asia going missing from factories in Jordan whilst sewing jeans
for Walmart; the violation of workers' right to association by
G-Star jeans suppliers in India; 52 deaths and over 1,000 workers
suffering lung and respiratory problems following the sandblast-
ing of denim in Turkey to give it the 'lived-in' appearance that
consumers love. Atrocities have been documented by advocacy organizations including the Institute for Global Labour and Human
Rights, the Clean Clothes Campaign, and Labour Behind the
Label. The worst recent example of worker exploitation in jeans
production was the horrific collapse of the Rana Plaza garment
factory in Bangladesh, which resulted in the loss of over 1,100
lives and caused 2,500 serious injuries. Rana Plaza contained
multiple garment factories which produced jeans for retailers,
including Primark in the UK. Akter Rojina, who was injured in
the collapse, earned just $65 a month as a sewer's assistant, which,
although above the $37 minimum wage for Bangladesh's garment
workers, still left her poor. 'We entered the factory because we
needed to be paid. But the government should have overseen
the construction of Rana Plaza; it was built on marshy land.'
Rojina noted that the top three floors were added illegally.[23]
Stories such as this rarely receive much attention and are quickly

forgotten when people go shopping for jeans. Researching labour conditions is very difficult; academics and investigative journalists have problems gaining permission and access. Likewise there are many barriers to practical action. National policies on labour are likely to be defeated by a lack of local political will, but even if they are robust regulations the lead design and retail firms from the global North are prone to see out their short-term contracts and relocate to another country where there are fewer barriers to labour exploitation. Policies put forward to protect workers' rights often show a complete lack of ambition in addressing global inequality and are at best tokenistic. The fight to improve labour standards in garment manufacturing is explored in the concluding chapter.

Advertising and retail

On average, consumers in the USA say they spend approximately $35 on a pair of jeans and own on average 6.7 pairs. Jeans ownership in the USA is actually down from a historical high of 8.2 pairs per individual in 2006.[24] The trade body Cotton Incorporated argues that the fall in ownership has been associated with economic pressure, as well as the fast-fashion phenomenon, which has compelled clothing retailers to reduce quality and cotton content. There is also a steady rate of discard as people get rid of old jeans. In the short term clothing prices are now generally likely to rise. At the same time, American shoppers have become concerned with declining quality and the reduced value jeans represent. Jeans suffered a similar setback in the 1980s with the rise of polyester and the popularity of tracksuits and joggers. Yet, despite the recent decline in the USA, the global market for jeans is booming, currently estimated to be worth around $60 billion, or an eighth of the total clothing sector. Jeans are not going away any time soon.

How we buy jeans is changing. Online retailers are growing
in popularity, either as digital storefronts for established names
like Gap and Zara, or as solely e-retailers like ASOS and Mr
Porter, the latter often specializing in rapidly bringing new fashion
trends from the catwalk to the customer. For many jeans shoppers either the mall or the supermarket is at the heart of their
retail experience, and this is where globalization, consumption,
identity and cultural politics collide. Supermarkets have been the
leaders in bringing ever cheaper denim to consumers. In the UK
sales of jeans increased in the 2000s as unbranded jeans retailed
in supermarkets, including Asda (owned by Walmart), brought
very cheap denim to market. While firms like Walmart primarily
generate profit on the basis of exploiting cheap Chinese labour,
they are also efficient organizations able to set themselves apart
from competitors through their effective distribution networks
and, like many supermarkets, the paying of low wages (the legal
minimum wage is currently £6.50 ($10) per hour in the UK,
whereas many workers in the USA earn under $10 an hour). When
jeans are purchased as an impulse or routine buy alongside the
grocery shopping they become an unreflexive part of life going on
as normal. Daniel Miller and Sophie Woodward even argue that
this type of banal shopping for 'denim is special, being as much a
refusal as an acceptance of capitalist pressures such as fashion'.[25]
However, this type of zombie-like shopping is not, in my view,
in any way a rejection of capitalism and shows compliance with
rather than rebellion against this mode of production.

Within malls specialist jeans retailers can be found alongside
fashion stores. Both are distinctive spaces engineered for consumption, and prime examples of how place is a source of potent
symbolism, infusing jeans with imagined values, depending on
how the garments are presented and the ways in which the store
itself is dressed. Levi's is one example of a company that has
extended its activities at the consumption end of the system of

provision with the vertical integration of Levi's branded stores. Levi's stores around the world emphasize their association with Americana culture, and denim is expertly presented in clean shops with an industrial aesthetic, making use of exposed steel and seasoned timber. Having its own stores allows Levi's to carefully control the merchandising activity and shape how its jeans are presented to the customer. As the lead firm in a complex system of provision it controls this key node which provides the most profitable business opportunity. Behind the branded storefronts and the neat displays of carefully folded denim is a whole complex of advertising. Studios in the heart of New York's garment district support Levi Strauss's marketing strategies and provide a stimulating environment to foster creative ideas. Advertisers work in close collaboration with designers and must perform the trick of convincing the consumer they have free choice instead of having their desires stimulated by marketing.

Advertising and merchandising contribute to establishing value in expensive jeans. Very few pairs of jeans cost more than $20 to manufacture, in rare cases $50; but even $500 designer jeans cost only marginally more to make than an average pair of Levis.[26] Designer brands invest in establishing advertising and marketing strategies. Capital is expended on renting the best retail space, fitting out shops in chic and minimalistic styles, buying glossy advertising space and employing top models in advertising. These costs are added into the retail price and the brand owners extract a surplus from all these different types of labour activity as well as the previous manufacturing process to amass a profit.

Today's jeans systems of provision

The label sewn in the back of jeans, which may read 'Made in China', actually tells the consumer very little about the origins of their garment. Starting from the cotton (which could originate

anywhere from Alabama to Zimbabwe) onwards, the production
of jeans is nigh-on impossible to audit. They are not made in one
place, but are constructed as a commodity with a particular set
of social values through a whole web of relationships. Consumers
do not only pay for the item, they also pay for advertising, design,
transport, packaging, wastage and profits. The fruits of production
are unevenly distributed. Diverse people involved in the growing
of cotton, or the stitching of fabric, or the marketing of jeans
receive different wages; meanwhile the managers, owners and
investors, who control the means of production, extract surplus
from both manufacturing and retail. Consumers' obsessions with
the relationships between commodities – how the jeans relate to
other clothes on sale, how they are advertised and marketed as
part of a lifestyle, and how they are priced – obscure the relationships between the people who labour to produce them and their
employers. Understanding the detail in such a journey is very
difficult, but if we step back from looking at individual jeans the
bigger picture is clearer. In the international clothing trade the
most profitable activities are concentrated in segments with the
highest barriers to entry. This can mean formal protection via
trademarks or patents, or softer barriers such as a close relationship
with the fashion press or a nuanced understanding of styles in rich
consumer markets. Identifying and forming trends are enabled by
the embedded cultural status stylists enjoy in London, Paris and
New York. Access to the market is also very important, and large
chain stores as well as supermarkets have an entrenched position
in the retail sector. In some jeans production systems, especially
for higher-value jeans such as Armani or Levi's, a lead firm plays a
key governance role that may be distant from the actual production
of commodities. A lead firm monopolizes the highly profitable
activities and can be a producer/designer and/or a buyer/retailer.

Across many jeans systems of provision the influence and
power of transnational firms from the global North who promote

markets for denim goods is near hegemonic. This alone does not preclude the emergence of powerful firms in the global South; nor is the involvement of transnational corporations always on rigidly exploitative terms. The reality of the multipolar global economy is more complicated, as is evidenced by the rise of China, the emergence of new hubs of accumulation in the global economy such as Dubai and Singapore, and the many transnational corporations based across both the global North and the global South. In the future new denim designer brands are likely to emerge from the global South. Indeed there is already evidence of this, such as the rise of the Mavi fashion brand from Turkey, as well as the influence of Brazilian jean styles on designers in the United States and Europe.

The mega-consumption of fast fashion reflects and reinforces socio-economic inequality whilst simultaneously degrading the environment. Buying new jeans in the global North is a type of consumption that intertwines with social aspiration through distinction-making. The quest for 'cheap' but serviceable clothes by consumers has led to the migration of industries from the (more expensive) global North to the (less expensive) global South, and to the inexorable depression of inflation-adjusted wage rates for many workers, whilst ratcheting up the pressures on farmland and water-scarce environments.[27] Consumption has become an incredibly important force in defining identity. Increasingly people are what they buy, which in particular places enormous financial and psychological pressure on the young to participate in what one might call a 'consumption arms race'. Teenagers have to buy the latest style to take part in distinction-making so they can simultaneously subscribe to current norms of behaviour and try to narrate their own identity.

But there is a second volume to this biography of jeans. Consumers in Europe and North America are involved in another concealed chain of activity, where the relationships between people and the creation and capture of value and profit are even more obscure than those that are hidden from view within the new jeans system of provision. Used jeans and other second-hand clothes are internationally recycled and traded from the rich to the poor. This second life cycle also stretches across continents and unequally connects diverse people. The story of jeans continues after the wearer has grown tired of them and donated them to a charity or recycler for reuse. From here they are resold to a commercial operator, processed, packaged and exported, resold again, and can be retailed in a market like the one in Mozambique seen in the introduction. Alternate trajectories for used jeans and other garments are picked up and discussed alongside the broader impacts of fast fashion throughout this book.

Theorizing production and consumption

There are two important lessons to learn from this chapter. The first is simple: there is a spatial division of labour in the clothing sector. Tasks are undertaken in places where they are enabled by different factors of production. Design takes place in studios in cosmopolitan cities, and cotton is grown where the climate and landscape allow, although, as we have seen, the story is more complicated than the natural environment and basic economic geography determining production alone. It is not nature that has led us to this geographical difference between spaces of production and places of consumption. Uneven development is the result of social cleavages that have divided society and is a historical and material process. This is explored later through evidence from across the globe.

The second lesson is that jeans and their constituent parts – like any commodities – are not just 'things', but are also a set of social relationships: a link between a farmer and a cotton trader, a connection between a factory owner and a sewing machine operator, or a cultural symbol purchased by a teenager. The social relationships, which are positions of power and dependency in economic transactions, are also in no way *natural*. To explain this we must examine how we use jeans. Jeans, like any 'thing', have a basic *use value*: on the one hand, they can be worn to provide warmth and protection; on the other hand, various types of jeans are considered to be more or less stylish, depending on the cultural context, which also affects their value. Frequently, the exchange of money which accompanies the movement of jeans between different parties in a supply chain is not directly associated with a labour activity that would make jeans *more useful*. In fact, social relations in market exchange are not connected with the material transformation of goods or an increase in use value. People get paid not for making jeans, but for making them into a commodity. It is wrong to take an element of economic activity, like the production of jeans, at face value. If we focus solely on the technical role of different types of worker in transforming material, we miss the other aspects through which value is derived. Value is socially determined and affected by factors such as advertising, fashions and trends, and not derived from the basic usefulness of a thing. The social forms of value inscribed in jeans arise from definitive contemporary and historical conditions, which can therefore by added to or eroded. A simple example would be to consider the different values which have been attached to flared or skinny jeans at various historical moments (this will become important to bear in mind when we consider the development of vintage fashions). People involved in the jeans system of provision, like designers, stylists, models and sales assistants, all play a social role in creating *symbolic value*, and the work they do is a product of culture. The reason why these well-paid jobs are carried out in the global North and not in the global South is the outcome of centuries of uneven development. This discussion of *use value* and the social determination of value is important; the

analytical context helps provide an understanding of how value
is captured and created in jeans and other new and second-hand
clothing commodities.

The arguments and theoretical framework presented in this
chapter are informed by a critical, political economy approach.
The discussion of commodities as social relationships in the
previous paragraph is broadly taken from Karl Marx's analysis of
commodity fetishism. In *Capital*, Marx illuminated how the veil
of market exchange hides the social and environmental relations
that conceal production from consumers. Producers and consumers are thereby alienated from one another. As Ben Fine succinctly
puts it, 'whilst capitalism organizes production in definite social
relationships between men, these relationships are expressed
and appear as relationships between things.'[28] This book is an
attempt to investigate connections between different types of
clothing, consumers and producers and thereby heeds the call of
the radical geographer David Harvey to 'get behind the veil, the
fetishism of the market'.[29] People buy clothes not knowing how
or where they are made; the fetishism of the commodity is such
that it even appears as if things have agency and exert control
over people and environments, rather than the ability to modify
conditions of production and consumption being central to social
relations under capitalism.

Studies of connections between production and consumption
have proliferated across a range of academic disciplines – including anthropology, business studies, cultural studies, economics, geography and sociology – and scholars have attempted
to research how commodities move between different places.
Journalists and documentary makers have also tried to map connections between production and consumption. This type of work
stretches between the developing and developed world and has
contributed to surveying the different contours of globalization;
for example, newspaper exposés of labour conditions in mobile

phone factories in China or documentaries on pesticide use on banana plantations in Nicaragua. Yet this type of research tends to be American- or Eurocentric, in so far as consumption in the global North is usually the entry point for most of these interventions. What is secondary is the consumer in the global South. This book begins to redress the balance through consideration of case studies from Africa and elsewhere in the global South which show how the poor are incorporated into cycles of consumption. Allied to this problem is the fact that many academics have been diverted by post-structuralism (a philosophical movement championed by critical theorists that examines the instability and complexity of human interactions), which has led them away from the grand economic theories of Karl Marx, David Ricardo and Adam Smith to a new group of approaches which privilege the role of individuals in determining commodity flows. Principally, post-structural commodity research often begins with the consumer and traces back to the connections between a specific good and individual producers. This book instead takes a more holistic approach, looking at how systems of provision have developed, and considering the relationships between production and consumption, which includes the hidden undercurrents of globalization.

This biography has sketched out the form of new jeans systems of provision. However, there are also other systems of provision that determine the flow of second-hand jeans around the world, and bring denim to Mario's stall in Mozambique. Second-hand clothes are the mainstay of many markets across the global South; chapters 3 and 6 explain how these little-known trade patterns have emerged. Mario's small business and his struggles to provide for his family, as well as the livelihoods of millions of other people involved in the making and selling of new and second-hand clothes are much more important and socially interesting than the particular origins and lifespan of a pair of Levi's 501s.

In that respect this is a book not about clothes but about people. To explore the full effects of the fast-fashion industry on billions of people it was necessary to think first about the manufacturing and retail of a new clothing commodity. The next step in understanding the relationships between clothes and poverty is to look at how and why the unequal geographical relationships in garment production and consumption have emerged. This necessitates a brief history of clothing and capitalism.

CHAPTER 2

Clothes and capital

Bra wars

Economic globalization has transformed the world. Making, trading and selling commodities like jeans is part of a dynamic global market system that shapes everyone's lives. What can be thought of as 'the official' or mainstream story of globalization begins with the line of argument that Britain – soon followed by Europe and North America – first adopted liberal free-market and free-trade policies in the eighteenth century to promote world economic development.[1] Liberal or laissez-faire approaches to trade involved removing barriers that constrain the free flow of goods and investment. Barriers to trade include duties (payments levied on goods), quotas (fixed numbers of imports) and protectionism (shielding domestic industry from foreign competition). According to popular history, liberal reforms by the early English pioneers of commerce removed trade barriers, freeing the market and enabling capital and products to circulate around the world. It was the superiority of these policies that led to the spectacular success of the global North. Free trade is commonly seen as the mechanism by which economic growth and prosperity are derived.

One of the main means by which laissez-faire approaches to trade policy are promoted today is the World Trade Organization (WTO). This global body represents 159 member states and both supervises and liberalizes international trade. A key function of the WTO is to resolve disputes between member states. Recent examples of quarrels include some curious-sounding cases: China and the European Union (EU) disagreed over duties relating to X-ray machines; Turkey banned imports of Hungarian pet food; South Korea disputed Japanese quotas on dried and seasoned laver (seaweed); and Costa Rica complained about Trinidad and Tobago's anti-dumping measures relating to macaroni and spaghetti. Among the varied disputes associated with barriers to trade are many examples relating to clothing products, including American textiles, Argentine leather, Australian boots, Egyptian apparel and Indian cotton. WTO dispute settlements are designed to ensure trade flows smoothly and so play an important role in governing the global circulation of clothing.[2] China was a relative latecomer to the WTO, joining in 2001 following difficult negotiations. In 2005, China and the European Union were involved in a major trade dispute over clothing. This clash garnered much greater public attention than their disagreement over X-ray equipment and exposes how, rather than promoting free trade and open markets, European states have actually hidden behind protectionism and long benefited from uneven terms of trade.

The so-called 'bra wars' were a dispute that erupted after quotas under the Multi-Fiber Arrangement (MFA), which restricted the imports of Chinese textiles and clothing to Europe, were removed on 1 January 2005. Contrary to the official version of globalization, European clothing and textile industries have always been safeguarded by trade barriers such as the MFA; indeed the long-term development of European economies has been preceded by centuries of protection for important industrial sectors, as will be expanded upon later. Many of the barriers to

garment imports were finally phased out in 2005 and the full costs
of free trade were suddenly to be borne by European factories.
However, across the continent manufacturers were not prepared
for the increased competition. Following their urgent complaints
some 80 million Chinese-made garments, including 48 million
pullovers, 18 million pairs of trousers and 11 million bras, were
blocked at European ports by new barriers to trade. In a gift to
headline writers the dispute was soon christened 'bra wars', as
clothing piled up in warehouses and customs checkpoints across
the continent. The flood of cheap garments was temporarily
stemmed, but many of the shipments had already been paid for
by retailers, who were enraged and faced the prospect of empty
shelves. Scare stories of a 'run on bras' soon circulated in the
tabloid press. Across the Atlantic, the administration of George
W. Bush imposed similar barriers restricting the import of bras
and other garments.[3]

This was not how free trade was meant to work. Wealthy
developed countries were implementing politically expedient
protectionism. Free-trade advocates saw this as kicking away
the ladder to prosperity – removing the steps up to industrial
progress that enabled the Western economies to develop. The
theory that free trade would enable civilization to flourish and
prosper via their comparative advantage was not being put into
practice. European intransigence meant that China was being
prevented from utilizing its huge modern factories and vast pool
of cheap labour to drive forward development.

European governments may have been united in the EU
common trade bloc, but were politically divided. France, Italy and
Spain, all with significant clothing sectors, called for protection,
whereas the more ideologically committed northern European
governments, especially Denmark and the UK, opposed barriers
to trade. The neoliberal (or 'new' liberal) right called for the
European Union to refocus on developing industries that could be ,

globally competitive and retraining former textile workers when
their jobs migrate. They argued that short-term protection of
dying industries would only harm low-income European consumers. Caught in the middle was the EU trade commissioner, Peter
Mandelson, a divisive British politician whose instincts led him
to the liberal right of centre. Following the customary 'gruelling
all-night negotiating session' Mandelson and his Chinese counterpart, Bo Xilai, brokered a complicated fix, which led to the bras
and other garments reaching the shops. The message which came
out of their meeting in Beijing was that the 'Textile wars have
been blown out of all proportion', in Mandelson's words, and that
moving forward the two parties would work to build stronger ties
as one another's first or second largest trading partner.[4] This was
a victory for globalization.

But who are the real winners and losers of a globalized economy
and free trade? Wages in China are a fraction of those in the
EU. Modern garments such as bras have complicated designs
made of up to forty-three different component parts and are
labour-intensive to produce, as delicate sections of fabric, elastic
and fasteners must be stitched together. Labour costs make the
difference in this relatively low-tech sector. The truce that came
out of the bra wars offered only temporary relief for European
manufacturers; since then jobs have been lost throughout the EU
clothing sector, while production in China has surged forward.
Governments play a key role in facilitating globalization as they
negotiate the liberalization of markets. The bra wars dispute was
a transitional step towards freer trade. Removing barriers to trade
enables the further spatial advance of capitalism, which must
be understood as the greatest force for transforming the world.
Capital and commodities such as clothing are the lifeblood which
flows through the body politic. Liberal economists and their
proponents on the political right would lead us to believe that
barriers to trade are deeply unhealthy for the global economy,

and that eliminating them will have an effect akin to coronary surgery to remove fatty deposits on the walls of arteries; dangerous blockages are avoided, and after convalescing the patient is restored to health and vitality. While offering a seemingly logical diagnosis, when we look at how tension is globally built up and released, we see that there is something diseased at the heart of capitalism; rather than moving towards an even and stable status, inequality and catastrophe are the unavoidable prognosis. The bra wars were a painful episode on the road towards a major crisis.

Crises of capitalism

One threat every business faces is the challenge of the falling rate of profit in established markets, for instance when clothing shops spread and saturate a territory.[5] So when people make money they look for new places in which to invest. Successful businesses are inherently expansionist. Clothing manufacturers look for low-cost locations to make garments and new marketplaces in which to sell their brands. Investors want to circumvent constraints on trade and compete in new regions. There have long been tensions between the state and business in controlling access to labour and the market, but the outcome persistently results in governments being overridden by the political rule of capital. Despite attempts to fence in production through protectionist measures, in the long run capitalism breaks free and stalks the earth in search of new territories to conquer. Daily life has come to depend upon the production of commodities through a system that has profit-seeking as its principal and socially accepted goal. Central to the vivacity of capitalism is the need for new investment opportunities to maintain profit growth. When too much capital is accumulated in one place it must be reinvested in a new area and therefore seeks out what is known as a 'spatial fix'.[6] Driven by the logic of maximizing profitability, investment spreads to occupy and seek a 'fix' in new spaces. It is this expansionist urge which has pushed bra production out of Europe and pulled Chinese factories towards the pre-eminent position in the global garment trade.

The need to expand and grow is at the centre of the capitalist mode of production and is linked to another important feature: the crisis-prone nature of capitalism. When we look back at the past two centuries we see clear evidence that capitalism is inherently ridden by crises. At a global scale these manifest as episodes of severe financial crisis, which occur when there is devaluation or a drastic loss of capital. Mega-events include the recent banker-led financial crisis of 2007–08, the oil crises of 1973–74 and 1979–83, the Wall Street Crash of 1929, the Long Depression of 1873–96, as well as the Panic of 1825 when the Bank of England was on the brink of collapse. In between the large worldwide systemic crashes, smaller crises occur on a regional scale. This happens when tension builds as capital encounters limits and barriers, such as protectionism, labour problems, technological failings, natural limits and a lack of effective demand, which can slow down or disrupt capital flows. There are multiple ways in which different crises can form in various historical and geographical contexts; the efforts of capitalism to overcome these barriers have become part of the history of economic development and change.[7]

In the short term investors can avoid the impacts of crises by taking advantage of the 'spatial fix', and flows of capital can be switched between places. Relocating factories enables businesses to temporarily overcome the falling rate of profit. Moving manufacturing to new lower wage locations mitigates the chance of a crisis of production in sectors such as clothing; hence garment manufacturing moved from Europe to Asia. Crises, though, can only be temporarily avoided. The spatial fix is not a real solution to the internal contradictions of capitalism; it merely moves the crises around, producing, as David Harvey explains, 'an uneven, unstable and tension-packed geographical landscape for production, exchange and consumption' that peri-odically erupts as a major global crisis.[8] Tensions build through unequal geographical development and bring about disruption and destruction to social and ecological systems, which are felt at particular places and times. The bra wars constituted one of countless historical moments when the switching of labour and capital resulted in a minor crisis, and were also a harbinger of the general global financial crisis of 2007–08.

Minor crises of capitalism have real human impacts. The bra wars did not cause long-term disruption to overall production and consumption of clothing, as these both expanded, but had social effects in different places. Following the bra wars, em-ployment in EU fashion manufacturing fell from 2.9 million to 1.9 million between 2004 and 2009, affecting some of the less prosperous regions of Europe.[9] Meanwhile, labour conditions in China involve the large-scale exploitation of predominately female workers. Crises have diverse social impacts and amplify uneven geographical development.

In spite of crisis, the market still operates. Rapid cycles of purchasing and disposing of garments continue and have severe environmental effects. The inherently expansionary logic of capitalism means profit growth in the clothing sector is based upon more and more consumption. Shopping for fast fashion is relentlessly encouraged. Retailers, somewhat unrealistically, suggest bras have a life expectancy of just 6–9 months and must be regularly replaced.[10] Bras are made of materials such as nylon and polyester, produced from petrochemicals that do not bio-degrade; spandex, which is energy-intensive to manufacture; and latex, which, although a natural material, is often produced using methods that result in deforestation and biodiversity loss.

The long history of changing modes of production and the global spread of trade are examined through the prism of the clothing sector in this chapter. We start with the development of weaving in early societies, then move on to explore the role of textiles and clothing in feudal kingdoms, colonialism, the Industrial Revolution and the expansion of capitalism up until the early twentieth century. Focusing on the social impacts of economic change, evidence will demonstrate how barriers to trade, including protectionism, were utilized in the textile trade to enable the economies of Europe and North America to grow. Uneven terms of trade helped produce the different levels of development in the global North and South, but protectionist measures in clothing production are now being overcome by economic globalization. Following the brief history of clothes and capital, the more recent story of twentieth-century globalization, including the negotiation of the MFA, and the growth of today's fast-fashion systems are discussed. Given the vast sweep of human history covered, the material is precised to offer just a keyhole look at massive shifts in political economy. Later in the book, as the hidden world of clothes unfolds, in-depth case studies of specific clothing systems of provision provide the story with far more nuanced human detail and give more examples of the crises formed by globalization.

The origins of clothes and uneven development

A history of early clothing begins with the origins of society and culture. People worked collectively in social groups to make garments that protect, cover and decorate. Like all 'stuff', clothing comes from the 'natural world' and could only be made once humans had mastered the ability to produce a permanent social surplus from nature – that is, reliably generating more food, drink and shelter than is needed to sustain life from the soils, water, flora and fauna. In the long run, by extracting surplus from nature, people also irreversibly changed the environment. Over time the expansion of human activity has transformed the planet, leading to global environmental change. Recently, humankind has transgressed planetary boundaries, most notably causing mass biodiversity loss, disrupting the global nitrogen cycle and transforming the global climate, to the extent that today there no longer exists a natural world outside of human interference.[11]

In ancient times, with the emergence of early societies, the production of surplus from nature enabled the division of labour. Some people came to live from the excess produce others generated, presenting new possibilities to organize communities into hierarchical social structures. Increased social diversification accompanied growth in production and population. New groups of people not directly involved in working with nature to produce surplus food and other goods for subsistence emerged, including teachers, rulers, priests, artisans and warriors. They engaged in new social, cultural and political activities, sharing knowledge, exercising power, forming religions and making art and war, while others became specialist craftspeople producing new goods or *use values*, such as weavers and tailors who made cloths and garments.[12]

The production of surplus from nature is necessary for the exchange of use values to occur, and then to enable production for exchange to develop. For instance, grain could only be exchanged for wool once there was a surplus of grain from farming. Throughout most of human history clothing has been difficult to access. Most people had few garments, as the overall surplus produced from the natural world was small, enabling limited production for exchange. There were constraints to human activity and clothing production was in essence ecologically sustainable. In societies where surplus production grew and social organization further diversified, production for exchange developed. Commercial activities and a market function separate from production grew to facilitate complex exchange transactions. Crucially money emerged to mediate the exchange of different types of commodity produced from nature. Money enabled the farmer to repeatedly sell his grain on the market, save up, and then later purchase a shirt from a tailor using the cumulative surplus earned from many harvests. The tailor could then return to the market and purchase cloth with the money earned to make new shirts, as well as buying bread to satisfy his own hunger.

The theory behind the development of the market is universal, but different environmental and cultural conditions enabled varied types of clothes making. Early societies across the world independently developed woven fabrics and used animal products to make clothing. The cultivation of clothing fibres accompanied the emergence of early cereal-based agriculture between 8,000 and 2,000 BCE, which originated in many different major cultural regions around the world. Early domesticated fibres included flax for linen grown in the Middle East and south-west Asia, hemp in China, and cotton in the Andes, Amazonia, India, Mesoamerica, West Africa and the Sahel.[13] Environments were important in enabling the development of plant agricultural and also animal husbandry, for hides and wools. However, one must not fall into the trap of environmental determinism and think that the physical environment alone, such as geology, landforms or climate, determines patterns of human culture and social development; the environment may set possibilities, but does not define culture. Rather, culture is defined by the opportunities presented and the choices people make in dealing with limits. There is no one habitable place or group of people innately more inventive in growing crops, rearing animals or making clothes, as all human beings share the same basic psychological capabilities.

Equally, agricultural systems and clothes-making did not 'diffuse' between places, like a contagious disease emerging outward from some permanent centre that represents a source or innate 'cultural hearth'; a place where land-use changes led to creativity and invention. Yes, ideas spread between neighbouring villages and tribes and endemic species were traded from their native areas, but at the scale of major cultural regions there was the independent invention of early technologies, including agriculture, money, sail, wheel and clothes-making. There is no innate 'modern' core and peripheral 'traditional' sectors to the world. Diffusionist beliefs, which predominate in environmental determinist accounts (like those of the widely popular Jared Diamond), stem from a colonial view of the world. Although colonialism itself *is* a diffusion process, diffusionism is misused to justify the subjugation and oppression that accompanied colonialism as somehow 'normal, natural, inevitable, and moral' because it bestowed 'civilization' on areas of the world considered 'savage'.[14]

Societies transitioned between different modes of production, from hunter–gather communities to feudal kingdoms and later to capitalist nations. Evidence points to the development of various capitalisms in merchant and maritime urban centres in dispersed cultural regions from Western Europe to eastern Asia and southern Africa. Yet there was not a straightforward teleological march through history from a less developed 'primitive' stage to today's globalized economy. Instead the interaction between communities and the differential levels of affluence and impoverishment experienced by varied groups across space led to patterns of uneven development, and ultimately to the geography of production and consumption in the global clothing trade.

European nations came to drive forward globalization and dominate world trade, including the clothing and textile sector, over the last 500 years. Differing theories explore how Europe came to dominate global trade, but one of the most convincing arguments is that an important factor gave Western Europe an advantage. The injection of gold and silver from the New World after 1492 provided resources in the form of *exchange value* (valuable currency) that propelled European merchant capital towards political power. Once emboldened by the power of transatlantic trade, capital wrested political control from Europe's feudal masters – the centuries-old dynasties of kings and queens which had monopolized legal authority – and then later destroyed political power and social groups elsewhere in the colonized world.[15]

Clothing in ancient society

The background history detailed above is important for understanding uneven development. However, as the political economy has got ahead of the social and cultural story of clothes, some infilling needs to be done to account for how garment production and consumption changed on a human scale.

Early people, 100,000 years ago, probably did not wear clothing at all. It was only when humans migrated from East Africa to colder (or possibly hotter) climates that people first came to clothe themselves using animal skins for protection. The origins of clothing remain speculative as there exists little evidence from the Paleolithic (Stone Age) period. However, archeological finds do show how Stone Age people used flint knives and bone needles to butcher mammals and to sew hides and leathers. Tools found in southern Africa for working hides have been dated to at least 61,000 years ago.[16] Weaving has been dated to around 27,000 years ago, significantly pre-dating the earliest records of cereal agriculture and sedentary farming societies. Textiles themselves do not survive, but impressions of woven twill plant fibre fabrics have been found on clay artefacts in the Czech Republic from the Upper Paleolithic period. Archeologists hypothesize that weaving using gathered plant fibres may date even further back and be found elsewhere.[17]

Wool was also woven to produce garments by early humans. Producing yarns from animal hairs enabled people to reduce the weight of clothes, in comparison to using hides. Tufts of sheep wool were likely collected from thorny bushes and experimented with; people could play with the hairs, spinning yarns between their fingers and later carded wool to form fibres more easily. After the development of permanent settled agricultural societies, sheep were domesticated. Grasses and leaves could be woven together. Flax underwent beating to separate the better fibres, which enabled linen yarns to be spun. With the production of permanent social surplus, the development of hierarchical societies provided an emphasis for clothing as it denoted status within tribal groups. In early history, garments made from plant fibres, skins or wool were likely highly prized as production was costly and laborious. Ancient garments were not poorly made; good-quality articles were produced making the most of carefully collected resources. Ötzi, a well-preserved natural mummy from 5,300 years ago discovered in the Alps between Austria and Italy, was found clothed in a cloak of woven grass and wearing items made of different leathers, including a coat, belt, leggings, loincloth and shoes. Petr Hlavacek, a footwear expert, re-created Ötzi's shoes, observing that 'because the shoes are actually quite complex, I'm convinced that even 5,300 years ago, people had the equivalent of a cobbler who made shoes for other people', suggesting he lived in a socially diverse community.[18]

With social development in early civilizations, different labour roles emerged for women and men. Yarn-making became a prized skill undertaken by females at the household level in the Middle East, as is eulogized in the highly gendered language of the Old Testament:

> Who can find a virtuous woman? For her price is far above rubies ... She seeketh wool, and flax, and worketh willingly with her hands ... She layeth her hands to the spindle, and her hands hold the distaff [a tool for spinning yarn]... She maketh fine linen, and selleth it; and delivereth girdles [wraps of clothing] unto the merchant.[19]

Hebrews as well as Babylonians, Celts, Egyptians, Greeks and Romans, along with other cultural groups around the world, developed different styles of dress that often involved variations on long tunics, togas, robes, wraps, kilts and trousers, the last of which were particular to Northern Europe. Finding evidence of early clothing is difficult as natural materials break down with age. Only in rare arid, waterlogged or frozen conditions can well-preserved garments be found. Examples from Europe include items of Bronze Age clothing found in oak-log coffins in Denmark; pre-Roman and Roman age garments preserved in acidic bogs in Denmark, northern Germany, the Netherlands and Sweden, in Villanovan tombs from Italy, and in Roman burials in France. Elsewhere there are frozen mausoleums in Central Asia and the Andes and arid tombs in the deserts of the Middle East.[20]

The examples discussed above are rather European- and Middle Eastern-centric, reflecting the balance of research that has been carried out in the field of ancient clothing. Elsewhere other patterns of dress and networks of exchange developed. Some of West Africa's early history of clothing production and trade is explored in Chapter 4. Detailing the changes in costume, the different materials used throughout the ages, and the styles of dress found across the whole world would involve a cultural history of every social group. Rather than offering the socio-cultural story of different local clothing systems of provision found in, say, the Inca Empire, Moorish Spain or the Khmer kingdom, the subject of the remainder of this chapter is the change from local and regional patterns of trade to the international circulation of clothing commodities, which was part of the transition to, and expansion of, capitalism.

Protected trade in the feudal era

This chapter opened with a contemporary case study of trade protectionism, yet barriers to trade are not a recent phenomenon; governments have long attempted to defend and promote special interests and indigenous clothing and textile sectors. One of the earliest well-documented examples of regulation comes from alliances between garment and fabric guilds and the Crown in England. Guilds were membership societies paid for by subscriptions that afforded their patrons specific benefits. Funds raised by the medieval weavers' guild of London were used to make a contribution to the royal Treasury, for which in exchange guild members were granted exclusive rights and privileges by the King. The first recorded payment was in 1130, and thereafter guild members were able to exercise powers such as punish defaulters in their own court who failed to pay subscriptions, or other weavers that encroached upon their trade. By the mid-twelfth century the guild had established a cartel and was very powerful as the cloth trade was the basis of England's economy throughout the Middle Ages. Their monopoly frustrated consumers, who were faced with high prices, as well as prospective producers outside the guild, some of whom moved overseas.

In 1321 the situation changed and freemen were allowed to set up looms and sell cloth, so long as the King received his tax. Edward III enabled expanded production as he realized the broader value of a managed cloth trade to the English economy. The weavers' guild lost its pre-eminence and other textile guilds developed, including the mercers, drapers, merchant tailors, haberdashers and clothworkers; descendants of many of these guilds survive today as the livery companies of the City of London. The King forbade the export of unprocessed wool and the import of foreign cloth, yet at the same time recognized the value of skilled immigrants. Flemish weavers, discontented with conditions in Flanders, were encouraged to bring their skills to England.[21] Additional protectionist barriers imposed by Edward III included restrictions on what normal people could wear, which remained in place until at least 1571 and the reign of Elizabeth I. Aside from the upper classes, everyone had to wear English-made woollen cloth. Dressing in purple, scarlet, crimson or blue cloth was prohibited as these fabrics were coloured with imported dyes. Constraints on trade and costume were also found in other feudal societies. Elsewhere in Europe, German towns such as Strasbourg enforced similar ordinances requiring people to wear local cloth, while in France there were attempts to control imports such as fabric from Flanders, lace from Milan and materials from China. Outside Europe, in seventeenth-century Japan efforts to control dress restricted ordinary townspeople to plainer cottons and silks, and the Ming, Qing and Manchu dynasties in China all had official styles of dress that signalled acquiescence to imperial authority.[22] These historic examples from feudal eras all share some basic similarity to the way that pre-2005 the European Union market was protected from Chinese competition by the MFA.

Protectionism was important in developing clothing and textile sectors. The transition from artisanal making to industrial cloth manufacturing centred on Europe, and in many ways this progression is archetypal of the continent's rise to the pinnacle of global power from the sixteenth century onwards. Especially significant in spurring the expansion of manufacturing were the colonial projects, which brought new raw materials and markets under European control. Colonial missions were initiated to further satisfy the personal desires and political appetites of feudal rulers. Before the Columbian exchange era was launched, luxury clothing for the elite was already traded over vast distances. Exotic fabrics from distant lands denoted wealth, power and status. The silk roads stretching from Europe to China via the Middle East and Central Asia became conduits for the exchange of ideas, goods and culture. Trade networks were also sources of conflict and tension, which prompted explorers to investigate new oceanic routes. Christopher Columbus's voyage to America was infamously motivated by a desire to find a new passage to

Asia to access valuable goods, including luxury silk and spices as well as satisfy the hunger for precious gold and silver.

At the same time as Columbus's great discovery other Iberian adventurers were voyaging out of Spain and Portugal. Key was the rounding of the Cape of Good Hope and the southern tip of Africa by Portuguese explorer Bartolomeu Dias in 1488 and later voyages by his compatriot Vasco da Gama, which opened up trade links with the Far East. Maritime exploration led to new forms of interactions between Europeans and the rest of the world and the era of colonialism began. Sustained contact in the long term meant new relationships in one of three modes: as relatively privileged foreigner traders in new lands (Jesuits in China and Portuguese in Japan), as conquers and dominators of existing societies (French in West Africa and British in India), or as invasive land clearers who decimated and supplanted aboriginal communities (British, French and Spanish in the Americas). The three types are a simplification; in reality different combinations, varieties and forms of interaction took place depending on context. China, for instance, although never formally colonized, was subservient to European mercantilist interests, especially after the British victory in the Opium Wars, which removed protection and opened up China to trade. European traders then benefited from a series of unequal treaties during the nineteenth and early twentieth centuries. Chapter 4 provides a detailed account of how formal and 'modernizing' colonialism worked in different parts of Africa, including the repugnant transatlantic trade in slaves. One of the most significant outcomes of the early colonial period was that it introduced the cotton trade to Europe. The international circulation of cotton and cotton products, while not the only material that played an important role in clothing and textile economies, became key to catalysing the Industrial Revolution in the North of England.

Capitalism and the Industrial Revolution

Mention of the Industrial Revolution conjures up images of brick-built factories, billowing tall smokestacks, heavy kinetic machinery and an army of industrial workers toiling away weaving textiles, none of which existed before the late eighteenth century. Like every major revolution it represented a qualitative and fundamental transformation in society. Arguably it is the most important global event since the establishment of hierarchical societies based on a permanent social surplus, and was certainly wider ranging than the more evocative American, Chinese, French or Russian Revolutions. The large-scale movement from handicraft tools to mechanized devices, which took off from about the 1780s with the increased use of machines like power looms in Northern England, transformed not only cloth production but social relations across industrialized societies. Machines began to perform work formerly done by self-employed artisanal labour, leading to massive increases in productivity. For instance, a human cotton spinner could operate one spinning wheel and use just one spindle to form cotton fibres in to thread, whereas the invention in 1764 of the spinning jenny in Lancashire helped revolutionize production so that eight or more spindles could operate in concert. Pivotal during this epoch was the transition of women and men from being sources of skilled motive power to machine operators. Labourers spent hours in dimly lit factories, listening to the constant clatter of machines and diligently watching woven material appear, then correcting mechanisms and mistakes. As Frederick Engels records in *The Conditions of The Working-Class in England*,

> The consequences of this were on the one hand, a rapid fall
> in the price of all manufactured commodities, prosperity
> of commerce and manufacturing, the conquest of nearly all
> unprotected foreign markets [by British made cloth], the sudden

multiplication of capital and national wealth; on the other hand a still more rapid multiplication of the proletariat, the destruction of all property-holding and of all security of employment for the working-class, demoralization, [and] political excitement.[23]

Factory employment necessitated widespread changes to work patterns, which redrew social hierarchies. Society became polarized between two classes: the wage-earning, hard-working proletariat and the vampire-like capitalist class of bourgeois industrialists. One sucked *surplus value* from the other in the form of profit. Now, it is worth briefly considering how wage labour is exploited to produce profit by capitalists. An hour's labour has, like any commodity, a value equal to the cost of its purchase; if one works for £10 an hour one's labour-power is a commodity that costs one's employer £10 per hour. In any profitable business the contribution made by labour-power to the value of a product is greater than the wage received for that work. All surplus value (or profit) is created by the *exploitation* of labour. This is best demonstrated by example. Suppose you work eight hours a day weaving cotton and make 100 yards of cloth, which sell for £160. The necessary labour to produce your wage is half a day's work as 50 yards of cloth is equal to £80 or eight times your £10-per-hour wage. Now assume the cost of maintaining the means of production – the cost of the cotton yarn and pro-rata investment in weaving machines and factory – amounts to a further £10. Therefore, for three hours each day you work for 'free' for the capitalist and they extract £70 of surplus value from your labour in the form of the profit they realize when they sell the 100 yards of cloth (£80 Wage + £10 Means of Production + £70 Surplus Value = £160). [24]

Rates of exploitation continue to increase as long as the socially accepted imperative of capital is to expand and generate ever greater profit. Competing and expanding firms seek to drive profits forward. There are two means to maximize the exploitation of labour. The first is by brute force: using exist-ing work processes and technology, more surplus value can be produced by increasing the length of the working day or simply cutting salaries. Second, via technological change the cost of labour-power can be reduced.[25] This was kick-started in the Industrial Revolution as labour was more finely divided into specific tasks, new machines and factories were used, and the pace of work increased. Technology was not the only leverage for increasing profitability, as brute force was also applied. Textile workers' wages were relentlessly suppressed in the eighteenth and nineteenth centuries. This was socially and culturally justified by the emerging bourgeoisie as low pay was deemed to increase productivity. As an English businessman of the time observed, extending working hours and suppressing wages could go hand in hand with crude attempts to justify social modernization:

> The manufacturer who can subsist on three days' work will be idle and drunken the remainder of the week... The poor in the manufacturing counties will never work any more time in general than is necessary just to live and support their weekly debauches... We can fairly aver that a reduction of wages in the woollen manufacture would be a national blessing and advan-tage, and no real injury to the poor. By this means we might keep our trade, uphold our rents, and reform the people into the bargain.[26]

At the heart of the Industrial Revolution, and its defining characteristic, was the factory-based system of provision, which facilitated exploitation and generated goods in such vast quantities and at diminishing costs that they formed their own markets for cloth products. But why did these factories emerge? The simple answer is profit; buying cheap and selling dear was the incentive. Yet why then? And why there? How were countless early British entrepreneurs to know that a radical shift in social organization would deliver great profits? Well, the Revolution did not have a definite beginning or end; nor did it have a revolutionary leader or grand architect. What came to be known as the Industrial Revolution occurred in Northern England because of the particular political context, and not due to a single event, intellectual refinement or technical innovation. Although technologies were a precondition, some industrial manufacturing approaches preceded the Industrial Revolution, and neighbouring France and Germany had made comparable scientific advances. Rather, the political context was the ultimate causal factor: Britain was ready and primed for an exponential growth in the capitalist mode of production as it was an expansionist nation where money talked and governed. The political system had long been influenced by commercial powers (like the earlier trading guilds), coupled to which maritime Britain was already the major colonial power. The political rule of capital propelled the Industrial Revolution.

The late Marxist historian Eric Hobsbawm recognized that two fundamentals preconditions were required in addition to the political context: 'first an industry which already offered exceptional rewards for the manufacturer who could expand his output quickly, if need be by reasonably cheap and simple innovations, and second, a *world* market largely monopolized by a single nation'.[27] The combination of political context and specific preconditions applied to Britain alone and most importantly in one industry: textiles. The cotton sector had developed with British colonial expansion overseas. The inhuman slave plantations of the West Indies first provided the bulk of raw cotton for industries in Manchester, Liverpool and other cities; thereafter English cotton cloth exports went to West Africa and the North American colonies. The colonial trade in cloth as well as garments proved to be highly lucrative and overseas markets expanded in a rapid and unpredictable manner, without ready limits. While individually the colonized areas of Africa, Asia and South America provided small markets for textiles and other

British goods, collectively a huge customer base was held in a near monopoly by the early nineteenth century. With the support of the British government the colonial market boomed. Expansion of trade was facilitated by policies such as those implemented in India, where the mercantilist interests of the East India Company systematically deindustrialized and underdeveloped the subcontinent and produced a captive market for Lancashire woven cotton cloth. At the same time protectionist laws enacted in Britain in the 1700s banned the import of textiles made in India.

The scene was set for social transformation and the expansion of capitalism around the world. To capitalize on the expanding foreign market early English industrialists had to use new technologies and were tempted to take risks to adopt revolutionary techniques in organizing labour, spurring the development of factories. Colonialism helped form the demand which pump-primed the emergence of industrial capitalism; once up and running, the age of industry gained its own momentum.

Capital and colonial expansion

Developments in English textile manufacturing had global impacts and helped propel British industrial supremacy in the nineteenth century. Once Britain had shown the way and demonstrated the profitability of the factory system, the approaches were rapidly imitated and skills and capital were imported by neighbouring countries. English experts and investment travelled to continental Europe and also moved across to North America, spreading the ideas and enabling factories to be developed in societies that shared some of the preconditions. Factories would later multiply out from New York across the 'Rust Belt' of the USA. Elsewhere in America, cotton sales influenced the trajectory of economic growth in the Southern slave states, including North and South Carolina, Georgia, Alabama and Mississippi. Raw cotton imports to the UK grew from less than 5 million pounds in weight in 1771 to 528 million pounds by 1841.[28] Ginned cotton from the South also became an important input into early industrialization in the northern United States and exports of cotton were sent elsewhere in Europe.

The effect of the emergence and expansion of capitalism and the factory were inherently spatial; while what would become the global North experienced economic development, the rest of the world paid the price. Colonized territories were drawn into the service of industrial economies. Africa, Asia and South America were underdeveloped as local artisan production declined in the face of competition and people were forced to supply raw materials for the industrial powers, which established the patterns of uneven development found across the world today. Marx, writing in 1867, observed these processes at first hand and merits quoting at length:

On the one hand, the immediate effect of machinery is to increase the supply of raw material in the same way, for example, as the cotton gin augmented [stimulated] the production of cotton. On the other hand, the cheapness of the articles produced by machinery, and the improved means of transport and communication furnish the weapons for conquering foreign markets. By ruining handicraft production in other countries, machinery forcibly converts them into fields for the supply of its raw material. In this way East India was compelled to produce cotton, wool, hemp, jute, and indigo for Great Britain. By constantly making a part of the hands 'supernumerary', modern industry, in all countries where it has taken root, gives a spur to emigration and to the colonisation of foreign lands, which are thereby converted into settlements for growing the raw material of the mother country; just as Australia, for example, was converted into a colony for growing wool. A new and international division of labour, a division suited to the requirements of the chief centres of modern industry springs up, and converts one part of the globe into a chiefly agricultural field of production, for supplying the other part which remains a chiefly industrial field.[29]

While textiles and clothing were not the only industrial sectors structuring the uneven development of the global economy, they clearly played a major role. The history of capitalism is bound up in the progress of textile and apparel production in Europe and North America in the eighteenth and nineteenth centuries. As the great nation-state powers of the colonial era expanded overseas, new territories were drawn into the capitalist mode of production, and market integration gradually drew nearly all society worldwide into one economic system. The Industrial Revolution brought the world's first global clothing systems of provision into operation.

Away from Europe and North America the influence of colonial powers – principally Britain, France, Germany, Italy and Portugal – alongside the cultural, political and economic weight of the United States, and the spread of Christianity, projected Western patterns of dress onto the colonized world. Not just cloth but also finished clothing was exported from the metropoles: key European industrial cities like Manchester and Paris to colonial capitals such as Delhi and Saigon. Colonial elites and assimilated populations purchased male buttoned dress shirts, cotton khaki trousers and leather shoes, alongside long ladies' dresses and embroidered lace. Native employees were dressed in formal service dress or industrial uniforms of caps, jackets, overalls and dungarees. In different regions the adoption or rejection of European styles of dress demonstrated acquiescence to or confrontation with different forms of authority, as people aspired to equality with, or exerted their autonomy from, the Western world. [30]

Later, dress became a key terrain for opposition to British rule in India. Foremost was Mohandas Gandhi's role as an anti-colonial leader and the pattern of dress he adopted in response to British oppression. For two centuries weavers throughout the Indian subcontinent had been driven out of business and into poverty by the expanding trade in English textiles. British business had even conspired with the colonial authorities to cut off the fingers of Bengali weavers and broken their looms to create captive markets. As Jeremy Seabrook documents,

> The future champion of free trade destroyed the fabrics indus-
> try in Bengal before Britain attained pre-eminence in textile
> manufacturing... As a result, the spinners and weavers of Bengal
> fell into the greatest penury. Dacca [Dhaka], centre of muslin
> production, became a deserted city: tigers and leopards roamed
> once-prosperous streets, and by the 1820s the city of men had
> become a city of animals. Weavers' dwellings were overgrown,
> the thatch alive with birds, snakes and insects... The first
> great de-industrialisation of the modern world had begun. The
> population of Dacca fell from several hundred thousand in 1760
> to about 50,000 by the 1820s. By this time, Manchester's rise
> had become irresistible. Bengal's abandonment of ancient crafts
> appears in Britain as a fable of our progress and entrepreneurial
> genius. To the desolate weavers, it meant the collapse of their
> world; and Bengal, famine-stricken, impoverished, reverted to
> agriculture.[31]

Capitalist expansion had brought crisis to India, transforming the economic geography and impoverishing the populace. India exported raw cotton to Britain where it was manufactured into clothing and then exported back to India; this process was effectively paid for by the export of other raw materials and created a relationship of structural dependency. British protectionism and trade policy blocked Indian industrialization in a process repeated across the colonized world.[32]

Gandhi recognized the tyranny at the heart of British Imperial policy and would come to play a foremost role in the independence struggle. Having previously adopted Western-style clothing when he studied law in London, Gandhi later became associated with a dramatically different costume. After graduating, and when working in South Africa, he engaged in radical politics. Gandhi began speaking out against minority rule and swapped his English suits for simple white cotton attire. On returning to India in 1915, Gandhi adopted his iconic loincloth and shawl, despite hailing from a prosperous merchant family. His style of dress was not widely imitated as he led the struggle for Indian nationalism; it was too closely associated with social egalitarianism and did not unite Muslim, Hindu and Sikh groups. However, Gandhi's costume formed part of a powerful cultural and economic protest movement. The loincloth was made from *khadi*, traditional homespun, undyed cloth, woven on a hand loom, which became a symbol for the independence struggle. Nationalists were encouraged by Gandhi to spin *khadi* daily for half an hour, partly as meditation and partly to provide competition for imported machine-made cloth. Boycotts of foreign goods became a core strategy of the Indian independence movement alongside non-violent protest. *Khadi* cloth cut in different ways, such as the Nehru jacket, would become de rigueur for Indian leaders for decades to come.[33]

Capitalism adapts in the twentieth century

The twentieth century was an age of extremes that saw rapid and fundamental changes to society in every corner of the world, from the cottonfields of rural India to the declining industrial towns of Northern England, to the rising suburbs of Middle America, and the booming industries of Eastern China. Rather than summarize the myriad transformations, some reflections on the reorganization of global political economy and changing patterns of dress are presented here.

At the turn of the twentieth century a major development spread across the industrialized world of North America and Western Europe. 'Fordism' was a term popularized by the Italian Marxist Antonio Gramsci to refer to a new approach to organizing industry for which Henry Ford's car factories provided the model. New production-line techniques were developed drawing on the ideas of Frederick W. Taylor, which promoted the scientific management of workers, who had to repeatedly perform static and standardized tasks.[34] Workers were assigned set roles in manufacturing processes to enhance the efficiency of production. A division of labour emerged between workers performing unskilled repetitive tasks and those in skilled and managerial roles. Ford and other industrialists began to recognize that they needed to stimulate markets for their products, to try to overcome the internal contradictions of capitalism. A link was established between production and consumption, and labour exploitation was relaxed as workers were paid salaries sufficient to enable them to consume the goods they were making. Life improved for labourers. The working day was shortened to eight hours, to create efficient workforces with stable family lives. Mass-manufactured, uniform, affordable garments, like Levi Strauss's five-pocket blue jeans, provided a new type of consumable clothing for the working classes. Capitalism could profit by creating standardized patterns of dress; new modern clothing systems of provision emerged.

It is instructive to look back at photographs and film from the first half of the twentieth century that show such relative uniformity in the way different sets of people dressed according to their place within a broader social system: for example, rows of English working-class men at football matches in flat caps and dark woollen suits, white cotton shirts and knotted neckties; Parisian bourgeois women parading along the Champs-Elysées in stiff long dresses in muted blacks, whites or subtle pastels with parasol shades; American factory workers emerging from plants in the Midwest in blue denim dungarees and shirtsleeves. Standardized costume denoted social class. For the poor this was partly due to the limited number of garments they owned; but it was also because Fordist patterns of production and consumption helped regulate and dictate dress and were forged through a particular system of provision that was part of the rise of modern ways of

organizing society – modern in the sense that society followed
centralized patterns of social and political control and accepted
scientifically rational norms. Progress occurred within limits and
was stabilized by the factory system of industrial production and
employment, and the operation of the market economy. Control
was exerted by the nation-state and mass democracy, although the
latter was only applied selectively in the global North; elsewhere
the colonial ideology was enforced by a specific and racialized
idea of modernity. The social practices of modernity set the tone
for the European-dominated world, which until after 1945 saw
the culture of the continent as the central axis around which the
rest of the world revolved.

During the post-war era the structure of the world economy
was steadily rebuilt. For around thirty years after the Second
World War the problems of capitalist expansion were solved
through the development of mass consumption in the global
North. A modern consumer class emerged as surplus extraction
further relaxed. People were organized in nuclear families, with
car ownership, televisions, refrigerators, and of course affordable
new clothes. Alongside the rising living standards in Europe and
North America, a global shift began to occur in manufacturing as
economies in Asia, the Middle East, South America and to a lesser
extent Africa were transformed. A mass migration of capital to the
global South began to take advantage of these countries as sources
of cheap labour for industry, rather than simply being suppliers
of raw materials and captive markets for goods from the global
North. Clothing was one of the first manufacturing industries to
spread as increasing wage levels in Europe and America and improvements in communication motivated capital to move clothing
production to economies where costs were lower, enabling greater
exploitation and accumulation of profits. The partial industrialization of some of the former underdeveloped countries provided a
spatial fix for capitalism and further opportunities for capitalists,

old and new, international and local, to expand the extraction of surplus value from wage labour.

Decolonization in Africa and Asia was important in stimulating industrial expansion. Beginning in the 1950s, many governments in the global South promoted basic manufacturing as a means to develop and modernize their economies, foremost among which were China and South Korea. A new international division of labour led to the long-term migration of factories from the old industrial heartlands of the global North to the developing world. Eventually some of the early clothing and textiles production regions, like the northern English cities of Liverpool and Manchester that had led the Industrial Revolution, would decline as they became uncompetitive. Clothing and textile industries took off in the global South. As poor countries gained political independence they adopted, first, import substitution approaches to industrialization (ISI), protecting their infant domestic industries from competition by foreign clothing, before progressing to export-orientated manufacturing. The technologies employed in clothing production up until the 1970s were similar to techniques that had been used for the previous century and a half. Within the global South labour conditions often echoed those found in eighteenth- or nineteenth-century Britain, rather than the Fordist mode of production. Workers were employed on low wages and for long hours – twelve to fourteen hours a day were not uncommon. Exploitative labour regimes in China are explored further in Chapter 5.

The Multi-Fiber Arrangement and the growth of fast fashion

Over the past fifty years there has been a steady realignment in the geography of global clothing production, but this has not led to unbridled free-market development. Equalization in the levels of development between the global North and South has partially been blocked by the inherited patterns of capital accumulation established in the colonial period and enforced through measures such as trade protectionism. Clothing trade patterns have primarily been structured since 1962 by the Long Term Agreement (LTA) regarding international trade in cotton textiles, and then from 1974 to 2004 by the Multi-Fiber Arrangement (MFA). Both agreements placed import controls, or quotas, on clothing and textiles, protecting certain markets. The LTA and MFA were intended to allow for steady and controlled development of the clothing industries and provide benefits for countries in both the global North and the global South. Access to European and North American markets was limited; it increased at around 6 per cent a year, as developed markets were partially protected. Bilateral arrangements between pairs of countries were negotiated to control the imports of specific types of clothing and textiles. Rather than liberalizing market access, this system constrained trade and was repeatedly renegotiated (in 1977, 1982, 1986 and 1991). The constraints on clothing imports benefited the rich countries as they were slowly able to adjust, rather than experiencing a 'shock' to their economies.

The quotas and controls relaxed further as part of market liberalization in the 1990s and early 2000s, bringing more affordable new clothing to the global North. The spread of fast fashion accelerated when the MFA expired in 2005, triggering the bra wars. European and American manufactures failed to compete with more efficient Asian producers who paid lower wages. As the clothing market has been increasingly liberalized, developed markets were inundated with affordable fashion imports. Clothing prices fell dramatically in the 2000s: by 26.2 per cent in Europe and 17.1 per cent in the USA. At the same time consumption boomed, with the number of items sold in the UK increasing by a third, leading to over 2 million tonnes of clothing being consumed every year.[35] Exports of Chinese clothing to the USA increased by 18 per cent per year, and to the EU by 21 per cent per year, between 2000 and 2007, and these economies went in to trading deficits in clothing, standing at around $81 billion per year for the USA and $60 billion for the EU in 2007. This resulted in local crises in clothes-producing regions.[36]

While in economics the world was undergoing a major restructuring through the second half of the twentieth century, there were also social and cultural challenges to the modern ways of organizing society. In the global North this happened across the full spectrum of cultural life, including art, architecture, film, literature, music and fashion. Old prescribed patterns of dress were destabilized through both cultural and social movements, such as the sexual revolution, anti-war protests and the end of segregation in the USA. In the 1960s and 1970s cheaper popular fashion first became accessible for youth markets. On the media scene female personalities like Jacqueline Kennedy Onassis, Jean Shrimpton, Audrey Hepburn, Twiggy and other fashion icons became household names, famous in part because of the way they dressed; as such they inspired new demand for clothing styles. Change, though, was not always 'radical' in the sense of a shift to the political left. Socio-cultural development often served the market as it was consonant with developing new modes of consumption that depended on expanding the exploitation of labour in the global South to bring cheap clothing into the market.

Fashion firms such as Sears and Marks & Spencer found new opportunities for growth by increasing the speed at which stimulated tastes and fashions change. Allied to clothing manufacturing is the influential fashion press and entertainment industry. Glossy magazines like *Elle* and *Vogue*, as well as advertising, fashion shows and later social media, promoted new trends, while celebrity culture supported the system of provision. Developments in transport and communication technologies, the spread of flexible production techniques, the breakdown in traditional autumn/winter and spring/summer fashion collections, and the increasing sophistication of advertising imagery have transformed the consumer landscape. New clothes are designed that are positional and will shortly become obsolete. In the 1990s the Spanish chain Zara pioneered a production approach based on short batch orders with a two-week turnaround from design to retail. Zara's business model is built upon producing a 'scarcity value'; the company launches 11,000 new items a year in comparison to the 2,000–4,000 of rivals like H&M and Gap. However, Zara's business model has inspired others.[37]

This chapter has briefly demonstrated how clothes-making moved from pre-modern artisanal production to the emergence of the fast-fashion system of provision. Across the long arc of human history the global circulation of cloth and clothing has been a key force in human development and economic globalization. As apparel is traded around the world it has contributed to the enrichment of the global North and the poverty of the South. Uneven development is a testament to humans' ability both to transcend and to despoil nature. The spatial impacts of industrial progress are irregularly distributed as concentrated patches of affluence and spaces of impoverishment. Rather than spurring general equilibrium between places as posited by classical liberal economics, uneven development is the defining characteristic of the spread of capitalism around the world. Some places are becoming ever richer – London, New York and enclaves of Beijing and Delhi – while billions remain impoverished as the gap between winners and losers in the global economy widens.

Governments, be they run by medieval feudal kings, colonized tribal leaders, imperial powers, democratic parties or the supranational EU, have long been pressured and drawn into disputes around access to the market due to the great tension between state and capital over who and what exerts political power.

Protectionism has served the development of clothing- and textile-based capitalism, most notably in the Industrial Revolution, but has also constrained free trade. The advance of capitalism and its pursuit of a 'spatial fix' led to the eventual deindustrialization of the global North and the relocation of clothing industries to China and elsewhere, as barriers to capital flows have been surpassed or crushed. One important question left unresolved in this chapter is why clothing production is concentrated in the emerging Chinese economy and other parts of Asia rather than the more impoverished societies of Africa? For one might expect the lowest labour cost to be found in the world's poorest continent, and the logic of the market to dictate that capital would relocate production there. The reasons behind the absence of clothing production in Africa are explored in later chapters.

In the present fast-fashion sector the rhythm of purchases far exceeds the tempo of fabric dilapidation. Much sound and light is focused on the continual cycles of new clothing purchases, which generate an increasingly large volume of old waste clothing as garments are discarded before they are worn out. Yet there is a counterpoint to the trade in new clothing, a dim silhouette that has escaped attention. Throughout history there have been other secondary hidden systems of provision that have clothed a significant proportion of the world's population. The next chapter draws attention to the neglected, yet globally important, shadow trade in used clothing.

CHAPTER 3

The shadow world of used clothing

Clothing in Papua New Guinea

For as long as clothes have existed, they have been borrowed, exchanged and swapped. One can easily imagine prehistoric people bartering used animal skins and furs for meat and flint tools. There is nothing new about second-hand clothes. Garments were likely shared between early people, as this is observable among present-day hunter–gatherer communities and other isolated tribal groups. Papua New Guinea is a remote country; a mainland of mountainous rainforest surrounded by scattered tropical islands, located between the Indonesian archipelago and the north coast of Australia. The main island of New Guinea is home to some of the world's most inaccessible communities, many of which have had limited contact with the modern world. Although notions of present-day tribes of 'stone age people' are inaccurate and unhelpful, many New Guineans do live in subsistence societies; as well as tending vegetable gardens, they have livelihoods that include elements of the hunter–gatherer approach – shooting birds with bow and arrow, and collecting plants from the bush.

Communities in the remote Western Highlands province can only be accessed by hiking for days or taking a flight in a cramped

Cessna light aircraft. Flights pass over steep mountain valleys and ravines and the small planes touch down on grass landing strips in forest clearings. To reach the most isolated groups visitors must continue by foot and trek over the Bismarck mountain range. In remote villages clothing is very basic. Many men wear stretched and stained shirts and long trousers that have been ripped or worn down to shorts. Others have pieces of fabric knotted around their waists like loincloths. Women may wear *lap-laps*, simple wide pieces of fabric tied around the midriff, and maybe a *meri* blouse, a basic dress or top introduced by missionaries to encourage them to cover up. The material is often old, little more than rags, worn down by hard wear in tropical conditions. Everyday clothing for most rural Papua New Guineans consists mainly of second-hand items which have come from Australia and the United States. Some even show logos from their earlier lives, ranging from the dress shirt of an officer in the Australian Royal Air Force, to the T-shirt of a waiter at Chili's Grill and Bar (a fast-food chain originating in Dallas, Texas). Imported modern clothing is hard to come by; the few items held in rural communities may be shared around, because people have so few material possessions. However, during *bungs* (tribal celebrations) everyone dons intricate ceremonial costumes which combine feathers, wood, bark and animal skins using techniques that are in all likelihood millennia old. Men wear fur headdresses, dyed grasses bound to their arms, and wraps around their waists woven from fine jungle vines; women wear seas shells traded from coastal regions threaded on necklaces and garlands of flowers; children have leaves tied to their elbows and feathers in their hair. Faces are painted red, white and black using natural dyes. Some people add to their traditional outfits with plastic beads and dayglo nylon fabric, precious new items that have been purchased in towns and carried back to near inaccessible rural areas.[1]

Furs, feathers and face paints are not everyday wear, but such dress patterns are a key part of cultural life. Isolated tribes cherish their limited clothing resources as modern garments are precious and difficult to obtain. The previous chapter showed how the clothing industry developed and spread around the globe. Across the world clothes manufactured using modern production techniques have largely replaced outfits made from materials like animal skins and vines. In Papua New Guinea, however, remote rural communities have little connection with the global economy. They are partially isolated from the capitalist market and therefore many traditional approaches have persisted. The few modern clothes that reach the Western Highlands province are mainly imported second-hand clothes from the global North. Used clothes are found throughout the developing world, from the Mozambican markets, introduced earlier, to the mountain communities of Papua New Guinea. Later in the book more examples from Africa, as well as Asia and Latin America, are introduced. Trade networks spread around the world, reaching even some of the most isolated corners, and there is a vast unseen circulation of second-hand garments from rich to poor countries. This chapter explores how used clothes have been shared, exchanged and traded between various communities at different historical moments, and how and why second-hand clothes are collected in the global North for resale to communities across the global South. An in-depth case study in the second half of the chapter uncovers what happens to clothes after they are donated to a charity or a textile recycler in the UK and shows how there is a hidden world of commercial, and even criminal, activity involved in the trade of used clothing.

Second-hand clothing in historical contexts

For most of history clothes-making has been time-consuming and garments difficult to acquire for all but the richest people. The re-wearing of clothes has existed for as long as humans have stitched together materials. Strong social bonds in close-knit communities meant that clothes were likely shared between people who had little, as they are sometimes in Papua New Guinea today. Limited evidence remains, but there is every reason to believe that rags and torn old fabrics were also recycled. The British Museum has a Roman doll filled with textile rags, found in Egypt, dating back to between the first and fifth centuries CE. Used clothing has also been traded commercially for many centuries; in the medieval period old clothing was taken from rich cities to be sold in poorer rural regions at markets and country fairs. In Europe the value of second-hand clothing changed from the preindustrial era to the post-modern contemporary era, as the tunics and breeches of the past were more readily re-worn than the T-shirts and board shorts of today. Good-quality second-hand clothes were prized, even being valuable enough to have served as an alternative to currency. Throughout pre-modern history wearable used clothes would never have been discarded, but instead passed between different social groups.[2]

Early accounts of second-hand clothing markets are hard to find, especially prior to the improvements in communication (literacy, newspaper printing, photography) that accompanied the Industrial Revolution. As is often the case, the history of the poor is fragmented; consequently the surviving record of how clothes were reused often focuses on the circulation of higher-end luxury garments. One example from Italy, in 1407, shows there were guilds concerned with the trade in high-quality clothes and other used goods in Florence. Formally established trading guilds dealt with items such as second-hand silk gowns and velvets, and lower-class, often female, itinerant vendors worked the street buying and selling old clothes of any quality from different classes of household.[3] Used clothes were also gifted between different tiers of society and passed from European feudal masters to their serfs, domestic staff and the local poor. Societal norms or formal laws, like those imposed by Edward III in medieval England, meant that lower-class servants were often unable to re-wear the same clothing as the aristocratic masters, so they resold luxurious garments. One main customer was theatre companies. For centuries travelling troupes of actors provided entertainment for the masses. In the Elizabethan period, Shakespearean plays were widely performed across England. Plays included a cast of rich and colourful characters such as Romeo and Juliet, Oberon and Prospero, for which actors would depend upon second-hand clothes for costumes. Bodices, cloaks, ruffs and stockings made of taffeta, silks and even garments with gold effects would be put to use to embellish thespian performances and create fashionable and fantastical outfits. Old clothes were readily sold on across Europe. Beyond the Western world examples of used-clothing markets are harder to find, which is not to say they were not traded elsewhere. One well-documented illustration from pre-modern Japan is the vibrant trade in used silk kimonos. These elegant garments with delicate and intricate detailing and flowing sleeves were as much objects of crafted art, which were – and continue to be – re-worn, and hence have encapsulated different values in specific times and places.[4]

The scarcity of clothes among pre-industrial societies ensured their careful safe keeping, whether it was actors looking after their costumes or the working poor preserving their best church-going clothes. Many people were what the French call *bricoleurs*: skilful or creative individuals who carefully reused textiles in clever ways. Clothes were repaired in the home; for example, women would spend hours darning, and tailors would let out trousers that had been outgrown. These domestic and local patterns of preservation and reuse continued until the development of cheap new clothing in the twentieth century.

Articles of used clothing have long had an ambiguous status as they are, on the one hand, items that are often given away as charitable gifts, while at the same time being commodities traded on the market. Recognizing this peculiarity, the Scottish economist Adam Smith wrote in 1776 of how the poor would receive the 'charity of well-disposed people' and that a 'beggar' would exchange gifts of clothing for more suitable garments or other items, or even sell them: 'The old cloaths which another bestows upon him he exchanges for other old cloaths which suit him better, or for lodging, or for food, or for money, with which he can buy either food, cloaths, or lodging, as he has occasion.'[5] Old clothes were often easier to obtain than any other form of charity, but the good intentions of donors were sometimes exploited. Organized beggars like the so-called 'shallow coves' – rascals who would go around English cities affecting shivers while exaggerating their poverty – visited homes half-naked asking for clothes. Barefoot 'limpers' specialized in collecting shoes. Donated old boots, shirts and waistcoats would then be sold on for a few pennies to the 'dolly shops', which, like today's thrift stores, sold old apparel, rags and other junk.[6] With the expansion of the Industrial Revolution new clothing gradually became more affordable and the value of second-hand clothes shifted as they became less desirable. In Charles Dickens's Victorian England it was common for out-of-fashion styles, worn clothes and stolen garments to be traded in open-air markets. For instance, when left with nothing but the clothes on his back, Dickens's most autobiographical character, David Copperfield, sells his waistcoat in desperation and struggles to secure a fair price. In *Oliver Twist* the infamous real-life Field Lane marketplace in London is described in detail as

> a commercial colony of itself: the emporium of petty larceny: visited at early morning, and setting-in of dusk, by silent merchants, who traffic in dark back-parlours, and who go as strangely as they come. Here, the clothesman, the shoe-vamper, and the rag-merchant, display their goods, as sign-boards to

the petty thief; here, stores of old iron and bones, and heaps of mildewy fragments of woollen-stuff and linen, rust and rot in the grimy cellars.[7]

In parallel with the development of industrial production of apparel, used clothing was gradually becoming something that was considered deviant, associated with crime and morally ambiguous processes on the fringes of society.

Damaged and deteriorating clothes that could not be re-worn were recycled, providing an input for early industrial processes. Marx discusses how female workers were exploited in the rag trade:

> One of the most shameful, the most dirty, and the worst paid kinds of labour, and one on which women and young girls are by preference employed, is the sorting of rags. It is well known that Great Britain, apart from its own immense store of rags, is the emporium for the rag trade of the whole world. They flow in from Japan, from the most remote States of South America, and from the Canary Islands. But the chief sources of their supply are Germany, France, Russia, Italy, Egypt, Turkey, Belgium and Holland. They are used for manure, for making bedflocks, for shoddy, and they serve as the raw material of paper. The rag-sorters are the medium for the spread of small-pox and other infectious diseases, and they themselves are the first victims.[8]

The nineteenth-century rag networks had a transnational geographical extent, which is paralleled in today's second-hand clothing systems of provision. Used clothes – including rags as well as re-wearable garments – have been traded around the world for more than a century; the emergence of these networks was both an outcome and a response to the changing nature of industrial garment manufacturing and the rise of capitalism.

With the growth in clothing manufacturing and the rapid development of North America and Europe in the nineteenth century, the availability of new clothing improved and second-hand distribution became increasingly formalized as a type of charitable handout. Old clothing passed down the social gradient from rich to poor as charitable donations. The ladies of the New York Clothing Society for the Relief of the Industrious Poor gave away 1,742 garments in 1837.[9] This type of gift-giving was often mediated through religious groups, which provided the urban middle classes with a virtuous outlet for unwanted clothing. By making donations to churches, respectable housewives had a way to get rid of clothing, avoiding direct contact with the undesirable underclass and criminal elements associated with the rag trade. Put simply, donors could feel good about themselves. The history of the second-hand clothing and rag trade as both a dirty and a deviant sector, and as a socially important means of charity, has influenced the development of contemporary systems of used-clothing provision, just as the social history of jeans influences how they are designed, manufactured and retailed today.

The advent of Fordist production and the 'golden age' of capitalism filled marketplaces with consumer goods and provided people with disposable income for consuming new clothing. This socio-economic system depended on people's ability to maintain a continuous cycle of consumption. In the modern world repair and reuse of clothing was discouraged, as conveyed in Aldous Huxley's dystopian modernist novel *Brave New World*. The protagonist Bernard Marx overhears elementary pupils rhythmically reciting: 'I do love having new clothes, I do love ... But old clothes are beastly ... we always throw away old clothes. Ending is better than mending, ending is better than mending, ending is better.'[10] People's relationships with clothing began to change. Business recognized that retaining clothes and wearing them out does not drive free-market development. There is an underlying need for capitalism to reinvent and constantly bring new products, often with simulated demands, to the marketplace. As B. Earl Puckett, a leading clothing retailer in the United States, said in

1950 when addressing 400 fashion experts in Manhattan: 'Basic utility cannot be the foundation of a prosperous apparel industry. We must accelerate obsolescence.'[11]

Manufactured obsolescence, promoted by migrating fashion trends and endless cycles of new production, brought more and more clothes to market, which transformed how people related to used clothing through the twentieth century. Clothes were less likely to be used again in the household and were increasingly exchanged in market transactions or donated for reuse. In American cities like Chicago and Philadelphia, prior to World War II, used clothing was traded away by hard-working housewives and domestic staff. Ragmen worked the urban neighbourhoods and exchanged unwanted clothes for new commodities such as pins, pans and needles. At face value this appeared to be a de-commoditized form of barter exchange; however, merchants actually made sophisticated calculations of the monetary value of used clothing and weighed this against what they paid in hardware. Ragmen sold on clothes to other, poorer, households or in street markets, and ripped and torn garments were wholesaled as shoddy for use in industrial processes, where they became machine wipers or were used to make other goods, for instance in furniture stuffing.[12]

The formalized culture of donating clothing for reuse also grew, and organizations such as the Salvation Army developed extensive networks for collecting and distributing second-hand clothes, providing an outlet for consumers who wanted to clear out their wardrobes. Later, in the second half of the twentieth century, charity and thrift stores like Good Will and Value Village in the USA and Oxfam and YMCA in the UK spread retailing used clothes at cheap prices. Throughout the twentieth century this served as a system of provision of clothing for the urban poor, providing low-value apparel to impoverished people on the margins of modern society. One of the particularities of the market is that everyone has the ability to consume something; there is differentiation in consumption and people become socially defined by their shopping habits. The purchasing of preconsumed used clothing at charity shops, thrift stores and yard sales is perceived negatively as undesirable, acceptable only for the impoverished and countercultural groups in Western society. Despite the current popular rise in household recycling and vintage fashion (discussed in Chapter 8), those who take an active role in the disposal and consumption of 'waste' are still normally viewed as outside the mainstream of society, as were the rag-and-bone men, the 'disease ridden' female rag-sorters, the rascals, the vagabonds and the thieves found in Smith's, Dickens's and Marx's time.

Waste and clothing consumption

The ways in which people thought of used clothing were transformed in the developed economies by the end of the twentieth century. Old clothing became a form of rubbish, often consigned to the dustbin alongside food waste and empty packaging. In the UK an estimated £1 billion ($1.7 billion) of clothing goes to landfill each year.[13] Generating household waste is integral to the economic system as it helps drive consumption forward. The growth of markets for new commodities depends on the disposal of old stuff. Purchasing and discarding objects are forms of freedom which override saving and repair. While old clothes are viewed negatively and past fashions often ridiculed, the new clothing sector and the fast-fashion system are positively associated with youth, independence and even female emancipation. This is a charade. Fashion, by its very nature, is effective in restricting social mobility and places consumers in a never-ending contest of purchases which contribute to expressing their identity. Everyone has some adherence to culturally constructed norms of dress, which evolve over time. Conspicuous consumption is not restricted to those who follow the latest fashions. Garments get ripped, stained and outgrown – all processes which diminish value. Clothing is often considered outdated or unwearable in the global North when it is still useable, because social pressure dictates the perceived obsolescence of clothes, ensuring that it becomes imperative to consume new garments regularly to maintain social status. Throughout the global North superfluous consumption has grown, driven by the falling real price of goods manufactured in China and elsewhere. Garments are priced far too low to reflect their true social and ecological value as capital mobility and excess global labour supply enable clothing firms to depress wages and avoid paying environmental costs. Consumers have responded to clothing availability and an environment of competitive consumption by purchasing increasing numbers of artificially cheap goods, and getting rid of old garments, in rapid cycles of acquisition and discard.

The continuous purchase of clothing is interlinked with the idea and practice of clothing disposability. Concurrent with conspicuous clothing consumption is the downgrading and throwing out of existing wardrobe items. As clothes age, they lose their aura of newness, becoming unfashionable or worn out in the eyes of the owner. Data suggests that up to 70 per cent of garments in home wardrobes may be inactive.[14] Clothes are purged periodically from the wardrobe, passed on to relatives or friends, placed in charity collection sacks, casually sold on eBay or at car-boot sales, or, most commonly, discarded with household rubbish. Disposing of things and creating wardrobe space for the consumption of new commodities is central to the maintenance of capitalist production. Meanwhile, in the global North the market for second-hand clothes has shrunk in volume in the last three decades relative to the mass increase in new clothing sales. However, the highly lucrative vintage fashion sector is booming.[15] The demand among the American and European poor for second-hand clothes fell away with rising affluence and the boom in affordable low-end value fashion sold by retailers such as Primark, Target and Walmart that encourages mass production by low-paid labour in the global South and continues to drive down real-term prices.

As more and more clothes are consumed, greater volumes of textile rubbish are produced. Waste old clothing does not just go away; it goes somewhere. New clothing consumption creates the preconditions for second-hand clothing systems of provision. The new and used clothing sectors are woven together. New purchases are interconnected to disposal; indeed imports of new apparel are a significant predictor of the export of used clothing from the United States to the rest of the world.[16] Transient clothing ownership produces a mass of used clothing, which is recycled in a second system of reproduction and consumption. Clothing donated to charities and textile recyclers enters a new economic network. Labour activities are undertaken and profits are accumulated by charities, firms and individuals as used clothes are traded to places like Mozambique and Papua New Guinea. But how does clothing go from the First World wardrobe to a Third World market? The remainder of this chapter explores how clothing is collected and processed in the developed world using a case study from England.

Second-hand clothing charities in the UK

Staines is a commuter town on the outskirts of London. Long the butt of satirical jokes, it is a dull, grey town that epitomizes Western suburbia. The high street has branches of chain shops along with a few small independent stores; away from the centre there is the Two Rivers Retail Park, which includes a Gap, a large Tesco Homestore, and the discount trader TK Maxx, three shops which represent mass market clothing retail. The YMCA shop in Staines is on a quiet end of the main street and has the typical appearance of a charity store, a slightly dilapidated retail space, with rails of random used clothing items hung in a disorderly way, and some crockery and toys scattered around the shelves alongside well-thumbed Dan Brown and Jackie Collins paperbacks. The YMCA is a Christian charity which supports young people; it has over 150 charity shops in Britain and programmes around the world. Clothing collecting agencies like the YMCA receive donations from households, which first select, sort and bag up clothes that can be worn again. Giving away used clothes does not fit within rigid definitions of materiality such as 'commodity', 'gift' and 'rubbish', yet donors expect their clothes to go on to make a difference somewhere. Some people find it hard to let go of their clothes, but charities like the YMCA are perceived as a good home.

Charities use promotional material to stimulate the donation of second-hand clothing. Some of this recalls the earlier social history of clothing being donated between different groups as well as emphasizing the environmental benefits of clothing reuse. Oxfam, the leading charity which fights global poverty, connects international development and environmentalism in publicity materials, with slogans such as: 'Having a clear-out? Reduce landfill and raise funds to fight poverty by bringing your unwanted items to Oxfam' and 'Save lives. De-clutter yours'.[17] Different ethical narratives and images are used in doorstep collection materials to stimulate donations. Sustaining this picture is an integral part of the system of provision and the material culture which surround the donation and consumption of used clothing. Charities such as the YMCA and others operating in the USA, like Goodwill Industries International, have become relatively effective in monopolizing collections for the specific historical cultural reasons that normalized the gifting of used clothing from the affluent to the impoverished in the nineteenth and twentieth centuries, and even earlier. However, this is not the full story: there is a darker side to clothing collections.

Used clothing collection leaflets continually arrive in letter-boxes across the UK. Many come from small local charities such as hospices and others from national NGOs like the NSPCC (National Society for the Prevention of Cruelty to Children). One leaflet distributed in Nottingham is a green and yellow flyer that shows an image of an Asian child in the aftermath of a disaster. Although the photo has no caption, an online image search reveals that it was a doctored picture of an earthquake in Sichuan, China. The text states 'All clothes are shipped to under-developed countries to improve their lives and welfare', but there is no mention of how this will be achieved or of the names of any charities or organizations linked to the Chinese earthquake.[18] The only identifications are false company registration and mobile phone numbers. Another example from Nottingham is a leaflet with pictures of helicopters, which gives the casual observer the impression that donations will benefit a local air ambulance charity. Careful inspection of the small print reveals that this collection company has no direct connection to any air ambulance service. Private organizations employ imagery that falsely suggests that donations will go to charity. There are many other examples of deceitful practices in the used clothing trade, including unlicensed collections by Ragtex in neighbouring Leicester.[19] In Richmondshire, Yorkshire, householders have been warned about the rise in 'bogus' charity collections by Councillor Jill McMullon:

> These leaflets are often worded to encourage people to assume that the items are collected for charity ... Unfortunately, these anonymous 'bogus' collectors try to exploit our generosity for their own gain. They may also steal donations left for collection for genuine charities.[20]

Research shows that, when alerted to the widespread illegal practices, donors are seriously concerned about the use of collection sacks and leaflets that imitate legitimate charities' brands: 'I think that [the use of the pink ribbon] is ... deliberately done to make you think you are donating to breast cancer.'[21] This problem is not restricted to the UK. It has also been reported in Canada, as a donor in Ontario expresses in disbelief: 'This bin is here and it's leading me to believe that it is part of a charitable organization. It almost even says so on it. So when I find out that it doesn't go to charity, I'm just flabbergasted that this can happen in my community.'[22] In California executives from Goodwill, the most established US clothing collection charity, have raised concerns about commercial operators using colours that evoke their branding of collection bins.[23] Brian Lincoln, regional manager of the YMCA, expressed anger about how many companies imitate charitable branding and expressed his belief that such operations are commonplace. The motivations for deception and theft stem from the large profits that can be made from exporting second-hand clothes.

The commercial trade in second-hand clothing

Leaving aside the 'fake' charity collections, many honest organizations, such as the YMCA and a number of legitimate commercial companies, operate in Europe and North America running clothing banks, carrying out domestic collections, and accepting donations directly to stores. These donations are then transformed into marketable goods. Second-hand clothing is big business in the UK, although measuring the size of the sector is difficult and up to date statistics are hard to obtain. The most recent estimates from the Department of the Environment and Rural Affairs show that 523,000 tonnes of used clothing items were collected in 2008 by the secondary textile industry. This reuse figure is equivalent to 23 per cent of the 2,266,000 tonnes of new textiles that were consumed during the same year.[24] The total volume of clothes recycled has undoubtedly increased since. Similar processes occur in many countries in the global North, including Australia, Canada, Germany, the Netherlands, Spain and the United States.

Donated clothes are transformed from waste into re-sellable commodities by collecting charities and commercial recyclers in the global North that sort and grade used clothes for onward sale. This process begins, for example, in a back room at the YMCA shop in Staines. Labour processes (sorting, unpacking, sometimes cleaning) and pricing and marketing are undertaken by waged or voluntary workers. This work activity is needed to turn the gift into a commodity. High-quality second-hand clothes are retailed in stores like the YMCA in Staines, although local shoppers are more likely to be found at the Gap, Tesco or TK Maxx in the nearby Two Rivers Retail Park. The YMCA shop generates only a small amount of revenue through retail sales, although such high street stores do have the additional purpose of raising the organization's profile. Due to the weak local demand in Staines, Brian Lincoln's colleagues sell on the surplus stock to a textile merchant, Choice Textiles, which deals with all their unsold shop waste (including bric-a-brac, electronic items and furniture). There are significant price fluctuations. For example, in 2001 the 'market almost collapsed' and went 'down to 10p a bag'; in contrast, by 2009 rag merchants' purchases were a 'very important revenue' source.[25] Brian said he was unsure exactly what happened to the majority of the wholesale used clothing, but was sure 'most of it ends up in the Third World'. Choice Textiles sells wearable used clothing to overseas markets and worn-out items for recycling.

This pattern is replicated across the country. A far greater volume of clothing is donated than is actually retailed in the UK's

9,000 charity stores. Obtaining exact national figures is not possible, but estimates indicate that only 10–30 per cent is retailed in
the UK; this is similar to the situation in Canada and the USA.[26]
The largest clothing collector in Britain is the Salvation Army,
which accounts for approximately 15 per cent of the total volume
of used-clothing collections.[27] They also have a large presence
in Australia, Canada and the USA. They are major suppliers to
both Mozambique and Papua New Guinea. Most of the clothing
they collect is for export or for sale as recyclable material, with
only a very small proportion being sold in their fifty or so UK
shops, or is used to support their local programme work – that
is, it is provided free to homeless people. Despite accounting for
only a small segment of the total used clothing market, charity
shops are important as the public face of the second-hand clothing
trade. They are a symbolically influential part of the image and
material culture of the used clothing system of provision, which
encourages people to associate clothing donations with local
charitable retail.

Many charities also operate in partnership with commercial
operators who pay a royalty fee to use the name of the charity and
collect second-hand clothing donations directly from the public.
Licensing charitable branding allows companies to expand their
involvement in the system of provision and increase their profitability. The UK charity Help the Aged operates two different
models of collection. In total they distribute 30 million collection
bags per year: 13 million from an internal business run by Help
the Aged staff and volunteers to stock the Help the Aged shops;
while 17 million bags are distributed by Precycle, which uses the
Help the Aged name as a licensed operator, and pays 50 per cent
of profits to the charity.[28] In the latter model, clothing donations
are collected from the doorstep and taken to the Precycle depot
in Reading; they then go by road to grading and sorting plants
in Poland where they are categorized: A-grade items are sold

in Polish shops; B grade are exported to Africa; C grade are exported to Iran, Iraq, Syria, Jordan and Pakistan; and other grades are recycled for industrial use. As with the tracking of new jeans production, tracing the transactions is difficult since the donations go through processes of amalgamation and separation from other used clothing collections.

There is controversy around the activities of some companies that operate entirely for-profit collection schemes, or that make 'token' donations to charities, as well as NGOs that have little positive social impact. In the USA Planet Aid, which has clothing banks in eighty cities across twenty states, is nominally a non-profit organization. Planet Aid has been heavily criticized in newspaper reports for a lack of transparency and insufficient spending on programme services: 'the most recent federal tax return from non-profit Planet Aid, which operates donation bins across the country, shows that just 28 per cent of its $36.5 million in spending went to its international aid programs in 2011. The bulk of its spending went to collect and process clothes for recycling.'[29] The lines are becoming blurred between charity and commerce in the second-hand clothing sector. In another example, typical of small British charities, the Rainbow Hospice entered in an agreement to receive a minimum of £40 ($67) for every tonne of used clothing collected by its commercial partner, when the market value of collected used clothing was £600–900 ($1,000–1,500) per tonne.[30] The British Heart Foundation has estimated that 'in some cases as little as 5 per cent is paid to a charity who is working with a commercial company.'[31] There is also competition between charities and commercial collectors. Brian Lincoln claimed that the YMCA had had 'problems from other charities' stealing their collections and that 'Great Ormond Street Hospital just blanket an area' with collection bags.[32]

A long-standing issue in the second-hand clothing sector is the outright theft of used clothing. Steve Wooldridge, head of property and stock operations at Help the Aged, said that when the price for used clothing is high, at around £900 ($1,500) per tonne, there is a problem with the theft of donation bags. Their drivers have been threatened, demands made for maps of their routes, and collection vehicles followed by unmarked trucks, to enable theft of donated clothing. Help the Aged suggested that those acting illegally are frequently Eastern Europeans. Similar problems have been experienced in Canada, where violent attacks have been reported in turf wars between clothing collectors. As an industry insider reported, 'People are getting beat up because these things work as a territory [different organizations control certain areas].... We have orders from the company, like don't let competition around you.'[33] This is not a new phenomenon; criminal elements have long been associated with the used clothing trade. In 1939 in the United States, for example, the Salvation Army complained that bags from door-to-door collections were being 'kidnapped' and 'hijacked'.[34]

The profits accumulated by legitimate commercial operators can also be viewed negatively as they violate the 'spirit' of the gift and distort donors' intentions. Shea and Brennan, who carried out focus group research with UK households, found that the majority of households were 'unaware that all goods collected door-to-door do not necessarily go straight to charity shops ... When made aware of commercial partnerships with charities and charity shops, many respondents' initial reaction was negative/ unhappy with the idea.'[35]

Partnerships formed between charities and textile merchants because they recognized that as the established market in the global North was becoming less profitable, developing countries offered more profitable new markets in which to expand. A used clothing system of provision which connects charitable donations to efficient commercial operators has emerged to maximize profit generation from the second-hand clothing trade. The actions of clothing processing charities and companies can be understood within the free-market social relations Adam Smith mapped out in the eighteenth century, described earlier. Both the companies' and the charities' objectives are to realize the latent value in used clothing and sell them for the maximum price, even if this is not achieved through using the donated clothing in the manner intended by the donor. Paul Ozanne of the Salvation Army believes that people are quite comfortable about giving clothing to the Salvation Army knowing that only a small proportion will directly be worn again by people in need (e.g. the homeless) or sold locally, and 'makes no bones about' the fact that the majority is sold overseas to generate profit.[36] However, the evidence from Shea and Brennan suggests otherwise.

Charities are responding to the transformations in the clothing sector. On one hand, in the global North demand for good vintage clothing has increased and charity shops and retro stores are raising the prices of fashionable vintage items to levels that are proving unaffordable even for some consumers. On the other hand, overall demand in volume terms for the much larger amount of lower-quality donated garments has fallen away as average incomes have risen and more and more affordable new clothes are available. This has led to new markets being identified in the global South, which have provided expanded business opportunities. Second-hand clothes have long been exported on a small scale; the 1980s saw supply grow as a disaster relief measure. Organizations such as the Red Cross shipped donations of clothes to provide warmth and protection following catastrophes such as earthquakes or wars. This was the case in Mozambique where used clothes are still known as *roupa da calamidade* (clothing of the calamity). Elsewhere the fall of the Berlin Wall and the collapse of the USSR opened up new second-hand markets as Czechs, Poles, Lithuanians and others in former communist countries grew hungry for the styles of the West; as they could not afford new clothing, used garments began to flow east. The broader-scale demand and need for clothing and the potential for a commercial market in poorer countries were recognized and the trade developed as the supply grew. Once the trade shifted from a local scale to international export, charities were unable to connect supplies and markets; they thus built relationships with commercial traders. In the 1990s, on an ever expanding scale commercial operators began exporting clothes to Africa, Eastern Europe, Latin America, the Middle East and Asia in what has since become a highly lucrative wholesale international trade. Globally the second-hand clothing trade was valued at over $4.3 billion in 2013, according to published UN statistics, which likely underestimate and undervalue the total trade due to the prevalence of smuggled and stolen clothing. The scale is more effectively demonstrated by the official total volume: 3.9 million tonnes of old clothes were recorded as being exported globally in 2013, which is equivalent to 7.5 billion pairs of jeans or 31.8 billion T-shirts.[37] This total does not include domestically traded second-hand clothing, such as the worn garments and vintage fashions resold in American thrift stores or British retro stores.

International traders connect used clothing supply in the UK to demand in countries that include Lithuania, Nigeria, Pakistan and Poland. Migrant communities often play a key role as they possess the entrepreneurial skills and contacts which charities lack and are able to amalgamate and split supplies to achieve critical economies of scale. The UK is the second largest exporter in the world. In 2013 it exported $612 million (or 350,000 tonnes) of used clothing, the top five destinations for which were Poland, Ghana, Pakistan, Ukraine and Benin. In the United States, the world's largest used clothes exporter, items are collected by small, often family-owned, firms. In all there are nearly 3,000 such businesses, in what is a very competitive industry.[38] Clothes worth $687 million (or 780,000 tonnes) are exported, the main destinations being Canada (primarily for sorting and re-export), Chile, Guatemala, India and the United Arab Emirates.[39] Karen Tranberg Hansen, who worked on tracing second-hand clothing exports from North America to Africa, found that diasporas play an important role. Many players are 'recent immigrants who know the potential of the second-hand clothing trade from their former homes in Third World countries', including people of 'Jewish and Middle Eastern background with long-term involvement with the textile and clothing trade, and more recently established firms with backgrounds in south Asia, particularly India and Pakistan, some of whom are recent immigrants to Europe and North America from Africa.'[40] The importing of second-hand clothing to Africa is explored in depth in Chapter 6.

Oxfam Wastesaver: processing clothes for export

Clothing is processed before being exported to the global South. Sorting, grading and packaging is undertaken in large industrial units. Oxfam is the second largest collector (accounting for approximately 3 per cent) in Britain, and retails used clothes through 700 charity shops. It differs from most charities and has its own processing plant, Wastesaver, which is, as general manager Tony Clark says, 'Oxfam's rag merchant in crude terms'.[41] Located in Huddersfield in the north of England, Oxfam Wastesaver is at the heart of one of the largest used-clothing export networks in Europe. The Wastesaver plant receives 200 tonnes of unsold goods from Oxfam shops per week, which accounts for 74 per cent of all the charity's donations.[42] Wastesaver sorts and grades clothing for export (60 per cent), recycling (25–28 per cent) and niche product lines for retail in the UK (8–10 per cent), with the remainder being waste.[43] Different categories vary dramatically in value. Recycling grades are worth £25 ($42) a tonne, whereas the UK retail category includes high-end vintage fashions valued as high as £20,000 ($33,000) or even £30,000 ($50,000) a tonne.[44] The plant has the appearance of a factory; there are conveyor belts dictating the tempo of work, time cards regulating employees' working days, and gantries and offices for managers overseeing the labour process. All are features of modern factory architecture, long exploited by capitalists in new clothing production to enforce discipline and enhance systematic production. The main labour activities of sorting and packaging are comparable to static work in new clothing production lines. Oxfam workers carefully sort clothes into 200 different categories, such as men's white T-shirts, ladies' button blouses, silks and fancy-dress outfits. Matching articles are weighed, labelled and bound into tightly packed bales. These bales are new commodities produced from a labour process that harnesses the material value still embodied in waste clothing. Wages are paid (although some work is done by volunteers), new labour costs that are contained within the final price for consumers in developing countries.

Oxfam has two different models of clothing export; the majority is channelled through normal market exchanges. Clothing is sold in 40 ft or 20 ft shipping containers. Each 40 ft container holds approximately 550–600 45 kg (100 lb) bales. This is standard practice throughout the used clothing trade, including by exporters in North America as well. Clients in the global South purchase a container with a mix of different bales, as Clark explains: '35 bales of men's T-shirts, 2 bales of bras and so on'. They sell to African companies, which are relatively small, 'what you would call an entrepreneur'; each importer takes between four and twenty containers a year. Dealing with African customers has created challenges for Oxfam; it now requires 'payment in advance', as it 'used to have people walk through the office with £20,000 in cash in an envelope'. Oxfam ships mainly to West Africa where 'markets are more stable and governments are more stable ... [in] Ghana, Togo, Benin, Gabon, Senegal'.

Oxfam also exports a 'second pick for Eastern Europe'. This comprises items not suitable for the African market, rather than secondary in terms of quality. Lower-quality items go to the Middle East, from where they are exported on to Central Asian countries, including Afghanistan and Uzbekistan. Oxfam's role as a campaigning organization advocating for change in the cotton sector sits uneasily with its position in the second-hand clothing system of provision. Clark commented that '[i]t was quite an eye opener for me' speaking to colleagues within Oxfam who are campaigning against US cotton subsidies and promoting fair-trade clothing. 'Oxfam was reluctant to talk about clothing ending up in countries they worked in ... which could affect local industry.' Aloysius Ihezie, the Nigerian director of Choice Textiles, explains that there 'are two schools of thought. One is that it is killing the local economy' by destroying clothing industries, and the other is that it has benefit of creating local jobs. These debates are explored further later.

In an effort to address some of the ethical issues that surround the trade, Oxfam has started exporting by means of a second method, which attempts to provide more local jobs and create income-generating opportunities. Large 450 kg bales of 'tropical mix' are sent to its own sorting plant in Dakar, Senegal. This commercial social enterprise, which aims to support Oxfam's in-country programme, sorts and grades used clothes and sells them to local traders. It employs twenty-five or so people. Oxfam is trying to link the operation to its work on livelihoods. There are difficulties in Senegal, however, as Clark further explained: 'We can't shift everything from a commercial basis to an ethical basis 'because the risk is too great ... It's not easy ... [we] invested £300,000 [$500,000]; you've got to have that level of investment ... [we are] paying full duty, putting us at a commercial disadvantage in-country.' The disadvantage is in relation to unethical commercial operators who may pay bribes to avoid duties:

'African markets [have] got a [reputation] for bending the rules' (the smuggling of used clothing is discussed further in Chapter 6). Oxfam is proud of its Dakar operation: 'That's our unique selling point.' It is 'sustainable' and 'as ethical as you can get these days. We're leading edge.' However, this is a small part of the charity's business, accounting for only 10 per cent of exports. Clark added: 'There is the international division which spend the money [Oxfam programme staff who work on international development projects] and others which support it [Wastesaver and the Oxfam Shops]'. Each is 'specialist'; 'they get on with what they need to do and I get on with what I need to do.' This shows the disconnect between Oxfam's campaigns and advocacy programmes, and the impact of its own commercial trade in used clothing.

One of the largest markets for British used clothing exports is West Africa, mainly Ghana, Benin and Togo, because, as Ihezie explains, 'the West African market has been in the trade for years, since the 1950s and 1960s.' Imports from the UK are found across the continent. Despite the large scale of African markets the British branch of the Salvation Army chooses not to export used clothing to Africa. It has a limited number of large buyers in Eastern Europe, including Bulgaria and Estonia. Multiple reasons were given for not trading with African merchants. There is an issue with clothing types, as 'overcoats and puffer jackets [are] unsuitable for the climate', a problem which has been accommodated by Oxfam, which has a different product line for Eastern Europe. Ozanne from the Salvation Army argued that, if they are not handled correctly, imports could damage local manufacturing in Africa. He believes Africa suffers from 'political unrest' and there are ethical considerations with providing 'financial incentives for senior officials', which 'is an issue for an organization with Christian values'. The Salvation Army had made an exception and exported bras to Africa, when they responded to a need identified in Malawi for women's underwear. They campaigned to collect additional bras in the UK. But there was a conflict between the Salvation Army's Christian values and the local cultural context. Malawian women were utilizing the bras not as undergarments in the service of modesty, but ostentatiously to display the figure and flaunt female sexuality. Unhappy with this, the Salvation Army halted the export programme.

Exporting second-hand clothing raises different ethical concerns for some NGOs. UK-based charities like Help the Aged and the YMCA are concerned with raising funds as part of their domestic charitable work and to enhance their local reputations, and do not focus on the downstream impacts of the second-hand clothing trade. As Clark observed, 'The difference between [Oxfam and the] YMCA is that the rag trade isn't going to impact their work.' Oxfam had prioritized fundraising, but was beginning to engage with the ethical impacts of the trade, especially as it potentially contradicted the charity's recent core programme work, including campaigns on trade justice, because imports can out-compete locally produced goods. As a large international development NGO, it occupies a broader geographical space than many other UK national charities and so is responsive on a different scale of accountability. The Salvation Army also took a broader scale approach to morality. But, as the example from Malawi illustrates, its actions were ultimately informed by 'Christian values' rather than the immediate needs and desires of people in the global South.

The second-hand and new clothing trades in global context

This chapter has traced how the history of the second-hand trade has been important in structuring the contemporary systems of used-clothing provision. The long traditions of donating and gifting used clothing and today's cultural pressures in the global

North that compel people to dispose of wearable clothing provide
the preconditions for a highly particular and well-organized global
circulation of used commodities that is not paralleled in other
sectors, such as second-hand books, furniture or other household
goods. There is a hidden professionalism to the used-clothing
trade. UK-based second-hand clothing organizations such as
Choice Textiles, Oxfam Wastesaver, the Salvation Army and the
YMCA, and their counterparts in the USA like Goodwill and
Planet Aid, have highly organized corporate business models, of
which donors are frequently unaware. Second-hand clothing is
sold as a commodity in market-based transactions and primarily
bought by the poor in the global South. Consumption is served
by the market.

In the used clothes market, the position and activities of those
involved in producing clothing commodities is concealed. Ben
Fine discusses how capitalism hides social relations in refer-
ence to Marx's theory of commodity fetishism: 'money provides
a common measure across commodities ... [it] seemingly sets
aside the underlying social relations, structures and processes
by which use values [goods] are made available for consumption.
The fashionable trainer does not display the child labour upon
which it depends.'[45] Equally the clothing collection bank or used
jeans do not display the economic pathways followed by donated
clothing. The labour activities associated with the collection,
processing and export of second-hand clothes and the complex
interactions between waste-making, donations and environmental
acts are hidden in contemporary society. Across the global North
and South the linkages between new clothing consumption and
used-clothing origins and markets are therefore often unknown by
those who donate, purchase and wear used clothes, as patterns of
capitalist exchange obscure and confuse the connections.

New clothing production is dominated by the marketplace
in the developed world. Retailers maintain cycles of production

by manipulating demand for unnecessary goods. The excessive consumption of new clothing in the global North provides a vast surplus of used clothing. By disposing of clothes through donations, people in the global North reinforce a series of connections. How second-hand clothes end up in the global South and what impacts they have on local economies and culture will be examined in Chapters 6 and 7 using case studies from Mozambique and elsewhere in Africa. To fully explain the diverse impacts, it is necessary first to understand the African clothing sectors, which are themselves interlinked with the affluence of the global North. The next two chapters present, first, an in-depth analysis of why the cotton sector is connected to poverty in Africa, followed by an investigation of how the rise and fall of clothing industries and the increasing engagement of China in Africa have affected economic development in the world's poorest continent.

CHAPTER 4

Cotton is the mother of poverty

Africa and global markets

The great Zambezi river flows across southern Africa, draining parts of Angola, Botswana, Malawi, Mozambique, Tanzania, Zambia and Zimbabwe. A delta at the mouth of the river opens into the Indian Ocean in northern Mozambique. Moving upstream, the Lower Zambezi receives the Shire river, bringing water from the majestic Lake Malawi. Further west the powerful channel is dammed at Cahora Bassa, a massive hydroelectric project built by the Portuguese during the turbulent era of decolonization to calm the waters and modernize the Mozambican state. Passing through spectacular scenery and wondrous wildlife, the middle river extends back, forming the border between Zambia and Zimbabwe. Water thunders over the Victoria Falls near Livingstone, the tourist centre named after the Scottish explorer who was the first European to set eyes upon the world's greatest waterfall. The Upper Zambezi curves round eastern Angola and the river rises in north-west Zambia in marshy woodland near the border with Congo. Along the river's course, tributaries fan out as the catchment area forms some of southern Africa's most valuable agricultural land.

On a Friday night in central Zambia, at the heart of the vast Zambezi basin, Pieter, a heavy-set white South African, relaxes after work, lounging in Tuskers bar. He calls over to the waiter: 'My friend, tonight the beers must flow like the waters of the mighty Zambezi!' Pieter manages a large cotton estate and needs to slake his thirst with cool Mosi lager after a long week delegating tasks and shouting orders on the farm. South Africans throughout the continent often fill managerial roles in the service of foreign capital, facilitating the accumulation of profit in agricultural and natural resource sectors. Cotton has become an important crop in Zambia, attracting new investment. It draws on water from the Zambezi catchment. Water is important in cotton growing and hydrological resources have to be carefully managed. Local agricultural labourers also need to be supervised; they work hard sowing seed, growing the shrubby plants and harvesting the cotton balls. Pieter explains how many of the short fibres from these plants are exported to China and go to make the thread for khaki materials and denim fabrics.

Across Africa, the warm climate and fertile environments offer good conditions for growing cotton. North of the Sahara, cotton is cultivated along the banks of the Nile. Egyptian cotton cloth, woven using local and imported fibres, has become a byword for fine, high-quality fabric. In francophone West Africa, cotton is found in Benin, Burkina Faso, Chad, Côte d'Ivoire, Mali and Senegal, and is a key export in all these states. Some East African economies have important cotton sectors, such as Tanzania, but other agricultural products, including tea in Kenya, and coffee in Uganda, play a greater role in countries with cooler, high-altitude farmland. Moving south, cotton has been important in the economic histories of Angola, Mozambique and Zimbabwe as well as Zambia. Today in Malawi some farmers are switching from tobacco to cotton crops as the market for cigarettes contracts. International cotton markets remain buoyant, driven by demand from Chinese and other Asian textile manufacturers, and ultimately retail markets in the global North. African cotton is woven into clothes that are sold around the world, after travelling though the complex systems of provision encountered earlier in the biography of jeans.

Malawians and Zambians, alongside other African farmers, are currently expanding production, but there is nothing new about cotton agriculture or textile and clothing production in Africa. Cotton is endemic and has been grown south of the Sahara since at least 3000 BCE.[1] Large-scale artisanal clothes-making was to be found across Africa prior to the arrival of Europeans. In the east, Mogadishu had a weaving industry in the twelfth century that produced coarse cotton goods and camel-hair cloth, which was traded in Egyptian markets thousands of miles away. Further south in 'Bantu Africa' – roughly the present-day southern African region and Congo Basin – production was less established and cotton cloth was found only in towns and around gold mines at the time of the first Portuguese contacts.[2] The story is very different in West Africa. Vibrant trade networks involving textiles and indigo dyes, as well as iron tools, were part of the culture of the Upper Guinea coast prior to the arrival of European traders. Cloth was both imported overland from Sudan and North Africa and manufactured in Guinea and Yorubaland (southern Nigeria). Interestingly, cotton cloth was even used as a form of currency known as *panos*. As historical geographer Linda Newson explains: 'A *pano* was a piece of cloth measuring about one by two metres … Cloth money was used in many parts of Africa in pre-colonial times, notably in eastern Africa, the Congo, and the savanna area south of the Sahara.'[3] Clothing trade networks extended from urban centres to small villages. Later, when intercontinental trade first took off in the sixteenth century, Portugal initially imported textiles from West Africa to sell in Europe, a pattern which would be reversed in the following centuries.

Coastal societies around the Gulf of Guinea were gradually challenged and changed by European mercantilism, the economic system where national strength was maximized by exporting goods and restricting foreign imports. Slavery formed part of this trade pattern. Local leaders succumbed to economic pressure and a manipulative African ruling class collaborated with the Europeans in exploiting the African masses through the trans-Atlantic slave trade.[4] The discovery of the Americas and the demand for labour in Brazilian gold mines and Carolina cotton plantations forced African feudal leaders, kings and merchants to provide more and more enslaved people on a horrific and insatiable scale.[5] West Africans were skilled and experienced in tropical agricultural and mining, and superior to European workers in equatorial climates. In the seventeenth century, enslaved African labour was exchanged for imported manufactured goods – cotton cloth, metal hardware and guns – produced in Britain, France, the Netherlands and Portugal, often using raw materials from the new American colonies. Portuguese traders led the way, practising methods that brought 'order and clarity to complex sets of transactions', as a precursor of, if not a direct prerequisite for, the emergence of modern capitalism.[6] Trade between West Africa and Europe developed and textiles were increasingly imported to ports around the Gulf of Guinea. Yet the process was not as straightforward as European goods entering captive markets, as Newson observes:

> The importance of cloth and clothing indicates that commercial relations between Africans and Europeans in the early seventeenth century did not consist of a simple exchange of imported goods for slaves, but rather that both parties participated in an active trade in local products. It also demonstrates that far from being dependent on Europe for textiles and clothing, as has sometimes been argued for Africa in general, the demand for these commodities in Upper Guinea in the early seventeenth century, at least, was largely met by its vibrant local textile industry.[7]

Although pre-European locally produced commodities also formed patterns of exchange in the seventeenth century, eventually the balance of trade would shift decisively with greater European engagement in West Africa, not just by the Portuguese, but by other powers which followed in their wake. As the Industrial Revolution took hold in Britain in the early eighteenth century, there was a co-evolution in the expansion of factories in Northern England and the extension of colonial rule. The emergence of capitalism and the business mentalities it produced in the form of autonomous enterprise, and the separation of ownership and management in joint stock companies, enabled Europeans to dominate more profitable trade networks. Cheaper mass-manufactured imports emerged from the early development of textile factories in Britain, France and elsewhere that undermined local African production, which restricted the further development of early artisan manufacturing such as fabric weaving, explaining why industrial capitalism failed to develop in West Africa.

Independent African feudal leaders across the continent were subsequently supplanted. Superior arms, communications and other technologies, along with capital for investment and new business approaches, enabled Belgians, English, French, Germans, Italians and Portuguese first to establish and grow trading networks, and later to extend administrative and governing powers across Africa; authority gradual extended across the continent through the diffuse and exploitative influence of colonialism. Foreign sovereign powers spread out from port cities and co-opted local chiefs and kings or violently wrestled executive powers from rulers. Some former feudal leaders held on to authority under colonial protection, enabling them to maintain rule over indigenous communities. Revenue was raised by institutionalizing the extraction of surplus value through both taxation and new capitalist labour regimes that produced export commodities. The culmination of the nineteenth-century 'Scramble for Africa' was the Berlin conference in 1884, when the continent was carved up by German chancellor Otto von Bismarck and representatives from the other European powers. Eventually nearly all of Africa fell under European control, if not formal colonialism, as was the case with Liberia and Ethiopia. Colonization transformed the mode of production as local economic systems built on tribute and tribal loyalties were forcibly integrated into a global, European-dominated capitalist political economy.

Colonialism had different effects on women and men. Cash crops such as cotton, as well as cocoa, tea, palm oil and rubber, were often cultivated by women, but they did not control the income generated from their labour. Meanwhile men were more likely to undertake waged employment in colonial economies. As well as this gender division of labour, all Africans encountered racism and discrimination when serving the interests of Europeans. Exploitation was based on cultural difference, and through a cruel new mode of production surplus value was extracted from the labour of native people, by the colonial rulers paying low prices for crops, providing low wages for workers or enforcing high taxation on Africans, which left the continent severely impoverished.

Cotton was just one of many African goods produced for the advantage of the colonial powers. Cocoa in Côte d'Ivoire was processed and retailed in France; Eritrean coffee was roasted, ground and brewed to make Italian espressos; Ghanaian gold, Kenyan tea and Nigerian palm oil have all been exported to Britain; and Congolese rubber went to Belgium to be moulded into tyres under one of the most brutal colonial systems. Such patterns of trade were established in the colonial period and relationships of exploitation continue today, although the companies and nations involved have changed. Many tropical products and prized minerals have long been exported from Africa, and profits accumulated in Brussels, London, Paris, New York and Milan and Beijing can now be added to this list. Export trade is not in and of itself a problem – indeed it is vital for growing economies in an international capitalist economy – but the flow of commodities out of Africa has long been of low-value primary goods. African minerals and tropical plants are manufactured into more complex consumable goods elsewhere, some of which are obvious, such as jewellery (gold), furniture (tropical hardwoods), cotton (jeans), and others less so, like oil (plastics), soaps and beauty products (palm oil), and mobile phones (coltan). Value is added in downstream industrial and service sectors outside of Africa. Labour in the global North enjoys higher wages; for instance Italian waiters earn more than Eritrean coffee growers, although both sell their labour power on the market to bring the espresso to the customer. The African labour that goes into producing primary products receives only a tiny proportion of the final sale price, whereas shareholders and managers gain far more from these enterprises. Surplus value is extracted from African labour by the firms which make the more complex goods, as well as transport and warehousing companies and final retailers, all of which take a slice of profit. Merchants in particular appropriate surplus value by purchasing commodities at below market value, and this includes the large American and European supermarkets, which sell cheap tropical products such as fresh bananas, canned pineapples and freeze-dried coffee.

Extensive and complex networks of international trade are involved in systems of provision that bring cotton jeans and other goods to consumer markets. Agricultural labour in the global South is structurally abused throughout many trade networks, and exploitation is in part a product of history. In nineteenth- and twentieth-century colonial Africa, cotton farming involved horrific labour practices. Agricultural communities were transformed by imperial greed, leaving a scar that is still visible in present-day societies. As Marx argues, '[Women and] Men make their own history, but they do not make it just as they please; they do not make it under circumstances chosen by themselves, but under circumstances directly encountered, given and transmitted from the past. The tradition of all the dead generations weighs like a nightmare on the brain of the living.'[8] It is important to understand the past role of colonized peoples in cotton production to begin to explain why cotton farming remains an exploitative labour practice, not just in Africa but elsewhere in the global South. Unequal exchange is embedded within the 'historical materialism' of cotton production, founded on historical modes of production. The former southern African Portuguese colonies of Angola and Mozambique, among the poorest countries in the world, had some of the worst examples of colonial labour abuse.

Cotton in colonial Mozambique

Prior to Portuguese colonialism, Mozambique was home to layered and complex societies. East African culture was not simple and uniform. There were different patterns of productive work; the past was not a pre-capitalist paradise. Indigenous societies had their own injustices, but colonialism led to a new level of severe oppression.[9] Portuguese engagement in Mozambique began with the voyages of Vasco da Gama and the golden age of lusophone exploration in the early sixteenth century, but impacts were minimal until after the Berlin conference of 1884. Colonialism began to expand markedly as each European power felt the need to demonstrate and prove that they were the 'legitimate' rulers of their agreed African dominions. Imperial expansion grew in Mozambique with the arrival of greater numbers of Portuguese settlers, more conflict and warfare, the establishment of government legislative power and the creation of new taxes. The impacts of Portuguese colonialism were especially severe, as Portugal was a relatively poor European country, whose desire to prove its right to occupy vast areas of Africa led to harsh and punitive demonstrations of authority. As the Portuguese state lacked capital, it could not fund the initial investment required for economic colonization. Therefore the Portuguese established large chartered companies, including the Nyassa Company and the Mozambique Company (similar to the British East India Company), that were allocated administrative jurisdiction over vast swathes of territory. Charter companies were mainly funded by non-Portuguese investors; although mandated to develop regions, their primary motivation was to realise profits, overcoming the crises of overaccumulation associated with falling long-term profit rates at home.

Portugal and her colonies were ruled by the autocratic prime minister António de Oliveira Salazar from 1932 until 1968. Salazar stated that colonies must 'produce raw materials to sell to the motherland in exchange for manufactured goods'.[10] Mozambique produced cotton, which was exported exclusively to Portugal until the early 1970s. Cotton prices were fixed and production patterns dictated by the colonial government through a marketing board, the Junta de Exportação de Algodão Colonial (Colonial Cotton Board).[11] Cotton was sold to the concessionary chartered companies with monopoly rights below the world market price. In 1930 Mozambicans were legally obliged to grow cotton. Every man between 18 and 55 and his family were expected to cultivate at least 2.5 acres of cotton, and each single woman and man aged between 56 and 60, 1.5 acres of cotton. Commercial agricultural production was expanded and the proportion of agricultural products used and consumed in Mozambique reduced. Rural life deteriorated as food production fell and famines occurred. By the mid-1950s between half a million and a million women, men and children worked in the sector, producing 140,000 tons of cotton and receiving an average income of only $11.17 per year. Portuguese administrators ensured that cotton was presented for sale to the chartered companies and farmers were not allowed to take their crops to alternative buyers. Police harassed families and ensured that men, women and children were all out tending cotton crops every day throughout the cotton season. Cotton farmer Gabriel Mauricio Nantimbo recalls life on the cotton farms in the 1960s:

> The time of cotton growing was a time of great poverty, because we could only produce cotton; we got a poor price for it, and we did not have time to grow other crops. We were forced to produce cotton. The people didn't want to: they knew cotton is the mother of poverty, but the company was protected by the government. We knew that anyone who refused to grow it would be sent to the plantations on São Tomé where he would work without any pay at all.[12]

Rebellious peasants were exiled to São Tomé on the fringes of the Portuguese colonial empire, but the valuable cotton they produced was at the heart of the European economy. Angolan and Mozambican cotton provided 82 per cent of inputs for the textile factories of Lisbon and Porto. Portugal successfully developed an industrial clothing sector, which in the 1960s employed a third of the industrial labour force and accounted for a fifth of Portuguese exports.[13] This helped grow the Portuguese economy throughout the twentieth century. Portugal has developed from being a poor state in the 1930s to a high income country today. Growth in the Portuguese clothing sector was dependent on having a secure supply of cheap cotton and colonies also provided a captive monopoly market for Portuguese clothing production. Meanwhile, peasants in Mozambique were forced to grow and sell cotton in a brutal and exploitative system of production. Economic life in Mozambique served the metropolitan power throughout Salazar's rule.[14]

Cotton and structural adjustment in Côte d'Ivoire

One of the key policy instruments of the colonial state in Mozambique was price control. The price paid for cotton was below the world market rate; thus labour was structurally exploited for the advantage of the colonial state. However, state price controls of agricultural products have not always been rigidly exploitative. In the post-independence era many African states inherited agricultural marketing boards that set prices. Once free from French colonialism, successful early economic development in Côte d'Ivoire was based on expanding export crop production, predominantly of coffee and cocoa, but also cotton. The state marketing boards (Caisses de stabilisation) extracted surplus from smallholders, who made up 70 per cent of the population. The differential between the lower national price and the global value of agricultural export products provided half of government tax revenue in 1980.[15] Caisses surplus subsidized government wages, social investment in urban areas, and industrial development,

FIGURE 1   Cotton prices, 1950–2000 (US$/kg)

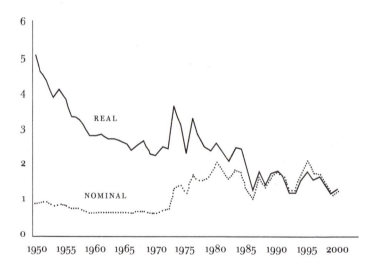

Source: John Baffes, *Cotton: Market Setting, Trade Policies, and Issues*, World Bank, Washington DC, 2004, pp. 62–3; www-wds.worldbank.org/servlet/WDSContentServer/ WDSP/IB/2004/06/03/000009486_20040603091724/Rendered/PDF/wps3218cotton.pdf, Real prices have been adjusted and deflated to 2003 prices.

but also facilitated rural agriculture through the provision of extension services and subsidized farm inputs, such as fertilizer. Additionally, marketing agencies could accumulate surplus funds to support prices when the global market value of agricultural products dropped.

Cotton and other export crops were providing revenue to help government development strategies in many independent African nations in the 1960s, 1970s and early 1980s, but growing tropical agricultural commodities did not lift African countries out of poverty for two interconnected reasons. The real price of cotton declined throughout the second half of the twentieth century from an inflation-adjusted $5.05 per kilogram in 1950 to $1.34 in 2000 and prices were also volatile (see Figure 1). Commercial agriculture was susceptible to fluctuations and crashes in international prices.[16] The dual problems of declining and fluctuating agricultural commodity prices were part of the reason for persistent poverty not just in Côte d'Ivoire but throughout Africa. However, a further shock imposed upon the continent would have widespread and devastating impacts.

In the 1970s, Côte d'Ivoire had been undertaking unsustainable government spending maintained by expanding borrowing, based on inaccurate future export crop revenue predictions. Côte d'Ivoire and other African nations had been encouraged to borrow money from global markets. A funding crisis developed and Côte d'Ivoire struggled to keep up with debt repayments. In 1981, under pressure from the international community, structural adjustment programmes (SAPs) were implemented based on a World Bank stabilization loan that was tied to reduced investment and a freeze on government salaries. The SAPs had calamitous effects. Sadly this blow to development was not unique to Côte d'Ivoire.

Across much of the global South in the 1980s and 1990s, SAPs were widely imposed on highly indebted countries and these programmes had a very negative effect on social and economic development. Drawing on the liberal traditions of Adam Smith and David Ricardo – hence the term *neo*liberalism – the theory was that freeing economies from the control of the state would enable growth. A naive faith in 'the magic of the market' was projected upon already impoverished nations as a condition for restructuring loans. SAPs were designed to limit government expenditure, remove state intervention in the economy, and promote liberalization and international trade. Conservative neoliberal leaders such as Margaret Thatcher and Ronald Regan inspired these programmes. Throughout much of Africa the impacts were great, bringing hardships to some of the most vulnerable communities, including the urban poor, who faced increased prices for basic necessities. African nations could not compete on the world market and SAPs hampered agricultural and industrial development as domestic markets for local produced goods lost protection. These crude programmes provided a shock to fragile economies, leading to stagnation.

In Côte d'Ivoire, SAPs were implemented through the 1980s and 1990s.[17] SAPs liberalized markets for agricultural products, removing marketing board price controls and exposing farmers to market price fluctuations, compounding the effects of a sharp recession. Development gains were lost and social impacts included a reduction in investment in rural health care. In the mid-1980s new SAPs aimed to shift economic policy in favour of export crop producers, but the policies were only partially implemented, and occurred against a background of further recession, followed by drought in 1983. Under SAPs the promotion of export crops was purely an economic policy, not supported by extension services or subsidized farm inputs. Technical assistance for farmers declined, and after 1990 there were mergers and redundancies at extension agencies. The costs of SAPs were increasingly borne by export farmers whose produce entered a world market beset by overproduction and declining prices. The tendency for profit to fall under capitalist competition in an increasingly liberalized market required producers to cut labour costs, creating a process of de-proletarianisation in some areas. De-proletarianisation meant that landless wage labourers who lacked opportunities to work in other sectors or the mobility to search for jobs elsewhere took positions as unpaid forced labour in a form of 'modern slavery'.[18] Life worsened for most Ivorians, as increases in the cost of living easily outstripped any growth in income that resulted from liberalized crop prices. For example, the costs of insecticide rose faster than increases in cocoa and coffee prices.[19] Smallholders producing cotton in the savannah region of northern Côte d'Ivoire suffered some of the steepest declines in income and experienced increased tensions with pastoralists.

The examples from Mozambique and Côte d'Ivoire illustrate some of the economic hardships Africans faced in the twentieth century. Throughout most of European rule the development of industry was deliberately restricted. African dominions served as suppliers of agricultural and mineral products for their colonial masters. European economies gained a head start in their industrial development at the expense of Africans, who were doubly disadvantaged – receiving low prices for their primary goods and being denied the opportunity to develop clothing factories and other manufacturing sectors. At the time of independence, inherited marketing boards, which had been used by colonial governments to extract surplus from colonies, enabled some independent African nations to generate revenue, yet declining terms of trade and the erosion of the value of tropical products limited this opportunity. Crucially, global recession in 1979–83, triggered by the oil crisis, led to the growth of indebtedness in Africa as another crisis of capitalism amplified uneven development. In exchange for further borrowing, African governments were forced to accept the SAPs championed by the World Bank and the IMF (International Monetary Fund). The conditions

associated with lending involved a suite of policies which further
inhibited national development: state companies were privatized,
public spending reduced, currencies devalued, public-sector pay
cut, and subsidies and price controls removed – all in the name of
increasing economic liberalization. The punitive impacts of SAPs
on cotton farmers and other smallholders were harsh, social crisis
spread and, critically, the decline in price support reduced rural
incomes as protection was lost when the volatile world market
price for cotton fell.[20]

Economic liberalization and cotton subsidies

Conditions in the 1990s and early 2000s improved for some
farmers in West and Central Africa, which led to reductions in
poverty. Despite the positive trends, concerns have been raised
about the continuing volatility of cotton prices, which are heavily
influenced by US subsidies as well as the long-term downward
trend in commodity prices. Oxfam has raised these issues in
regard to Mali, Africa's second largest cotton producer and one of
the poorest countries in the world. Trade-distorting subsidies and
pressure from the World Bank and the IMF to increase the role of
the market are leading to the destabilization of rural livelihoods.
Reforms centre on the continuing liberalization of price-setting:

> While reform may create economic opportunities for cotton
> producers, such as the chance to negotiate a higher share of the
> world price and participate in the management of the sector,
> producers cannot manage the risks associated with depressed,
> volatile, and generally declining prices. Transferring the risks of
> a highly volatile world market down to the bottom of the chain
> may benefit the ginning companies and exporters, but only at
> the expense of poor farmers. It also begs the question of why
> those least capable of managing these risks are increasingly
> expected to pick up the responsibility. At the very least, price
> risk should be shared between the farmers, the ginning compa-
> nies, and the traders.[21]

This example illustrates how other parties involved in the clothing system of provision, including ginning companies and traders, extract surplus from cotton production as vulnerabilities to price fluctuations impact upon impoverished Malian cotton farmers.

Economic liberalization and the removal of price controls are policies promoted by decision-makers in the global North, especially bureaucrats in Washington, who advocate free trade as a solution to the problem of poverty in Africa's rural communities. Price controls are viewed as market distortions. The argument follows that once free from the constraints of state interference in their livelihoods, entrepreneurial farmers should be able to develop and expand their agricultural businesses. In principle this libertarian approach to governance is appealing, yet it is a policy prescription based on a lie. The inconvenient truth is that the USA was until recently the world's largest dispenser of cotton subsidies and price support. Large industrial farms are the primary recipients of US government subsidies, which shield them from price volatility. US subsidies distort the world cotton market, deflating international prices and enabling American farmers to maintain their position as the largest exporter of cotton. World cotton prices are reduced by an estimated 10 per cent due to the effect of US subsidies.[22] Developing countries have applied through the World Trade Organization (WTO) to reform the programme, and the WTO has twice judged US subsidies to be illegal, but the US government has failed to act. Lobbying by Brazil through the WTO, along with domestic US political pressure, appears to be leading to a reduction in subsidies, but this is unlikely to dramatically transform the economic climate for Africa's farmers, as a new hegemony is emerging in world cotton markets.

Beijing is becoming increasingly dominant in controlling world cotton prices. In 2009–10 China overtook the USA as the largest dispenser of cotton subsidies; China is also the world's largest

importer of cotton, accounting for 36 per cent of all imports
(followed by Bangladesh, Turkey, Indonesia and Vietnam), and
holds half the world's stockpile. Cotton production in Africa is
increasingly influenced by Chinese market dominance: China is
the primary destination for African cotton. The International
Centre for Trade and Sustainable Development argues that
Chinese trade regulations negatively affect African cotton farmers
as China 'imposes import duties from 5 percent up to 40 percent
on cotton imported outside of the annual 894,000-ton import
quota related to WTO obligations. If China were to allow entry
of African cotton free of duty, such cotton would therefore gain
some competitiveness versus other origins of cotton.'[23] As the
global significance of US cotton production declines, both in
volume terms and as a payer of subsidies for cotton production,
China's role in the sector is expanding. China's ascent in cotton
mirrors the broader-scale rebalancing of the global economy as
we move further into a Chinese-dominated twenty-first century.

China now takes centre stage in clothing and other major
economic sectors, whereas African countries are often on the
margins of global trade. Taking the long view brings a different
perspective. Rather than being peripheral to world economic
affairs, Africa has played a pivotal role in the emergence of international trade patterns. Prior to the encounters with Portuguese
and other explorers in the sixteenth century, there were flourishing clothing sectors in some parts of Africa, which attracted
European interest. The establishment of trade between West
Africa, Europe and America in slaves, cloth, cotton, gold and
other commodities set the conditions for centuries of exploitation. Trade centred on the Atlantic enabled the emergence of
mercantilism, or merchant capitalism, which provided one of
the preconditions for the Industrial Revolution and development
of modern capitalism, the powerful force that has transformed
societies and the environment around the world. Capitalism and

colonialism spread together hand in glove across the African continent. Foreign rule drew new populations into the service of capital and led to the structural exploitation of African labour for the benefit of European powers, helping them to become some of the richest nations on earth. With independence the cotton sector in some countries has shown both stagnation and improvements. Economic development has been hampered by the long-term decline in terms of trade, economic liberalization and unfair subsidies paid elsewhere, in the USA and now China. In tandem with the difficulties in the cotton sector, African nations have largely been unable to develop industrial bases that would enable them to produce more complex and valuable commodities, such as manufacturing finished clothes from locally produced cotton. Some clothing and textile factories were established in the last half-century after African nations began to win political independence, but they have struggled to compete with production elsewhere. Understanding the reasons behind this requires careful attention. Furthermore, it is interlinked with the emergence of China as the dominant player in world clothing production.

CHAPTER 5

Made in China and Africa

Chinese economic expansion

The Zambia China Mulungushi Textiles factory stands semi-derelict on the northern outskirts of Kabwe, a city in the centre of Zambia. Set back from the main North–South National Highway, the 1970s' factory is a large and imposing modern industrial plant. Bored-looking security guards can occasionally be seen patrolling the grounds and a reclusive Chinese caretaker is rumoured to live on the site. Paint peels from the buildings, plants grow up through the yard, and a couple of delivery trucks are gradually rusting away near the loading bay. It has been a long time since the power looms and sewing machines last produced a pair of trousers or a length of fabric. In recent years the Zambian government and its Chinese partners have tried to revive this factory, which for four decades was promoted as a focus for Zambian industrial development and an icon of Chinese–African friendship. Dreams have been shattered and blood occasionally spilt during the factory's troubled and violent past. The venture was a failed attempt at industrial modernization, proving uncompetitive in the global clothing marketplace.

Sadly, Zambia China Mulungushi Textiles is one of many failed African industrial projects and, as such, indicative of the broader malaise which has beset African efforts at economic and social modernization. Historically, Africa's role in clothing production and consumption has received little popular or critical attention. On a global scale sub-Saharan Africa manufactures a small proportion of finished clothes, and accounts for a tiny slice of new clothing consumption. Beijing's rapid rise towards the pinnacle of global power is evident throughout Africa and influences clothing production and consumption from Algeria to Zimbabwe. In addition to China being the largest market for African cotton, clothes from China sell in virtually every street market, and Chinese management approaches have been introduced in African textile factories. In recent years Africa has begun to provide a spatial fix for the overaccumulation of Chinese capital and a new place for investment. Capital is invested via huge sovereign wealth funds; annual trade between China and Africa is currently greater than US$160 billion.[1] Meanwhile, the imprint on African economies of the era of European colonialism remains, contributing to the absence of development in the garment sectors. Africa's experiences in the textile and clothing trade illustrate some of the reasons for the dire economic performance and the absence of development across the continent as a whole. The downward spiral of clothing industry performance is illustrative of the trajectories of other African industrial sectors and can help explain the causes and consequences of poverty.

In contrast to the experience of African nations, China has successfully established the world's largest clothing and textile sectors, which has helped drive national development. The emergence of China, not just in the apparel sector but across the whole spectrum of global trade, is without question the most significant economic transformation of the last four decades. China's influence over the global economy is huge and increasing due to three factors: a dramatic growth rate, a huge labour force and an increasing openness – on its own terms – to trade. The strategic integration of China into the worldwide capitalist economy is causing a global shift in circuits of capital and commodities. Global influence is being exerted not just through the export of cheap goods, but also via the ways in which Chinese firms and investors are determining the relative value of labour, flows of investment, and prices of financial assets. Most significantly, though, China has become the workshop of the world. The global cost of manufactured products, including clothes, has been reduced by Chinese expansion, affecting industrial development everywhere. China is competitive because it can produce labour-intensive products on a massive scale, drawing upon a huge population and the systematic exploitation of labour. However, very particular circumstances have enabled China to put a low-wage mass labour force to work in export-orientated factories.

China was an attractive destination for surplus capital investment in the 1980s and 1990s, as it had huge reserves of labour which would work for low salaries. But why China? Similar potential workforces could be found throughout the global South, not least in Africa. So what was it that made China particularly attractive for investment seeking a new 'spatial fix'? At a time when much of Africa as well as South America were straddled with SAPs and therefore experiencing social crises, the main draw of the Far East was the high quality of Chinese labour. Workers were comparatively well educated, healthy and had a capacity for self-management. Society had been shaped by the hierarchical and disciplined forms of social control, as well as the welfare advances established by the Communist Party of China (CPC) between 1949 and the late 1970s. The rise of China is not a simple story of an isolated communist regime suddenly opening up to international trade, resulting in free-market development. Instead the particular preconditions for growth in China depended on the existing political economy, the earlier progress in social development, and a managed integration within the global market. Economic success was not down to unbridled neoliberalism and a 'rolling back' of the state, but rather built on what is characterized by the sociologist Giovanni Arrighi as the 'extraordinary' social achievements of the Mao-era government before the 1980s. Foreign capital intervened later, on China's own terms, and took advantage of pre-existing social progress. This fact was even acknowledged by the World Bank in 1981, which recognized how the Chinese were much better off than the poor elsewhere in the global South, having employment, food supplies, school enrolment, basic health care, family planning and 'outstanding' life expectancy.[2]

China's economic development accelerated under the guidance of Deng Xiaoping, the reformist chairman of the CPC, who came to power in 1982. Famously in 1961, Deng had said 'it doesn't matter whether a cat is black or white; if it catches mice it is a good cat'. This enigmatic phrase was later perceived as a metaphor for adopting a pragmatic approach to modernizing the Chinese economy. He led a strategic opening up and liberalization of the economy, which included the 'one country, two systems' approach that would later see the reintegration of Hong Kong and Macau into China and the coexistence of capitalist and communist modes of production. Chinese reforms nurtured and protected the domestic economy, unlike the shock therapies externally imposed on Africa through the structural adjustment programmes, which suddenly and viciously cracked opened markets. Gradualism marked the transition to capitalism. China slowly allowed foreign capital to invest in the economy, enabling labour-intensive export manufacturing across different sectors, such as electronics, hardware and furniture-making, as well as clothing and textiles, to grow.

In addition to the high quality of Chinese labour, two further factors were important in catalysing the boom in the garment

sector. First, in the early 1980s the state sector played the dominant role in clothing and textile exports and helped establish
the industry in the first instance, and then private firms gradually took over. Second, important 'matchmakers' linked overseas
investment to the Chinese labour reserve. Diaspora Chinese
communities in neighbouring East Asia and the global North
used their cultural ties to help open up new territory for capital,
enabling new clothing factories to be built. Here timing was also
crucial. China's export surge came just after the East Asian newly
industrialized economies' (Hong Kong, Singapore, South Korea
and Taiwan) collective share of world clothing and textile production peaked in the mid-1980s. Entrepreneurs from these countries
with cultural links to China and experience in manufacturing
clothing for America and Europe were able to invest surplus
capital and develop business relationships that allowed them to
act as a bridge between the relatively isolated People's Republic of
China and consumer demand in the global North. China provided
the perfect spatial fix for capital in the clothing sector.

Textile and clothing industries were concentrated in the accessible coastal regions of Fujian, Guangdong, Jiangsu, Shandong
and Shanghai provinces, close to Hong Kong, Taiwan and South
Korea. The state established Special Economic Zones (SEZs)
along the eastern seaboard to provided tax inducements to attract
foreign investment. Factories were built, like China Galaxy, established in the Pearl River Delta (Guangdong, near Hong Kong),
which belonged to a Hong Kong company and had Hong Kong di-
rectors and managers, and produced for European and American
brand-name sportswear companies.[3] Another example is Fortune
Sports (FS) a subsidiary of a large Taiwanese sports shoe maker,
which, after establishing a profitable business in Taiwan in the
early 1970s, switched production across the Taiwanese Straits
to Fujian province in the late 1980s due on account of the lower
costs of labour, land, energy and transport. Through the 1990s FS

grew to become the second largest supplier for Reebok in China, employing over 10,000 workers and producing 10 million pairs of shoes per year by 2002. Senior management roles were filled by Taiwanese men, whereas the domestic labour force was 90 per cent female, largely 18- to 30-year-old unmarried women from poor rural provinces, employed on insecure annual contracts. The manufacturing process at FS was labour-intensive; employees undertook particular work activities on finely divided production lines to maximize the extraction of surplus value.[4]

In the early 1990s it was not uncommon for female textile workers to spend seven days and seventy hours a week in factories. Furthermore casual labour systems were widely used, which provided little employment security and paid low wages. Pay averaged just 10–15 yuan ($1.20–1.80) per day or $30–54 per month, from which 100 yuan could be deducted for food and dormitory accommodation.[5] Between 1980 and 1994 China's exports of clothing and textiles increased eightfold.[6] Following rapid growth in employment in the coastal provinces, shortages of labour developed. As China is so large, with varying labour costs between regions, textile and clothing exports were able to remain competitive as production could expand and migrate to low-cost areas, or, as happened more often, low-wage labour moved to the coastal factories. Unskilled migrant labour from inland provinces such as Sichuan was drawn into the service of capital, allowing the continued expansion of profit. Work for migrant employees was hard, conditions were difficult, tasks were repetitive and often physically demanding, and industrial accidents were commonplace. The young women were separated from their families and lived in dormitories, with six, eight or more to a room, often sharing one toilet.

Labour exploitation in China was not just driven by foreign management. Initial investors from East Asia led the way; then privately owned Chinese companies grew. Chinese factories came to manufacture most Western-branded clothing goods and serve the fast-fashion markets in Europe and North America. Despite the constraints of the MFA, China managed to continue to increase exports through the late 1990s and 2000s, as steady trade liberalization in the global North provided improved access to markets in Europe and North America. Production was further boosted by the opportunities provided by the end of the MFA in 2005, and after the bra wars most protectionist measures were removed.

The labour system in the Chinese garment sector was cruel and depended on mass labour exploitation, but it also led to industrial growth; furthermore, remittances from urban areas helped support rural development. Parallel to the economic development of China there has been a limited degree of social and political change. Protests calling for political freedoms and the massacre in Tiananmen Square in 1989 drew attention to human rights in China and have been influential in framing how the CPC is viewed overseas. The social impacts of China's rapid expansion in clothing production began to be reported on in the West. In 1992 the *Washington Post* ran a watershed article on Levi's jeans being manufactured by Chinese prison labour. Public concern in the global North about labour conditions in Chinese clothing factories spread. Levi Strauss reacted immediately by drawing up a code of conduct. Media exposés led to the word 'sweatshop' becoming a ubiquitous phrase synonymous with poor labour standards in Chinese clothing factories. Following further outcry from NGOs, churches and student groups, Western clothing companies began to introduce codes of conduct and apply some ethical standards to the factories of their suppliers. Codes usually specify that forced, bonded or child labour must not be used and that adequate wages and benefits are paid without discrimination, that overtime is not excessive, and that health and safety measures are followed. Despite the existence of codes of conduct, research on clothing workers at China Galaxy and another firm, China Miracle, found that employees in 2003 were earning 600–700 yuan a month ($75–90), which did not meet the legal minimum wage.[7] In 2005 wages at FS were 470 yuan ($60) – too low to support workers' basic needs or provide for their families. The FS factory had followed Reebok codes of conduct, but the improved labour standards still failed to meet minimal criteria. Harsh labour exploitation continues in China. While the codes of contact have produced some minor improvements to work practices, evidence indicates that transnational clothing companies have no genuine concern for labour rights.[8]

Developing a labour-intensive and exploitative clothing industry fuelled China's rapid growth and at the same time drew millions of workers into oppressive employment. The Chinese experience is in no way unique; labour exploitation has been at the heart of many boom periods in both clothing production and national economic development. South Korean economist Ha-Joon Chang recalls how in the 1970s teenage males and females in Seoul worked in conditions reminiscent of nineteenth-century English textile mills, 'spending 12 hours or more in very hazardous conditions for low pay. Some factories refused to serve soup in the canteen, lest the workers should require an extra toilet break that might wipe out their wafer-thin profit margins.'[9] China today, South Korea in the 1970s, and nineteenth-century England have all exploited labour to establish mass clothing production, which contributed to economic growth and aided economic diversification and development. Many African countries also attempted to use clothing industries and other labour-intensive manufacturing activities to spur economic expansion in the last half century, but usually they tried to follow a different path, which has not led to industrial development. The reasons behind this failure, as well as some of the local-scale impacts of Chinese engagement in African clothing industries, are explored in the rest of this chapter.

African attempts at industrial modernization

Newly independent states across Africa in the 1960s and 1970s anticipated that once free from colonialism they would be able to develop and modernize their economies. Foremost among their independence strategies was the development of basic industries such as agricultural processing plants, furniture manufacturing and clothing factories. Following economic theories drawing upon the experiences of Europe and America, and both the Industrial Revolution and Fordism, modern clothing production was believed to offer an engine for economic growth and social transformation. Across Africa, small and fragile infant clothing sectors were nurtured and new factories established to produce clothing for national markets as well as exports. Kenya built a large clothing sector in the 1960s under an import substitution industrial strategy; Nigerian clothing manufacturing employed 200,000 workers at its peak;[10] Zambia had over 25,000 workers in the 1980s, including in the important factory Zambia–China Mulungushi Textiles (ZCMT).

In the 1960s, China also began to establish links with Africa, at a time when, under Chairman Mao, Beijing was committed to spreading communist ideology. The zenith of this early era of co-operation was the massive Tanzania–Zambia railway (TAZARA) linking the Zambian copperbelt to Dar es Salaam in Tanzania, built with Chinese aid.[11] China also supported the development of integrated cotton and clothing production programmes in eight countries, each of which employed thousands of workers.[12] One of these was the Mulungushi textile factory, constructed between 1977 and 1981. The project included support for small-holder farmers and involved a fully integrated chain of clothing production, from cotton growing to ginning, spinning, weaving, stitching and design. Although associated with China since its inception, ZCMT originally operated from 1982 until 1996 as a

Zambian state-owned enterprise. It was the largest textile factory in Zambia and, alongside nationalized copper mines, was an icon of modern industrial development.

In the post-independence era, Zambia was a model for African development, moving towards economic and political independence through industrialization and attempting to track the pathway and approaches employed by the global North. Zambian state-owned corporations reflected the government's developmental philosophy. Workers principally in the mining sector, but also those at Mulungushi textiles, received relatively high wages, and there was a 'cradle to grave' welfare policy which supported employees and dependants with housing, education and health care.[13] The pattern of production was similar to the Fordist model of industrial development found in European and North American clothing factories in the 1950s and 1960s. This institutional pattern brought economic growth to the advanced capitalist countries in the post-war boom, in the period before the rise of competition from East Asia and China, and provided a model for labour regimes in Zambian state-owned industries.[14] From 1982 to the early 1990s the 'Fordist' jobs at Mulungushi provided secure employment, company housing and medical care. Social benefits were as much a part of the factory's industrial landscape as the clatter of weaving machines and the bolts of colourful African fabrics which emerged from the production lines. Industrial work at ZCMT conferred prestige, which saw the predominately male industrial workers anticipate progressing towards a 'modern' life.

Zambia, alongside other African countries such as Kenya and Ghana, attempted to follow a different development model to that of China's low wage levels and exploitation of labour. So why did Zambia try to introduce a 'high' wage regime? There are two possible explanations. The first involves a reification of culture, which posits that Victorian English textile mill owners, or 1970s'

South Korean industrialists, or today's Chinese factory managers have an inherently exploitative and cruel relationship with labour, whereas Zambian bosses do not. This theory provides an intuitive explanation: evil managers treat workers badly. However, this answer vilifies culture and does not explain the structural role of capitalism in commodifying labour. Bad Korean, Chinese or English managers have treated their workers poorly, but so have Zambians at other times. Management is only the immediate conduit for oppression; it is capitalist social relations which enable labour exploitation. Ultimately it is unbridled market forces and not innate human cruelty that drive the value of labour-power down to a minimum.

The second explanation is to consider the advantages for capital of *not* exploiting labour. First, high wages in Fordist production systems have to be put into perspective: they are relative and not solely altruistic on the part of capitalist enterprise. The perceived 'high' level of wages rests on socially constructed expectations; workers may feel they enjoy a good standard of living, but this is a standard of living the management thinks is most appropriate for the method of production at that particular moment.[15] Among Ford's key management principles were ensuring a stable family life for workers and fostering a consumer class. Second, 'high' wages and social welfare are instruments used to select and maintain the skilled labour suited to a particular system of production. Workers who are compliant in industrial practices are content and efficient, and welfare benefits ensure the social costs of reproducing the labour force are met. However, on a global scale the use of Fordist production approaches in clothing industries was becoming increasing uncompetitive by the 1980s and 1990s. High production costs in Europe, North America and Africa were undercut by cheap manufacturing in China and elsewhere. At the same time Zambia and other African economies underwent economic liberalization, which transformed their labour practices and exposed their industries to increased domestic competition and reduced the local market for clothing.

In Zambia the experiment with Fordist-style modernization broke down during a period of national economic crisis in the late 1980s and early 1990s. Mines and other state enterprises were privatized. Casualization became a feature of wage employment, which enabled greater surplus accumulation from workers' labour. Salaries decreased under casual conditions and other costs such as health care were avoided when economic liberalization was promoted under SAPs.[16] The Mulungushi clothing factory was beset by financial difficulties, including increased competition, and began to decline from the early 1990s; it was first forced to close in 1996.

The failure of clothing factories was not a specifically Zambian problem, but was a process sadly repeated across Africa textile industries in the 1980s and 1990s. The decline of clothing industries across Africa was shaped by the continent's neoliberal transformation. As African countries accumulated debts in the 1980s and were forced to implement SAPs, a new political economy orthodoxy spread across the continent. Governments were forced to adopt a model based on laissez-faire free-market economics. Within this neoliberal model industrial development was only presumed to be possible by reducing state control and liberalizing markets. In reality these structural changes actually disadvantaged most African clothing manufacturers as governments were no longer able to protect textile factories and thus local markets contracted. For example, in South Africa the clothing industry declined as local retailers took advantage of market liberalization under the ANC government after 1994 and sourced clothing from Chinese and other Asian producers.[17] In Kenya, clothing manufacturers faced weak markets in towns and cities due to declining urban incomes.[18] Across Africa reduced demand for locally manufactured new clothing in the 1990s was combined with competition from more affordable new, but also importantly used, clothing (explored in the next chapter). Since the implementation of economic liberalization policies in the 1980s and 1990s, the predominant trend has been decline within the African clothing industry. In Ghana textile and clothing employment fell by 80 per cent from 1975 to 2000; in Zambia it went down from 25,000 to below 10,000 in 2002; and Nigeria's 200,000 person workforce all but disappeared.[19]

China's new investments in Africa

Economic liberalization transformed African economies and opened them up to new investment opportunities for foreign capital. In the late 1990s and early 2000s Chinese engagement in Africa began to grow and has rapidly become a major area of interest for policymakers and scholars alike. Investment from China has led to new exploitation of natural resources, such as Zambian copper and Sudanese oil, and Chinese aid has built Mozambique's new national football stadium and Malawi's parliament building. Foreign direct investment and trade between Africa and China have grown tremendously; however, many have questioned Chinese methods in this new era of engagement in Africa.[20] Research has focused on the continental level; many authors have rushed to make bold statements about the impacts of Chinese investment in Africa, as if 'China' and 'Africa' could be reduced to single homogeneous and reified cultural entities. African populations have diverse perceptions of Chinese investment, but many populist media and NGO reports, in both the global North and Africa, contain negative portrayals of Chinese people in Africa, which often appear to be unsophisticated or even xenophobic 'China bashing'.[21] Western critiques of Chinese corporations, over issues such as human rights, may conceal anger at the comparative economic advantage they frequently enjoy over their Western counterparts.[22] Attention has also focused on controversies surrounding natural resource extraction and workers' safety. In Zambia, two major incidents at the Chinese-owned Chambishi Copper Mines stand out: an accident in 2005 that led to fifty-two workers losing their lives; and a wildcat strike the following year, during which two protestors were shot dead.[23]

As part of the opening up of African economies Chinese and other Asian investors began to enter the clothing sector. Incentives were provided by the Chinese state, which encouraged clothing firms to expand overseas as part of a 'going global' initiative.[24] Furthermore, trade rules were evolving that provided new catalysts for expanding export-orientated clothing manufacturing in Africa. The MFA had been developed in response to competition from Asian manufacturers and quotas, but prior to 2005 special trade preferences were given to Africa through the EU Lomé arrangement and the USA's African Growth and Opportunity Act (AGOA), which gave African clothing products tariff-free access to the global North.[25] Chinese companies invested in at least fifty-eight clothing manufacturers between 1979 and 2000, including four of the major programmes established in the previous era of Chinese engagement in Africa. In Guinea, Uganda, Mali, Mauritius and Niger, and elsewhere across Africa, Chinese firms formed new ventures and invested in privatized factories and textile mills.[26] Alongside Chinese companies other new East Asian investors arrived, including ethnic Chinese from Taiwan and Hong Kong, in Madagascar, Mauritius, Lesotho, Swaziland and South Africa, to take advantage of Africa's special access to European and American markets. One area of Chinese investment was the resurrection of ZCMT. The following in-depth case study illuminates how Chinese engagement in ZCMT between 1997 and 2006 both exemplifies the challenges of establishing clothing production in Africa and demonstrates the might of Chinese economic power. It also highlights the impact of labour casualization in global clothing industries.

Casualization and labour abuses at Mulungushi Textiles

In 1997 an agreement was reached between the Chinese and
Zambian governments with the Qingdao Textiles Corporation – a
Chinese state-owned enterprise – providing new investment to
rehabilitate the Mulungushi factory, forming the Zambia–China
Mulungushi Textiles Joint Venture Ltd as a company owned by
Qingdao Textiles (66 per cent) and the Zambian Ministry of
Defence (34 per cent). Qingdao also took complete ownership of a
nearby cotton ginnery. Qingdao Textiles hails from Qingdao city,
a centre of intensive clothing manufacturing in Shandong province on China's eastern seaboard. For the Zambian government,
China's unparalleled rise in the global economy and leading role
in clothing manufacturing gave it credence as a model and partner
for development. Moreover, Chinese investment in Mulungushi
had come at a time when other international investors were reluctant to commit to the Zambian economy. With Chinese assistance
the Mulungushi factory's machinery began to spin and weave
once again, producing 17 million metres of fabric, and stitching
100,000 items of clothing a year for domestic consumption and
export.[27] However, struggles between workers and the Chinese
management, along with competition from international clothing
and textile sources, rendered the business unsustainable and the
plant closed again in 2006.

Qingdao's investment in Mulungushi was welcomed in 1997.
The arrival of Qingdao offered a fresh opportunity for development. Thomas Muwowo, secretary of the Kabwe Chamber of
Commerce (KCC), commented: 'We are very impressed with the
Chinese investment. We need it. We have no option if this town
is to survive.'[28] There was optimism among employees at Mulungushi, who were 'excited', 'grateful', and 'very happy'.[29] People
were desperate for gainful modern formal employment, including
salaries and working conditions similar to those experienced in

the previous era of Zambian management. However, the Chinese investors did not live up to expectations: as a weaving machine operator observed, 'the way we were seeing there'd be a future, but what happened is a hell'.

In industrial societies the workers in clothing factories are split into two social groups: managers and the managed. At Mulungushi the division was not based merely on this dimension of the organizational structure, but also on race and culture, as Chinese people constituted a specialist management class. The management regime adopted by differing cultural groups can be influenced by the wider institutional patterns prevalent in the given society.[30] Chinese managers organized work in a radically different way to their Zambian predecessors and were influenced by the evolution of the Chinese economy and society. In her case study of clothing factories in Tanzania, C.K. Lee discusses how Chinese managers had been influenced by reforms to socialist models in China, which saw changes to the labour regime, including the casualization and strict disciplining of workplaces in centres like Qingdao. These labour reforms, rather than welfare policies combined with a high-wage model, are subsequently seen as the key to running an efficient capitalist enterprise and a prerequisites for the development of profitable clothing businesses. Lee also records how the Chinese managers to whom she spoke believe workers must make sacrifices for the sake of national economic take-off and industrial development.

Qingdao Textiles transformed the social organization of the Mulungushi factory, which involved implementing new work patterns, casualizing and disciplining the workforce, and allowing safety standards to decline. Chinese management changed the way long-serving labour experienced the factory environment, and introduced a new group of industrial workers to oppressive and exploitative employment conditions. The workforce expanded from approximately 600 (pre-1997 under Zambian management) to between 1,200 and 1,800 employees and workers were divided into 'permanent' and 'casual' categories. In 1997, 600–700 mainly long-serving, skilled former Mulungushi Textiles employees were rehired on permanent terms; alongside them approximately 1,000 new workers were employed on a casual basis. There was a large difference between the monthly pay of casual (K60,000–120,000 ($16–33)) and permanent (K180,000–350,000 ($50–97)) workers. Furthermore, most permanent employees also had housing provided.

Casual conditions of employment are common throughout clothing industries in the global South. Employers pay low wages and do not provide social welfare benefits in recognition of workers' basic rights. Casual workers at ZCMT lost money for days taken off for illness and could be fired without notice for not reporting for work, or indeed for getting pregnant. Similar conditions of employment are prevalent in factories in China.[31] ZCMT employees spent up to ten years working on casual terms, even though, legally, after six months they should have been granted permanent status.[32] Casual workers found their wages were not enough to maintain a livelihood: 'the salary, it was too low for us to sustain our working … It was like slavery. It was just survival of the fittest… In Zambia there is unemployment. If you left this job you would not get work elsewhere, that's why you would keep doing this work.'

Complaints about low wage levels were not confined to casual workers; permanent employees were also very unhappy, as an office secretary commented: 'No, it [the pay] was very little compared to the work I was doing.' The wages paid to both casual and permanent employees were well below those required to support basic needs in Zambia. Employees could not properly provide for their families; the wages were therefore just part of a household's livelihood survival strategy. The capitalist mode drives wages down to, and even below, the subsistence level. Work in clothing factories in the global South thus often does not provide sufficient income for people to support dependants.[33] Employees at ZCMT would seek alternative means to supplement their wages, such as taking on other paid work outside of the factory or selling goods.

Companies form and tailor a labour force according to their own requirements.[34] For the Qingdao Textile Corporation, new to Zambia, the Mulungushi factory was an opportunity for expansion, a spatial fix and further capital accumulation. Qingdao's managers would have been influenced by their experiences of employing casual labour in China and knew the advantages of a large low-skilled and low-paid workforce in the labour-intensive textile industry, and therefore did not subscribe to the Zambian vision of a modern Fordist industrial society. The workforce at ZCMT became increasing casualized between 1997 and 2006 as the Chinese managers gradually retrenched permanent employees, putting great pressure on workers' and their dependants' livelihoods. Working in the clothing factory in the 1980s had been something to be proud of, but it was now a cause of shame, as a young worker recalls: 'I would even hide it [the job at Mulungushi] from my friends.'

Discipline and profit

Changes to the work patterns at Mulungushi involved more than lower wages and casualization; they included increased discipline and surveillance, new shift patterns, a greater degree of target setting and reduced safety standards. Chinese managers changed behaviour to increase profits at ZCMT. Employees were closely supervised and movement severely restricted. Most workers were casual machine operators toiling on ranks of weaving and spinning machinery, performing low-skilled and highly repetitive jobs to produce bolts of textiles. They were not allowed to talk or stand up and had to get permission to visit the toilet. Some felt they were treated as 'schoolchildren' or 'slaves'. Strict work-place disciplining enforces respect for regulations and increases speed and output, generating greater profit. The automation of machinery was used to dictate work patterns: 'The work was very hard'; 'It was difficult to cope with the machines'; employees worked 'under pressure' and often 'the [targets] margins were too wide'. A production supervisor discussed how automation acted on workers' minds and bodies, as control over them became inscribed in the mechanics of the productive process itself: 'When you work for the Chinese you become like a machine. You can't take a rest. Only when the machine has [a] fault can you take a break.' The Chinese management ran the factory twenty-four hours a day, with three consecutive eight-hour shifts. At the end of each six-day working week, machine-operating employees would swap shifts, which was very unpopular. Keeping the machines running constantly dictated the rhythm of workers' lives. Machines lose value whenever they are not being put to work by labour; the shift system increased the rate at which machines transmitted value to clothing products.

Workers were further exploited through an unsafe working environment, operating machines without adequate safety equipment and training. Industrial accidents caused injury and disability, and ruined future livelihoods. A casual machine operator who lost his lower right forearm in a machinery accident was interviewed:

> I was involved in an industrial accident. [After the accident] the Chinese visited the hospital and made some promises to ensure my wellbeing... Unfortunately after I was discharged it was a different story... The management at the company contrived with the hospital to destroy or hide the file... Without this information it is very difficult ... for me to be compensated in the future ... maybe the company wanted to run away from its responsibilities...

After the accident this worker was re-employed and continued to receive casual wages and have his medical treatment paid, but he never received any compensation payment. Horrific injuries were common and other ex-employees have also been left maimed.

Global capitalist competition in the clothing sector leads to a continuous downward spiral in conditions of work.[35] Chinese managers, having introduced labour reform in their own textile and clothing industries, were a conduit for neoliberal globalization and introduced the new harsh working regime to Africa.[36] Labour exploitation enabled them to extract more surplus-value from the workforce. In the Chinese production system the maintenance of a productive workforce at ZCMT did not hinge on the physical condition of individual labourers, and in a context of high unemployment and weak legal protection incapacitated or unproductive workers could readily be replaced. To expand production and suppress costs, Chinese management drew upon prior experiences with Qingdao Textiles in eastern China. Hence a Chinese manager in a textile factory in Tanzania thought African workers had a 'backward' work ethic and believed they were unwilling to make sacrifices to break out of poverty – suggesting the racial stereotyping of Africans.[37]

Qingdao's investment failed to lift Zambians out of poverty; the Chinese employees, who lived in an isolated compound in Kabwe, became categorized as 'bad' and 'racist'. Workers complained that the Chinese management were 'not proper investors' and that 'they should go back to their own land'. Zambians were used to a less disciplined organization of labour and became discontented; they articulated this as a dislike of Chinese people. The anger felt by ZCMT workers may have been greater than equivalent groups of workers in China who grew up under the CPC. Differing social experiences can influence whether cultural groups are satisfied or dissatisfied with a particular work process and organizational structure.[38]

The negative views of Zambian workers towards the Chinese were produced as a consequence of ZCMT's organizational structure. The tense Chinese–Zambian racial division at Mulungushi may appear superficially to be an entrenched difference, but the racial schism was socially produced. As fabrics were woven and cloth stitched together, understandings of racial and cultural difference were also manufactured at Mulungushi. It was a function of the social and economic relations that marked the work experience. Similar patterns have been found with Chinese and Taiwanese managers in South Africa and in Tanzania.[39] As C.K. Lee explains,

> [Chinese managers] have come to Africa with life long experience in state owned enterprises, and have now basically rejected the socialist firm as a viable form for economic development. They often attribute China's lift from backwardness and poverty to its abandonment of the iron rice bowl mentality and practice [a social safety net]. They demand of their African workers the same work ethics and sacrifice they believed have allowed the Chinese to develop, and have yet to be found among the African workforce.[40]

China has followed a model of rampant capitalist development dependent on the exploitation of labour. This world-view is not confined to the Chinese of course; it has become the globally dominant ideology and is found throughout the clothing manufacturing sector in the global South today.

Labour discontent and the closure of Mulungushi Textiles

Workers organized collectively to struggle against their ill-treatment by the Chinese management at Mulungushi. Although permanent employees were formally represented by the Zambia China Mulungushi Textiles Union, it failed to negotiate improvements in pay and conditions. Casual workers attempted to negotiate directly with Chinese managers. Workers complained that labour leaders were intimidated during negotiations and ineffective, so the workforce took part in strikes 'every year'. Up until 2006, these sporadic labour disputes had little impact, as one disillusioned ex-union member explains: 'There was a strike; we really fought hard to rectify the problems. Nothing happened.' Employees were unable to challenge the management regime forcibly and the pressure to maintain a livelihood compelled them to resume work. This type of dispute is not unique to Zambia; in Lesotho and South Africa workers have struck over wages and working conditions in Taiwanese-managed textile factories.[41]

Serious labour disputes erupted at ZCMT when the state introduced a national minimum wage in June 2006, requiring all employers to pay at least K268,000 ($74) a month,[42] which ZCMT refused to pay. Workers now had a new incentive to strike aggressively against labour practices legally recognized as exploitative. Violent disputes broke out and strikers blocked the main highway outside the factory, throwing petrol bombs from the barricade. There were pitched battles with police, as a former casual worker explains: 'We had made [a larger strike]. It was broken up by the police. They came with tear gas when we organized that strike.' Protests extended beyond complaining about the Chinese management to directing anger towards the perceived failings of the Zambian state and politicians. The factory became increasingly crisis-ridden. Mulungushi ceased production in December 2006.

The closure of Mulungushi was likely due to a combination of factors: market forces, financial difficulties, the pressure for a higher level of wages, and the violent discontent of workers. Trade agreements such as AGOA also began to expire in 2005 as the MFA drew to a close, exposing African production to competition from cheaper imported, particularly Chinese, clothing in both home and foreign markets. This had a disastrous effect on textile production across Africa, spreading further crises.[43] The macroeconomic climate made ZCMT uncompetitive, although the ex-workers believed the factory 'made a lot of profit' and that it was '[t]he strike [that] led to it shutting down'. In contrast Che Ming, the Chinese managing director, is reported to have said that ZCMT had problems paying the minimum wage of K268,000 and that it was this that led to the closure in January 2007.[44] Many ex-employees have since struggled to find formal employment, and hence to sustain their livelihoods; yet others have managed to secure alternative means of subsistence and even found that life is better, feeling a sense of liberation from exploitation, with one remarking that 'It is very different. I'm free now. I was suffering too much.'

Zambians' experiences of working for Chinese managers at ZCMT left them deeply dissatisfied with their encounters with an exploitative labour regime. In simple terms Mulungushi may not have been able to compete in the global clothing sector and pay workers adequate wages in a liberal free-market economy. The production costs for ZCMT are not available, but evidence from Lesotho compares the costs of manufacturing jeans in sub-Saharan Africa and in China. For jeans that would retail in the USA for $20–40, the cost for fabric, buttons, zippers, denim wash and finishing, overheads and labour, and excluding any duties and freight, has been calculated as $7.49 for Lesotho compared to $6.51 for China; however, when current duties (at 16.08 per cent for China) and freight costs (similar for both countries) are factored in, the bottom line is that the 'total landed cost' is very similar for Lesothan ($7.78) and Chinese ($7.84) jeans.[45] These figures are only a rough approximation, and costs in Zambia may be very different, but they at least illustrate that African production may be competitive, although throughout fast fashion supply chain firms do relentlessly squeeze margins to maximize profit.

Firms in the clothing sector continue to seek out the lowest cost locations for production possible.

Peter Gibbon, who has written extensively on the African clothing sector, has posed the question, 'Does it make sense to demand wage levels whose implementation, given local capabilities and distance to market, would probably lead to a shift of orders to lower-cost locations?'[46] From the perspective of businesses and policymakers operating within the rules of contemporary capitalism, the only logical response would appear to be 'no', but really the answer is immaterial. Gibbon's question recognizes that businesses will take advantage of a spatial fix when faced by the challenge of increased salaries. Instead of debating the consequences of wage suppression for one set of clothing workers (such as those from Mulungushi) compared to those in another location (be it eastern China or elsewhere) in a temporary stalling of a race to the bottom for labour standards, the problem of the uneven development of capitalism needs to be confronted. The immensity of this challenge and the alternatives to labour exploitation are contested in the Conclusion. Before reaching that point, the other side to Africa's engagement with the clothing sector, one of the most hidden aspects of the global garment trade, which also affects the competitiveness of clothing industries, is opened up and explored, as the focus shifts from clothing production to the impacts of second-hand clothing consumption in Africa.

CHAPTER 6

Second-hand Africa

Super Bowl's other winners

On 2 February 2014 the Denver Broncos and Seattle Seahawks met in New York to contest Super Bowl XLVIII, America's annual football spectacular. This Super Bowl was special. It was a long-awaited appearance at the Big Apple, and as the first ever played in an outdoor, cold-weather location the game was being called the 'Ice Bowl' ahead of the biggest weekend in the US sporting calendar. In the end temperatures were not as freezing as expected, but more surprisingly the Seahawks, against all expectations, defeated the Broncos 43–8 in the largest margin of victory in a Super Bowl for twenty-one years. Millions were glued to the most watched programme in US television history. Jubilant quarterback Russell Wilson lifted the Vince Lombardi Trophy up high to the crowd as confetti fell all around him, wearing a 'Seattle Seahawks Super Bowl Champions' T-shirt. Banners, caps, sweatshirts and other merchandise were ready and waiting for Wilson's teammates and the Seattle fans.[1] Tens of thousands of souvenirs were sold in the following days. But what would have happened if the Broncos had lived up to the expectations of millions and won Super Bowl XLVIII? Surely there were celebratory T-shirts awaiting them too? So, what became of all that unwanted gear?

Every year a large surplus of unwanted championship merchandise is produced. National Football League (NFL) rules bar the sale of losing Super Bowl apparel in the United States. Rather than destroying the merchandise, the evangelical Christian charity World Vision, which has operated in partnership with the NFL for seventeen years, accepts all the losers' championship clothing, which it freely distributes overseas. In 2013 over 100,000 items from losing finalists the San Francisco 49ers were donated, for which the NFL got a hefty tax deduction. Similar arrangements exist with Major League Baseball, the NBA (basketball) and the NHL (ice hockey). For example, in 2010 defeated Indianapolis Colts shirts were supplied to Haiti; in 2008 Pittsburgh Steelers jerseys went to Armenia, Nicaragua, Romania and Zambia; and in 2007 Chicago Bears caps went to Chad and Romania. Alongside other companies, NFL gifts in kind distributed by World Vision have apparently been worth in excess of a scarcely believable $1.1 billion.[2] Promotional images show grateful Africans and other poor people proudly wearing counter-factual champions' clothing. Stories periodically appear in the mainstream media such as Bloomberg, CNN, ESPN, the *Huffington Post* and *Time* magazine; indeed the Super Bowl donations receive more publicity than any other story relating to unwanted or second-hand clothes in the USA. In the post-Super Bowl hubris they make for a diverting human interest feature and generally provide positive publicity for the NFL and World Vision.[3] Sometimes commentators engage with the subject critically, questioning if the donations are really 'bad aid', as these clothing items are all readily available in the countries that receive donations. The argument follows that gifts undermine local clothing markets and contribute to forging relationships of dependence, depriving poor people of work and dignity. Alternatively these overvalued donations are viewed as a curious PR sidebar and tax dodge, which accompanies the carnival of excess consumption (clothing, drink, food, multimillion-dollar commercials, etc.) that Super Bowl represents.

The donation of unwanted sporting goods is really just the barely visible tip of the iceberg of a much more widespread commercial trade of unwanted clothing from the global North to the global South. World Vision intends to donate all the apparel for wearing, but inevitably some is resold by recipients who would rather have cash than clothing. Most receiving countries already have established second-hand clothing marketplaces; hence the donation of unwanted championship sports apparel is completely atypical. The Super Bowl story provides a diverting curiosity which belies the much larger hidden for-profit second-hand clothing trade. The NFL/World Vision system of provision, is comparatively small scale; yet it does play an important role in legitimizing the broader culture of donating second-hand clothing. In viewing this pattern of clothing distribution, people in the main unquestioningly accept that it can only bring benefits to poor people in the global South, which reinforces the popular idea that clothing donations must be doing good. The reality, though, is not so straightforward.

Second-hand clothes in Africa

Sub-Saharan Africa became one of the major marketplaces for second-hand clothing imports in the 1980s. As the previous chapters have demonstrated, weak domestic clothing industries lost protection as economic liberalization was introduced via IMF- and World Bank-sponsored structural adjustment programmes. As incomes declined, the availability of cheap used clothing provided relief from price inflation for the poor. Imported used clothing, as well as cheaper new garments and textiles from East Asia, outcompeted locally produced goods while factories closed across the continent. Money previously spent on domestically produced goods was diverted to purchases of imported clothing, and profits flowed out of African economies to the commercial exporters and charities operating in the global North as well as Chinese and other Asian manufacturers. Used clothing provides the major source of garments in many African nations, for example accounting for 81 per cent of clothing purchases in Uganda.[4] The trade is important in most of Africa, including Kenya, Malawi, Mozambique, Nigeria, Rwanda, Senegal, Swaziland, Tanzania, Zambia and Zimbabwe.[5] However, it notably constitutes a far smaller proportion of the market in South Africa, Africa's largest economy, where imports have been restricted.[6]

From thriving West African coastal cities like Accra (Ghana) which capitalize on the transatlantic trade, to depressed rural areas such as the inflation-hit highlands of Zimbabwe, the economic and social impacts of second-hand clothing imports have been felt across the continent. Different groups of Africans, including second-hand clothing traders, textile workers and impoverished consumers, have had varied experiences, but their individual interests should not be considered in isolation. Some people have gained whilst others have lost. The argument is frequently made by charities and companies that second-hand trading provides jobs; it is therefore promoted as a positive activity. Compartmentalizing the different experiences of various groups of the poor gives a fragmented view of society and can serve to embed the view that inequality and uneven development are somehow natural, rather than the outcome of capitalist enterprise. For instance, while informal street traders may gain, simultaneously the broader possibilities for the development of modern clothing industries are foreclosed. Therefore this analysis of the second-hand trade must be linked to a discussion of industrial decline and clothing culture in Africa.

Vast container ships ply the Atlantic and Indian Oceans filled with mixed cargos, including thousands of tonnes of used clothes bound for African ports such as Abidjan, Cotonou, Dakar, Dar es Salaam and Maputo. Export destinations are influenced by the cheapest shipping routes to available markets and depend on existing trade geographies (see Table 3, p. 187, for examples from around the world). Used clothing is often exported as return cargo in otherwise empty vessels, which have brought valuable primary products such as coffee or hardwood timber from Africa to the global North; as part of triangular trade patterns; and as mark-up cargo (additional cargo added to fill excess capacity and charged at a lower cost). Containers heading for Africa can transit via global hubs such as Dubai or export-processing zones in India, which conceal their final destination from exporters, as well as their origin from downstream purchasers.[7]

Transport geographies are influential in forming trade patterns, but markets are also determined by economic and political factors. Charities and companies in the used-clothing trade need to be constantly adapting, as African markets are very volatile. For instance, in the 1990s in Rwanda and Zaire (Democratic Republic of Congo) civil unrest and warfare disrupted trade, impacting on the import of second-hand clothing.[8] The degree of protection or other import restrictions can also change rapidly. For example, due to market instability and changing regulations, Oxfam ceased exporting used clothing to East as well as West Africa, which it now favours. Fluctuating geographies are difficult to map, especially as official trade statistics have many missing records or inaccuracies. The used-clothing system of provision is a shifting *process*, rather than a *structure*. Firms and charities respond to changing conditions as well as import legislation, and utilize existing global trade infrastructure. The importance of African markets shifts, and they become more or less profitable, but across Africa demand usually exceeds supply. American and European exporters look for the best market and switch trade routes. As the British exporter Intercontinental

Clothing explains: 'it is certainly not competitive as far as selling is concerned because you always have (if you are any good) more customers than you can supply.'[9]

Evidence from different African markets shows that people often do not know the origin of second-hand clothes. Used-clothing vendors in Soweto market, Lusaka, Zambia were confused as to where old clothes came from. They believed the garments were German when the clothes were recognizably – through the names of brands and logos – items from Britain.[10] In Maputo several vendors at Xipamanine market thought used clothing came directly from China, because of the 'made in China' labelling. Market traders knew the clothes had been previously worn, but were unaware that they came from Canada or the United States. Throughout Africa used clothes are given different labels and names in various languages, which pertain to their ambiguous identity. In Zambia used clothing is *salaula*, a Bemba word meaning 'selecting from a pile in the manner of rummaging'.[11] In Lagos, Nigeria, second-hand clothing is named *kafa ulaya*, 'the clothes of the dead whites', and *okirika*, 'bend down boutique', as well as 'London clothes';[12] in Congo-Brazzaville it is *sola*, 'to choose';[13] in Zimbabwe the term used is *mupedzanhamo*, 'where all problems end'; and in Kenya and Tanzania *mitumba*,[14] a Swahili term meaning 'bundles', is widely used. All these names conceal or obscure the true heritage of the clothes. It is not surprising that vendors do not know clothes' origins, given the plethora of terms for them and the difficulty in accurately mapping trade patterns. Tracing where clothing comes from and how it gets to market is methodologically challenging for any researcher.

In 2004 the journey of a single blouse was followed from the UK to Zambia; although this example is anecdotal and the tracing of the journey of one item difficult to replicate, this case study is illustrative of international trade routes. The blouse was first donated at a Scope (the organization for people with cerebral palsy) clothing bank in a supermarket car park in Ashby-de-la-Zouch, Leicestershire. The bank was owned by Ragtex UK, which collects about 95 tonnes of clothes a week from around 200 recycling banks in the Leicester area. Ragtex donates £100 ($167) a year per licensed bank to Scope for the use of their name. It also collects for other charities (including Rainbow Hospice, mentioned in Chapter 3). Scope likewise works with other companies.[15] The blouse went to Ragtex's textile recycling plant in Leicester and was packed into a 45 kg bale containing similar blouses; it was then loaded onto a Maersk shipping container and exported aboard the *Sealand Michigan* to Beira, Mozambique. In Beira port the container spent a week in customs before being taken by road to Chipata in Zambia. The bale was then acquired by Khalid, an Indian clothing wholesaler who is one of around a hundred merchants in Chipata who come from the same part of Gujarat, Khalid buys twenty container-loads of clothing a year and then sells the bales of clothing on to small traders. The bale containing the blouse was finally purchased by Mary, a Zambian market vendor, and sold in the open-air Kapata market in Chipata.

This example illustrates the multiple actors involved in this system of provision, with different cultural heritages, trading assets and levels of capital including: Scope (a UK disability charity), Ragtex (a long-established British rag merchant), Khalid (an Indian expatriate wholesaler), Mary (a Zambian market trader), along with the transport operators (including the American-owned Maersk container and *Sealand Michigan,* a vessel from the same fleet as the MV *Maersk Alabama*, the hijacked ship famous for the heroics of Captain Phillips). Auditing the economic and social impact of the donation of this blouse or other clothing items is incredibly challenging. This donated blouse was likely combined with both other charity donations and non-charitable collections. The blouse could even have been mixed in with illegally acquired clothing, as Ragtex has been prosecuted by North West Leicestershire District Council after carrying out house-to-house collections without a licence.[16] A clothing item donated at another time to a different Scope bank could have followed a completely different route to its final market. A multitude of different counter-factual pathways can be imagined. This type of network has little coordination, and frequently retailers – like Mary in Zambia – have little information about where the bale of second-hand clothing comes from or what quality of clothing it contains, which creates problems for those at the end of the supply chain.[17]

Used-clothing assignments

Clothes which sell well in Africa include women's light short-sleeved cotton tops, men's rugged cargo shorts and colourful children's T-shirts – apparel that suits the predominantly tropical climate and a youthful population, garments that are hard-wearing and well made, but also have some appeal to local fashion. Such desirable goods are not always in ready supply. One factor which determines profit is the make-up of cargo assignments. African clients have to accept a mixed packing list of different categories of 45 kg clothing bales in container shipments.[18] They are not permitted to select the items they would prefer. For instance, a batch might contain, say, desirable warm-weather items such as T-shirts and shorts, as well as less popular heavy coats and suits. Notably, undesirable used curtains, overcoats and nightgowns sell for low prices in Mozambique, Kenya, Malawi and Zambia. The market conditions, where demand normally exceeds supply, are taken advantage of by organizations like Oxfam, the Salvation Army and Ragtex, enabling them to profit from less desirable bulky cold weather and unfashionable items and accumulate a greater total income. Controlling the packing list allows suppliers to maximize profitability and demonstrates how exporters in the global North have ascendancy over their customers in the global South. Additional money is made from passing on inferior stock, which includes unpopular items as well as lower-quality, torn and soiled clothing. As Simone Field, who carried out research in Britain, found, because 'of the high returns from quality clothing and the limited availability of high quality donations in the UK, it is common for textile merchants to include a small proportion of low-grade clothing into a higher-grade category in order to maximize profit'.[19] Furthermore, the exporter Intercontinental Clothing stated that 'If you do the grading properly (like we do) then there is not vast profits. Whereas if you put things in that people will just about accept without complaint then there is more money to be made and obviously you get a lot more for it.'[20] Business strategies in the global North increase the profitability of exports, but reduce the opportunities for African companies to accumulate capital from the import and sale of second-hand clothing.

Olumide Abimbola has extensively researched the second-hand clothing trade between the UK and West Africa. He argues that, in general, there is 'information asymmetry' between exporters and final retailers, but some systems of provision are more co-ordinated. Igbo apprentices from West Africa who serve importers based in Benin work in many British second-hand clothing firms to assist the sorting of second-hand clothing. They create 'standardized goods' for export:

> Large-scale importers of second-hand clothing send an apprentice to the British exporting company, where the apprentice would act as a quality assurance person. He makes sure that what is sent to the West African market is what the people would buy. At the same time, he also helps his boss overcome the information asymmetry problem that is stacked against him by inspecting what is actually exported to him.[21]

This arrangement is mutually beneficial. Exporters utilize the free expert labour of a worker who is aware of the styles and preferences in the African marketplace. Importers maintain a degree of influence over the grading process; the apprentices have the experience of living in the UK and acquire skills and capital, which enables some of them to start their own businesses when they later return to West Africa.

The role of Igbo apprentices illustrates how some used-clothing trade networks are highly coordinated and export processing is undertaken for a specific retail market and client. However, this pattern of trade is unusual. Abimbola argues that these relationships are connected to a deeper Igbo culture of apprenticeships. Furthermore, it is not consumer demand alone that shapes this system of provision, as the styles of clothing from which the Igbo apprentice in Britain selects are supplied through the uncontrolled donation of unwanted clothing. West Africans' influence over provision and their ability to co-construct or (re)produce desirable second-hand clothing goods is dependent on donations. When selecting garments, apprentices are also reacting to the *stimulated* demands for certain fashions which are formed both internationally and in Africa.

Firms require expertise, money and critical assets to establish themselves in the used-clothing trade. One of the largest private companies in Tanzania, Mohammed Enterprises Tanzania Ltd (MeTL) was an early entrant. MeTL was already established as a manufacturing company producing textiles, clothing, soap and bicycles. The company supplies printed African fabrics to neighbouring parts of East Africa and is the largest textile manufacturer in sub-Saharan Africa.[22] In 1985, following Tanzanian trade liberalization, MeTL met with American used-clothing exporters. Ten years later it had grown to import 4,000 tons (4,064 tonnes) of used clothing per month via Dar es Salaam. MeTL was one of the first businesses in the trade, because it had sufficient capital as well as an existing warehouse and distribution network. There were few barriers to entry for Tanzanians at that time, especially as many had diasporic connections in the United States and Europe who could link MeTL to supplies of used-clothing bales. These cultural networks built trust between supplies and markets and helped decrease exports of low-quality stock.[23] MeTL is a further example of how second-hand and new clothing sectors are linked.

The importance of immigrant communities and long-established networks of trust demonstrates how used-clothing systems of provision cannot be explained by a strictly classical economic model of market equilibrium, the so-called 'invisible hand' of the market. Firms and individuals invest in building relationships and may depend on family or kinship ties rather than just minimizing costs. Neither is there clear correspondence between supply and demand, as sourcing used clothing depends on the uncontrolled donation of unwanted clothing (albeit stimulated, for example by leaflet drops and the positioning of clothing banks). The importance of history and institutions, especially the role of charity in stimulating donations, is key to these trade patterns. Trading relationships are built on shared cultural heritage and international links, such as the legacy of British–West African colonialism, Igbo traditions of apprenticeship, networks of Tanzanians in America and long-standing Indian trading families in southern Africa. Connections and personal ties can help ensure profitability. Established and embedded networks are difficult to compete with, even for well-capitalized organizations, which is what Oxfam found in Senegal.[24] Equally, it is often the African final retailers who find it hardest to make a living from this trade. The business environment is competitive, but there is a further issue which effects profits and trade patterns to discuss: the widespread smuggling of second-hand clothing. Nigeria, Africa's most populous and pivotal country, is the epicentre of illegal imports.

Nigeria: economic turmoil

It is a cliché of travel writing to call a country 'a land of contrasts'. Everywhere has diversity: people who are richer or poorer as well as cultural differences and social inequalities. Uneven development at the scale of individual cities is as much an inevitable outcome of capitalism as the divergence between global North and South. In Lagos, Nigeria, there is not a steady social continuum, but a harsh duality and great divisions between the affluent and the impoverished, who live separate lives. Victoria Island and Lekki are elite enclaves accessible by bridge from other parts of the city; they are frequently guarded by paramilitary checkpoints. Amid the embassies and five-star hotels the mega-rich enjoy luxury hyper-consumption, driving top-of-the-line SUVs with darkened windows, wearing designer labels from Europe and heavy gold jewellery. Many have countless millions hidden away in foreign bank accounts. Across the lagoon in mainland Lagos poverty is everywhere. Shacks and slums are built alongside the water; people are packed in tightly together and diseases like cholera can spread easily. The iconic image of Lagos is of lines of yellow buses queuing in never-ending tailbacks. Among the disorderly and chaotic streets are hundreds of informal marketplaces selling contraband 'London clothes', second-hand garments coming from the UK and also elsewhere in Europe and America. Traders make a living selling to the poor, and hawkers take advantage of the long traffic queues, carrying loads atop their heads and trying to tempt passengers with their wares. Walking past a luxury Jeep or Toyota Land Cruiser in a traffic jam is as close as they are ever likely to get to the super-rich lifestyle.[25]

Affluence in Nigeria primarily comes directly or indirectly from the vast oil reserves, which have been pumped out of the Niger Delta for five decades and account for 90 per cent of export earnings.[26] Oil wealth has brought little meaningful development to most Nigerians, leaving them as poor consumers who live in poverty and often wear second-hand clothes. Despite economic growth in the last five years, fuelled by increasing oil prices, the quality of life of the average Nigerian is extremely low. The persistence of underdevelopment in resource-abundant nations, particularly Nigeria and Africa's other 'petro-states', such as Angola, Equatorial Guinea and Gabon, has led to much debate as experts attempt to explain the apparent paradox of the coexistence of fossil fuel wealth and persistent poverty. Evidence suggests that in states with weak institutions and poor fiscal management the inflow of money from natural resource exports can weaken the state in a number of ways. Oil revenues reduce the impetus for domestic taxation, discourage discussion over how revenues are managed, and weaken the 'social contract' – the reciprocal responsibility shared by state and citizens which taxation embodies. Government institutions and bureaucracies lack authority, and the absence of reciprocity undermines the rationale for democracy. Control of state power guarantees access to oil wealth; hence Nigeria and other resource-abundant states have moved towards authoritarianism. Budgets are not managed transparently, which enables frivolous expenditure and the diversion of significant sums into the pockets of member of the political elite.[27] The extent of corruption and of the pilfering of Nigeria's oil wealth is quite staggering, with an estimated $400 billion 'disappearing' since Nigeria began producing oil in the 1960s.[28]

Oil shapes all economic activity in Nigeria. The state attempted to protect domestic clothing industries by restricting the import of used clothes, but the policies failed; this failure needs to be considered in the context of the oil-dominated political economy. In 1989, nearly 96 per cent of tariff lines for textiles and clothing were subject to import-prohibition regimes.[29] These import restrictions were part of a broader scheme to promote domestic manufacturing and wean the economy off oil dependency, by following an import substitution approach to industrialization (ISI). Import controls were never implemented effectively due to the weakness of state institutions and the fact that Nigeria is one of the largest markets for second-hand clothing in the world. Imports are partially accounted for in official import statistics: Nigeria ranked number 15 out of 50 African nations in terms of reported used-clothing exports sent from the global North in the 1980s and 1990s, despite the market being officially closed to used-clothing imports during this period.[30] This does not give the full picture, however. A far greater quantity of used clothes are imported than register in official statistics, as the large differences in import policies in neighbouring countries provides an impetus for smuggling. Aloysius Ihezie from Choice Textiles explained that although used clothing has been 'contraband for the last forty years' Nigerian borders are 'porous'; he estimates that '75 to 80 per cent' of the used clothing imported to West Africa is finally retailed in Nigeria.[31]

Several key West African countries import a disproportionately high volume of used clothing relative to the size of their populations. Between 1980 and 2010 the levels of official imports to Nigeria were very low in comparison to Togo and Benin, two much smaller neighbouring countries. Cotonou (Benin) and Lomé (Togo) have no restrictions on used-clothing imports; smuggling across the land borders to Nigeria of second-hand clothing alongside other goods formally banned or heavily taxed is rife. The Beninois economy is dependent on Cotonou acting as an entrepôt for banned and restricted goods entering Nigeria. Trans-border trading communities of Igbo and Abiriban merchants control import routes and their activities oscillate with the strength of Nigerian restrictions.[32] Firms in the global North are complicit in this illegal system of provision as they are fully aware that the mass exports sent elsewhere in West Africa filter through to Nigeria with its huge population of 160 million.

The relative poverty of most Nigerians, with their low incomes and weak purchasing power, means the consumer clothing market in Nigeria is serviced by illegally imported second-hand clothing. During the 1980s and 1990s, the Nigerian clothing and textile industry declined dramatically, and Nigerian textile firms continue to fail.[33] For Nigerians, used clothes represented a cheaper alternative to expensive domestically produced garments, even with all the inflated transaction costs associated with smuggling and the bypassing of import tariffs. The Nigerian example shows how an attempt to implement ISI to facilitate economic growth was undermined by widespread illegal trade practices, which illustrates how the second-hand clothing trade has had negative impacts on African development. Fault does not lie just with second-hand clothing traders, as the restrictions on used-clothing imports were not supported by robust customs controls. Institutions have been weakened and corruption has proliferated in the oil-dominated economy. Former Nigerian president Olusegun Obasanjo even accused the customs service of 'making nonsense of government's import prohibition policy'.[34]

Nigeria is not unique. South Africa, the other major economy in sub-Saharan Africa, has also tried to restrict the import of second-hand clothing to protect domestic industries. South Africa has been more successful than Nigeria, but used-clothing markets can be found in Johannesburg as well as Durban and Nelspruit close to the Mozambican boarder. South Africans visit market traders in Maputo to buy up used clothes, despite imports being severely restricted by government legislation. Clothing industries have declined in South Africa, although it is also important to note that South African firms have fared poorly primarily due to competition from imported new Asian produced clothing. Elsewhere, punitive tariffs were imposed in Zimbabwe in 1995 restricting second-hand clothing imports after local textile and clothing manufacturers had lobbied the government. However, widespread illegal informal sourcing processes continued.[35] So-called 'suitcase traders' skip across the border daily between Mozambique and Zimbabwe carrying stock, either masquerading as their own clothes or to which the customs officials turn a blind eye for a few cents. In Kenya Moses Ikiara, executive director of the Kenya Institute for Public Policy Research and Analysis, complained that 'New imported clothing comes in disguised as *mitumba* [used clothing] and it gets into the market, and of course without paying taxes, which makes it a big challenge for domestic textile producers to be able to find a market.'[36]

Customs officials are frequently complicit in smuggling and extract bribes from importers. Corruption is a reality of the socio-political context of many states in Africa, but is also an outcome of opportunities presented by the weakening of African governments in response to structural adjustment and destabilization caused by neocolonialism. Economic liberalization throughout Africa has tended to accelerate both pilfering of existing state resources and the diversification of the state bureaucrats into private activity, as formerly 'grey' areas of economic life have become seemingly legitimate.[37] There are external costs for others outside such privileged networks. The majority of Africans experience the detrimental impact of circumvented import costs and forgone government revenues, which reduces social expenditure and impacts upon economic policy, such as Nigeria's failure to protect domestic clothing industries. Economic liberalization has not provided opportunities for individual impoverished Africans to become entrepreneurs and rise out of poverty; it has instead served the interests of a narrow elite, such as the residents of Victoria Island in Lagos, while leaving most Africans only dreaming of economic emancipation. The evidence further demonstrates how the used-clothing trade is associated with deviant economic activity that continues the long-term connection with criminality. Due to widespread smuggling, accurate economic modelling of

the effect of the undocumented trade is very problematic, which
contributes to the difficulty of assessing the full impact of second-
hand clothing imports on the decline of clothing industries in
Africa.

Used clothing imports and the decline of African clothing industries

Used clothing has outcompeted and displaced African clothing
manufacturing in Kenya, Malawi, Mozambique, Tanzania, Zambia
and other countries which permitted imports of second-hand
clothing, as well as in countries like Nigeria where they are traded
illegally. Various African policymakers have accused second-hand
clothing importers of 'killing' local textile and garment sectors.
A report published by the World Trade Organization assesses
the impact:

> With the liberalization of the second-hand clothing market, the
> already deteriorating textiles and clothing industry was severely
> affected. The garments produced in Malawi have been found to
> be more expensive than second-hand clothing, and as a result,
> some of the major factories could not compete with the cheaper
> prices offered by the second-hand clothing industry and they
> were forced to close. Initially, the influx of second-hand clothing
> was seen as 'the best thing that ever happened to Malawi', but
> the consequences to the clothing industry were devastating.[38]

This argument may have been accurate for Malawi, but the
decline of African clothing industries is not due just to second-
hand clothing imports; this is an oversimplistic explanation for a
complex problem. The ultimate cause of crisis has been economic
liberalization, of which the increased import of old clothes from
the global North is a constituent part. Second-hand clothing
is dominant in many African marketplaces, but the reason for
the failure of clothing factories was not simply because poor

consumers switched from buying more expensive locally made goods to cheap imported second-hand clothing. As the previous chapter demonstrated, African clothing factories faced multiple challenges in the 1980s, 1990s and 2000s. Other factors operated in concert, with the import of second-hand clothing exacerbating the problem. Incomes declined, reducing Africans' purchasing power, which in turn depressed demand. Factories failed when state-owned firms were privatized and suffered from profiteering and poor management.[39] Clothes were also able to flow between African countries when SAPs weakened border controls, increasing competitive pressure for African producers in regional markets. For example, colourful African printed fabric featuring geometric and floral designs is manufactured in countries including Congo (DRC) and Tanzania and exported to neighbouring markets like Mozambique and Zambia. East African printed cloth now competes with cheap imports of printed textiles from China and India, as well as second-hand clothing. In these instances, imported new clothing may be displacing regional production in neighbouring countries.

Globalization opened borders and had unpredictable effects on African markets. In Mozambique and Zambia shoe-sellers combine imported new counterfeit Adidas, Nike and Reebok sneakers and cheap dress shoes with imported second-hand shoes. The new products can even be deliberately scuffed and tarnished to look like authentic original Nikes imported from North America. Robust shoes in good condition originating from the global North are highly prized and can sell for up to $20, much more than low-quality new imports. Traders mix up the stock to try to conceal the new shoes' heritage and deceive the consumer. The last example shows how individual traders are finding new ways to deal with the challenges of selling used items. More in-depth evidence is needed to illuminate how vendors make a living from this hidden trade network as well as revealing the interconnections with new clothing manufacturing. Research from Mozambique in the next chapter provides insights into how people struggle to make a living from the second-hand clothing trade.

CHAPTER 7

Persistent poverty

Growth without development in Mozambique

The former Secretary General of the United Nations, Kofi Annan, is one Africa's most celebrated statesmen. The Ghanaian led the UN between 1997 and 2006, during which time he was a co-recipient of the 2001 Noble Peace Prize. Respected for his even-handed decision-making, Annan is someone who knows African politics; his judgements are carefully considered and rarely controversial. His has been one of many voices to have highlighted Mozambique as a shining example for Africa. On a trip to Maputo in 2002 he said that 'Mozambique's continuing success story and the climate of trust it has generated is the best possible antidote to the sceptics and cynics about Africa', celebrating what he saw as development gains made in the decade following the end of the civil war.[1] Since Annan's visit this southern African country has consistently been held up by the main Western donors as one of the continent's major success stories. In 2013, Annan's successor as UN Secretary General, Ban Ki-moon, visited Mozambique and hailed the country as an 'important success story for the global community'.[2] Mozambique is widely championed as an example of a nation that has moved from warfare to peace and stability, as well as from economic stagnation to rapid growth, and is said to have achieved both these goals by following the dual Western policy prescriptions of democracy and pro-market liberal economic reforms.

This all sounds like good news, but if we look more closely at the experiences of most Mozambicans the harsh reality is much more painful; indeed evidence indicates that Annan, Ki-moon and the donors may well be wrong. It is true that the country has been largely peaceful for over twenty years and has experienced economic growth, but rather than an ongoing success story Mozambique is a place of persistent poverty where levels of impoverishment rival those of war-torn states. Mozambique has experienced a growing economy without a sustained and meaningful reduction in poverty. What is of further concern is how Mozambique's recent history is being twisted to support political positions. Annan's argument that this example can counteract cynics and Ki-moon's statement that it represents an 'important success story for the global community' are insightful. These platitudes are for an international audience. Mozambique is held up as a success story to show to other nations because it adopted the neoliberal development model and is one example that could – it is mistakenly believed – support the market-friendly policy prescriptions and SAPs long championed by the global North.[3]

Mozambique has been ruled exclusively by the Frelimo party since gaining independence from Portugal in 1975. Under the charismatic Samora Machel and his comrades, Frelimo led the freedom struggle and later fervently supported Mandela's ANC through the final years of apartheid. Like many of Africa's independence movements, Frelimo was once dedicated to Marxism, a legacy evident in the names of Maputo's avenues: Avenida Vladimir Lenine, Avenida Mao Tse Tung, and Avenida Karl Marx. Over four decades Frelimo has faced many challenges, which have made it difficult to steer the nation away from impoverishment and have led many of the party cadres to abandon their socialist ideology. Throughout the twentieth century Mozambique's industrial development was aggressively constrained, first by Portuguese colonialism and later by a devastating civil war fuelled by support for insurgents from the white minority regimes in neighbouring Rhodesia (present-day Zimbabwe) and South Africa. Insecurity restricted the emergence of industry, including clothes manufacturing. Mozambique was left desperately poor and severely indebted. Under pressure from the West a World Bank and IMF-inspired structural adjustment programme was implemented in 1987. The country was left as poor as anywhere in the world.

Following the fall of apartheid in South Africa and the subsequent ceasefire in Mozambique, peace was made in 1992, after which Frelimo embraced further free-market reforms under the guidance of donors. Elections have been held since 1994, which Frelimo has dominated. The hard-won peace is something that should be rightly celebrated. However, the country has not been successful in combating poverty. The peace dividend led to growth in the late 1990s and the establishment of an important aluminum processing industry, albeit one which employs few people. Recently, discoveries of coal and gas reserves have fuelled economic expansion, although financial gains are unevenly distributed. Nigeria's experience with oil offers a prescient and cautionary lesson for policymakers. Despite widespread optimism among the international community as well as Frelimo politicians, Mozambique remains one of the poorest countries on earth, as the African Development Bank notes: 'growth has as yet created limited jobs and has had a less-than-desirable impact on poverty reduction.'[4] In the Human Development Index, calculated by the United Nations, Mozambique ranked 185th out of 187 countries in 2014, below barely functioning conflict-ravaged societies such as Afghanistan and Mali. Figures from the World Bank illustrate that since 2003 GDP growth has averaged over 7 per cent per year; meanwhile the percentage of people living below the poverty line was stable at 54 per cent between 2003 and the last survey in 2009. Life expectancy is only 42 years and gross national income per capita is just $501 per year.[5]

In Maputo, the names of left-wing icons such as Lenin and Marx may still be found on the capital's streets, but Frelimo has moved in a dramatically different direction and fully embraced economic liberalization. Since the end of the civil war the state has not intervened to establish planned industry, as happened in China in the 1980s and 1990s, and South Korea in the 1960s and 1970s; it has instead followed a laissez-faire approach towards national development. New policies have not fostered the type of economic growth that is based on the establishment of old-fashioned labour-intensive industry, but instead have promoted the extraction of natural resources, providing GDP growth but limited employment. Sectors like the small clothes- and textile-making industries have fared poorly since collectivism was abandoned in the 1990s and the few state-owned factories were privatized with catastrophic effect. Private owners lacked capital, management capacity and competence. Unscrupulous bosses stripped clothing factories of assets to enrich themselves, buying BMWs and Mercedes and furnishing their houses. There are even examples, including in Nampula, where once the resources of clothing factories were used up the buildings had been transformed into warehouses for selling second-hand clothing. The pattern of deindustrialization was repeated in other economic sectors, including cashew-nut processing, flour mills and furniture manufacturing.[6]

Industry stagnated or declined; at the same time second-hand clothing and other consumer goods were allowed into the reformed market. The small clothing sector faced myriad problems because of the wider socio-economic impacts of SAPs in Mozambique. Urban incomes fell for many formal wage-earners and declining basic services affected businesses. In 1993 Texmoque, a privately owned textile factory, was forced to close due to a lack of materials and electrical power.[7] Challenges for the garment industry continued in the early 2000s, when clothing factories were left idle and 'mothballed'.[8] The failure of local manufacturing provided further opportunity for cheap imports of new and used clothing, as detailed in a report by USAID:

> Substantial imports of used clothing underscored the limited means of most Mozambican consumers. Thus, local demand for new clothing and the productivity and size of the apparel industry could not sustain the capital investments that a competitive spinning, weaving, and finishing industry required simply to survive. Saddled with debt, rising labour costs attributable to new regulations and laws, and a centralized industrial strategy that put wealthy consumers in export markets beyond their reach, Mozambique's textiles and apparel industries dwindled to a few small suppliers of local niche markets.[9]

On a very modest scale, Mozambique has experienced growth in the clothing sector since the mid-2000s, but total employment is only around 2,000 workers.[10] The Texmoque factory reopened in 2008 following investment from MeTL (the Tanzanian firm discussed in the previous chapter), and the Moxtex factory launched in 2009, and has since expanded from producing garments for South Africa to also exporting to the United States.[11] One of the reasons for the small growth in manufacturing is that export-orientated factories have relocated from South Africa to southern Mozambique due to lower wage levels.[12] This is another small-scale regional example of capital seeking a spatial fix. In South Africa, 'unrealistically progressive' labour market policies are making it difficult for clothing factories to grow profits, so entrepreneurs have tried relocating to lower-wage Mozambique.[13] While employment in clothing factories may bring work for a few Mozambicans, this is another example of a race to the bottom for labour standards in the garment sector. Under current economic policies most Mozambicans are unlikely to ever get jobs in industries like clothes-making, and many more have to engage in informal ways of making a living, such as selling imported second-hand clothes.

Second-hand clothing imports and wholesale

Second-hand clothing is found everywhere in Mozambique. In many instances, used clothes are the only garments available for the impoverished population, and are widespread even in remote rural areas. Maputo in the south, along with the port of Beira in the centre, are regionally important Indian Ocean trading hubs. Second-hand clothes come from Australia, Europe and North America, and are sold in Mozambique and exported to Malawi, South Africa, Swaziland, Zambia, Zimbabwe and elsewhere. Despite the liberal market reforms, arranging the import of second-hand clothing requires the right contacts. Imports get held up by the *alfândegas* (customs officials), who negotiate both *impostos* (import taxes) and additional *taxa* (informal charges). Corruption is commonplace in Mozambique. A continuing process of 'state capture' – the control of national assets and political posts for personal gain – by a narrow elite within Frelimo means that importers often have to make backhanded and under-the-table payments to ensure their goods are allowed into the country.[14] The misuse of state office has contributed to the rising inequality and helps explain why economic growth is not reaching the poorest Mozambicans. Used clothes are imported primarily by Indian traders with transnational links to the global North and connections to local politicians. Anne Pitcher believes that 'many African consumers as well as industrialists view Indians as parasites who undermine productive activities and charge high prices. Some argue that the government protects Indians because of their electoral support for Frelimo.'[15]

Used clothes are imported from the global North by firms such as AHP Commercial, Armazém Nguesse Commercial, Fatah Trading, Sabah Enterprises and UMUT World Connection.[16] UMUT has a warehouse close to the large Xipamanine market in Maputo where many importers are based. Twenty-foot shipping containers holding 250–300 45 kg bales are unloaded at the side of the street and carried into storage. Consignments of bales are determined by a packing list; as with Oxfam's clients, UMUT does not control what types of clothing are sent from the global North. UMUT is typical of the importers working across East and West Africa, importing on average two or three shipping containers per month. A supervisor at UMUT believed that most of their clothing originates from Spain and Germany, but his company procures it from Nigeria. Evidently someone associated with UMUT works in Nigeria and purchases the clothing from Europe.[17] AHP Commercial sources clothing from Australia: Australian Salvation Army-branded bales can be seen inside the warehouse. Sabah Enterprises and Armazém Nguesse Commercial both import used clothing from Canada. Bales of second-hand clothing are usually labelled with a description of the contents, such as 'LTS–LS–MIX' (ladies T-shirt, light/summer mix), as well as the origin. One label common in Maputo is from Canam International. Canam first exports clothing from North America to grading facilities in India and then re-exports processed second-hand clothing to East Africa. It employs 700 people in India, taking advantage of low labour costs and incentives in a special economic zone in Kandla. This west Indian port is a hub for the labour-intensive processing activity 'between' the collection nodes in North America and retail in Africa, even though it is thousands of miles from both continents.[18] The geographies of international shipping routes, including the access provided by the Suez Canal and shipping lanes which avoid Somalian piracy, make Kandla a strategic location. Similar hubs in the Arabian Gulf are used by firms exporting second-hand clothes from Europe to East Africa.[19] UN data show that $55.3 million worth of used clothing was exported to Mozambique in 2012, equal to 52 million tonnes of garments, or the equivalent of 99 million pairs of jeans or 423 million T-shirts. This is likely to be an underestimate of the total size of the market.[20]

Import firms in Maputo have specialist warehouses (*armazéns*) where second-hand clothing bales are stored and sold. Local market traders buy the intact bales and sell individual clothing items to consumers. Shipments of second-hand clothing are irregular and the inconsistency of supply creates problems. For instance, Paulo, a market vender who sells second-hand shirts, found that there had been a serious shortage of bales around the general elections in November 2009 when few boats delivered shipments into Maputo. At other times there can be a surge of imports and the cost of bales can decrease. *Armazéns* then send text messages to traders advertising new and discounted second-hand clothing bales. Across all clothing supply chains the rate of transactions is an important determiner of profitability.[21] As with fast-fashion firms in new clothing systems of provision, *armazéns* attempt to accelerate their rate of transactions in order to gain a quick return on their investment. They are helped in this process by local speculators known as *mamães grandes* (literally 'big mothers'), who try to control the movement of clothing bales and manipulate the market. *Mamães grandes* are favoured clients of *armazéns* who purchase large numbers (50–100) of bales, particularly desirable clothing, which allows *armazéns* to quickly complete sales. Individual *mamães grandes* or groups attempt to form oligopolies; these are especially active when there is a shortage of clothing bales. When they have control of the trade *mamães grandes* then charge a premium of around 300 Mozambican meticals (MZN) (approximately $10) for a bale to market vendors.

The two main risks in second-hand clothing trading are currency fluctuations and poor-quality clothing. Risks to profits are

TABLE 1   Types of 45 kg used-clothing bales advertised for sale by an importer in Maputo

Type of clothing bale	Price (MZN)	Price (US$)
Children's clothing (o to 7 years)	3,000	103.44
Mixed shorts	1,500	51.72
Pants (women's)	1,400	48.28
Pants (men's)	1,700	58.62
Skirts (denim)	1,800	62.07
Skirts (cloth)	2,500	86.21
Shirts (with collar)	1,500	51.72
Shirts (without collar)	1,300	44.83
Khaki pants (men's)	1,500	51.72
Khaki pants (women's)	1,800	62.07
Jeans (for men and women)	2,000	68.97
Underwear (men's)	3,500	120.69

Note: Prices recorded 8 June 2010.

passed from wholesalers to market traders, reflecting the power relationships in this system of provision. Importers' contracts with suppliers in America and Europe are agreed in US dollars. When the Mozambican metical weakens, importers increase prices. However, when the dollar falls against the metical, prices are not reduced by the *armazéns*. Market traders complain, but have been unable to end this practice. Sergio, who sells boys' T-shirts, argued that market traders are treated *sem seriedade* (without seriousness) by importers and local authorities, which may reflect the close ties between *armazéns* and Frelimo politicians. Price inflation is a common cause for complaint, but the greatest challenge is bad-quality stock. Used clothing is inherently variable; some items are clean and like new, others are rags that are falling apart. Stock quality is the major factor determining profitability, and there is an unequal relationship between importers and the market traders who retail clothes. Bales are sold 'blind': as sealed and unopened packages. Market traders only know what category of clothing – such as men's jeans, socks or floral dresses (see Table 1) – they are buying from *armazéns* and cannot examine the contents in advance. If they are lucky they can get many good items in nearly new condition, and which are stylish and the right sizes, or they may be unfortunate and open a bale to find items that are ripped or rotten, unfashionable or too large.

Maria sells used fabric and curtains in Xipamanine market. Visiting the *armazéns* takes her half a day. When she brings a bale back to Xipamanine she is always anxious and excited. Her stall is located towards the rear of the market. She makes sure her regular customers know when she is going to open up a new bale, as the first rummage through the stock always attracts a large number of clients keen for a prize purchase. A sharp knife is used to slice through the thick, tight plastic strapping, whereupon the bale sacking springs open to reveal the packed stock. Everyone bends down to pick through the textiles. She recorded her contrasting experiences on two consecutive days. The first day was 'not a good day because I opened a bale of curtains without there being one piece sold'; this failure meant she had to return and try a different importer the next day. This time she was luckier: 'I opened a bale of cloth. I sold 1,200 metricals' worth ($37.50). It was a good day.'[22]

Soiled or wet articles included in bales can damage a whole package, as mould, dirt and soiling permeate through the fabrics in the tropical heat. Hygiene issues are both a practical concern and a matter of dignity. In Ghana the government has taken the step of banning imports of second-hand underwear for this reason, to mixed reactions from consumers, who find used underwear cheaper and often of a higher quality than new goods.[23] This issue stands out as the exemplifier of inequality in global clothing systems of provision. In Maputo all the traders consider each bale bought to be a real game of chance, which is known as a *totobola* or lottery. A winning bale can be very profitable and can double or triple their income, whereas poor-quality stock will make it difficult even to recover the cost of the bale from retail sales. *Armazéns* do not offer refunds on bad-quality clothing. However, individual African traders are not completely powerless in the face of the larger international importers. For instance, Judite, who sells skirts, sometimes pays a bribe of a couple of dollars to a worker at the warehouse so they select a good bale for her, without the knowledge of the *armazém* manager.

Another problem encountered by traders in Mozambique is the size of clothing. North American clothing, especially, is often too large for Mozambicans. Mario and other jeans traders discussed how this creates a major problem for them. The diet and lifestyle of many Americans, which have led to mass obesity and a national health crisis, have resulted in jeans with a 42 inch waist or larger becoming commonplace in used clothing imports. Few Mozambicans are so big. If a trader opens a bale and finds many pairs of very large jeans, they are faced with two problems: first, the jeans are too large to sell; second, there will be fewer pairs of big jeans in a single bale (which are sold at set weights of 45 kg) so they end up with less stock. Super-size clothes sell for a low price, as they are less useful. Large jeans alongside other undesirable clothing, like ripped and dirty garments, are brought by specialist vendors who sell them at a very low price outside of the main market area to people in extreme poverty.

Every garment sold in the second-hand clothing markets is unique; each has its own biography and shows marks of its former lives. Market traders check and empty pockets, occasionally finding US or Australian dollar bills. Sales tags are sometimes left on items, including those of the Australian Salvation Army and Value Village used-clothing retail shops – indicating garments that had previously been marketed in these outlets but were not purchased and instead ended up being exported. Used clothes

also display names indicating where they were first consumed
in the global North: these may be sports teams, government
institutions or businesses – for example, 'Andalucía Volebol', 'New
South Wales Police Service', 'Walmart USA'. National brands are
sometimes identified: for instance, George at Asda and Marks &
Spencer from the UK, and Billabong, a popular and distinctly
Australian brand, which is also marketed elsewhere in the global
North. Other labels, such as Fruit of the Loom, H&M and Nike
are multinational brands, retailed around the world, reflecting
the internationalization of the clothing industry. New clothing
'seconds' (substandard products) are very occasionally found – an
example being tens of pairs of identical new Crocs sandals.[24] And
there have been reports of the unwanted championship clothing
from the NFL, discussed in Chapter 6, finding its way to market
in some African countries.

Work in the second-hand clothing sector

Few researchers have tried to understand the livelihoods of
second-hand clothes traders in Africa. The work that has emerged
has tended to paint a positive picture on account of the employment created.[25] For example, Simone Field, who undertook
research in Zimbabwe in the 1990s and Kenya in the 2000s,
considers that the business provided very valuable self-employ-
ment opportunities for informal traders, as well as advantages
for consumers and the economy as a whole. She describes the
local economic benefits, indicating the advantages for importers,
wholesalers, market traders, consumers and the state, as well as
pointing to other spin-off benefits. Field asserts that in Kenya
the second-hand clothing 'trade directly or indirectly affects 5
million people through employment and income generation', a
claim that is repeated by the UK-based Textile Recycling Association as evidence of the 'crucial contributions this industry

makes to the world economy'.[26] But researchers have to be careful
when making such bold claims. The total population of Kenya is
around 37 million people; therefore 5 million people represents
13.5 per cent – a very high proportion. Field does not state how
she produced this figure. There is, however, another source to
consider: a national survey by the Central Bureau of Statistics
of Kenya, which recorded that second-hand retailing accounted
for 8 per cent of the total number of small and medium-sized
enterprises and employed only 103,961 workers in 2001.[27] Even if
each person supported five dependants or indirect beneficiaries,
this would give a total of approximately 500,000 people, one-tenth
of Field's figure, indicating that her estimate is excessively high.
Nevertheless, a similar very large claim is made by the Salvation
Army: 'in Ghana it has been estimated that up to 20% of the
working population is employed in the used clothing chain'. The
source for this data is not referenced.[28] Again, when contrasted
with the 8 per cent of small and medium-sized enterprises (not
total working population) in Kenya, this figure seems unlikely.
To conclusively disprove these figures cited by Field and the
Salvation Army is difficult, given the weakness of employment
statistics in many African states. With regard to Mozambique, a
conservative estimate would be that the people employed in this
sector number only in the tens of thousands, and proportionally
far fewer than claimed by Field and the Salvation Army.[29]

In Maputo there are over 1,000 vendors selling second-hand
clothes in Xipamanine market and thousands of others at smaller
markets around the city. In Xipamanine traders mostly work
alone, selling clothes from small stalls a couple of yards square.
Stalls are built from odd lengths of wood, corrugated iron and
packaging from used-clothing bales. The market is a former
soccer field; the remains of the goals can be found in the dark
alleyways. The stalls are owned or rented and vendors pay a
small daily fee to the municipal council. Most vendors have been

selling for many years; indeed it is not unusual to find sellers who have been trading in used clothing for over a decade. People have drawn on friends and family for loans or obtained credit from moneylenders to start selling second-hand clothes. Others have taken to selling clothing using money earned from other types of trading, such as selling food, mobile-phone credit or soap. In a further example of the impacts of economic liberalization, some use redundancy payments from formal-sector jobs, such as at the train station or university, after the loss of employment due to structural adjustment programmes. Retailing used clothing is not an occupation people choose because they are interested in fashion or style; rather, it is a livelihood born of necessity.

Earnings in the market are very variable. Due to the low quality of stock it is not unusual for people to make daily or weekly losses as overheads exceed sales. Vendors risk capital on the lottery of new bale purchases. They have to work hard in the market to retail second-hand clothes to poor customers, attempting to maximize prices whilst maintaining turnover. Traders specialize, selling only certain types of clothes. They are risk-averse: once they know local preferences and prices they tend to stick with, say, jeans or T-shirts. Successful vendors may record short-term losses, but are able to take a long-term perspective on trading, constantly building-up, renewing and depleting stock and capital. Market traders have different strategies when pricing clothes. Sergio sells boys' T-shirts at fixed prices between 45 and 70 MZN ($1.40–$2.20). Others price items individually, like Maria, who sells curtains. Maria sometimes changes the quoted price of pieces of fabric over time as potential customers make repeat visits to her stall to negotiate a purchase. She will try to haggle for a higher price if she thinks a potential client is relatively well off. Customers with more money to spend pick out appealing items, especially young women and men who want to emulate international styles, like those associated with American hip-hop and R&B cultures. Young men favour clean and immaculate striped polo shirts and high-quality, loose-fitting cargo shorts, which traders market at high prices. By contrast, if a trader is in need of money and desperate for a sale – maybe if they are short of food at home or unable to pay the rent – they can price items artificially low (i.e. below market price). For a week Mario had to drop the price of jeans down to 85 MZN ($2.70), below his usual retail prices of over 100 MZN ($3.10), because he was short of cash to support his young family. These examples of variation in price show there is interplay between local fashions, clothing trends and the business models and livelihoods of second-hand clothing vendors.

To understand how much money different charities, companies and traders in second-hand supply chains make it is important to consider the rate of transactions, as the tempo of sales is a fundamental feature of profitability in capitalist trade. In Maputo, market traders can sell used shirts for twice the wholesale cost, a higher percentage mark-up than the *armazéns* gain from selling complete 45 kg bales. But it is just as important to consider the rate at which capital flows through the system of provision. Market traders frequently remain with the same stock for a long time and can go days with making a sale; thus they are losing money. The *armazéns*, for their part, experience the rapid sale of stock. In any trade system, sellers need their capital to be active and must have turnover, which enables them to achieve valorization (or an increase in value). Traders consistently reported how it is the day's relative *movimento* (the movement of goods) which determines their profit levels. Slow sales and variable quality limit their ability to profit from the trade and escape poverty. In order to fully map how much money different groups and individuals make from the entire second-hand system of provision, the cooperation of all the parties involved across the global North and South would be required, but this is unrealistic.

The average income of second-hand traders in Xipamanine is around 172 MZN ($5.40) a day.[30] In the context of one of the poorest countries in the world, selling used clothing can be the basis for a relatively good income for a single young individual, but it is harder for someone who is a household head to support a family on this amount. There are always tensions between reinvesting profits and using revenue to support dependants. Second-hand clothing vendors are poor, but they are not among the most impoverished of people in Maputo. They tend to own mobile phones, which are useful for contacting *armazéns* and regular customers, and often spend money on remittance payments or school fees to support their parents and children. Trading second-hand clothing represents a step up compared to other types of market work, such as selling vegetables or soap, but traders are still very poor and therefore experience hardships and difficulties. For instance, when trade is slow, they frequently go without meals; and people have been forced out of the business when a succession of bad bales has led to the loss of all their money.[31]

For all traders it is very difficult to expand their second-hand clothing businesses, because the inherent variability of items makes saving money hard. A bad bale can wipe out profits earmarked for expanding a business. Selling used clothing in Xipamanine market is, as Francis Wegulo found while conducting research among second-hand shoe vendors in Kenya, a way to escape 'sheer destitution' but not for traders to get beyond 'keeping their heads above the water'.[32] Vendors interviewed were not content with their livelihoods; they looked to the future hoping for better formal work outside the second-hand clothing market. Working in the market is an adaptive response which compensates for the absence of development and other opportunities in Mozambique, rather than a livelihood which should be celebrated as a successful entrepreneurial way to make a living. Older vendors, who had previously been formally employed in modern professions, were especially sad that they were left selling used clothes and working on the margins of the global economy.

The unusual case of Humana-ADPP

Most of the second-hand clothes in Mozambique are sold in markets, either large organized urban markets like Xipamanine or small informal stalls at the side of the road. However, one significant importer has a different business model and sells used clothing in its own shops. Humana–ADPP is an international organization that imports used clothes to Mozambique as well as to neighbouring countries such as Malawi and Zambia. ADPP (Ajuda de Desenvolvimento de Povo para Povo – Development Aid from People to People) is a Mozambican Association and member of the International Federation 'Humana People to People'.[33] In 2009, two Humana retail second-hand clothing shops were opened, in Maputo and Matola; in total there are twelve such shops in Mozambique, including four in Beira and others in Cabo Delgado, Nampula and Quelimane. An employee from West Africa, who had previous experience working for Humana elsewhere in Africa, emphasized in an interview that the Humana shop in Maputo, which sells approximately 300 items per day, provides poor people with the opportunity to purchase low-cost clothing: 'We do it because we need to help people and we also did it because people need work … It really is not a business, because business means that you buy and sell and have a lot of money. We are helping people as the clothes are cheap.' Profits are said to go to fund education and HIV/AIDS projects, and clothes are sometimes distributed directly to children or people impoverished by the disease.

Clothing sold by Humana in Mozambique comes from countries that include Australia, Italy, the UK and the USA. Humana or its affiliates collect the clothing themselves in the global North. They have been involved in some controversy. In the UK, for instance, the organisation TRAID, which currently has eleven stores selling second-hand clothing across London, 'worked with the Charity

Commission to close down Humana UK due to concerns over how the organisation was managed and funded. The remaining assets were used to establish TRAID in July 1999, [as] a brand new charity.[34] Media reports have covered the controversies. The charismatic leader of Humana is Mogens Amdi Petersen, who created 'the many-tentacled Humana People-to-People NGO, operating under a baffling variety of names and spheres of interest'.[35] In different parts of the world it operates under the names 'Gaia', 'Planet Aid' and 'Tvind'. The management of the organization has been associated with illegal activities in Africa, Europe, the USA and Mexico. In the USA, Planet Aid is a controversial collection agency linked to poor practices (discussed in Chapter 3). Another commercial operator related to Tvind, USAgain, works in states including Illinois and Washington. A former manager reported that USAgain 'never explained the for-profit nature of the company to owners of sites where boxes were placed'.[36] Controversies have also been reorted in the African press; for example, 'Employees at Development Aid from People to People in Malawi (DAPP) have turned against their employers, accusing them of secretly swindling money for unknown activities.'[37] Unethical practices extend much further; indeed Tvind has been likened to a manipulative cult. A group of investigative journalists have set up a website, Tvind Alert, which makes allegations that this 'charity business' runs scams, embezzles cash and its leaders enjoy luxurious lifestyles.[38] These claims cannot all be substantiated. Nevertheless other reporting suggests that Tvind/Humana may be connected to illegal activity elsewhere. What is clear is that Mogens Amdi Petersen is a wanted man, a warrant for whose arrest has been circulated around the world by Interpol. The suspected cult leader went underground in 2006 and is believed to be on the run in Mexico. He was sentenced *in absentia* to a year in prison in 2013 by the Danish authorities for embezzling millions of kroner from a Tvind fund in the 1990s.[39] The network of organizations which make up Humana clearly require further investigation, but full explanations as to the origins, history and practices may have to await the apprehension of Petersen. The malpractices Tvind, Planet Aid and others linked operations have been associated with once again highlight the concealed trade practices and criminality that are prevalent in the international second-hand clothing trade.

Shopping for second-hand clothes in Mozambique

The poor in Africa cannot dwell on the controversies associated with used-clothing systems of provision. Poverty frames their purchasing decisions. Second-hand clothing is frequently preferred by consumers not just on account of the lower price, but also as it is of a higher quality and will last longer than new garments. Used and new clothing are both on sale in Xipamanine market, but tend to serve discrete market niches. New clothes are more aspirational in style, including for instance counterfeit English Premier League soccer shirts and versions of the tight-fitting ladies' tops retailed in more expensive stores in central Maputo, such as Logas das Dames. The new items are often of low quality as they are made to narrow cost margins to be sold at affordable prices to poor people. In contrast used clothes are locally less fashionable as they are typically clothes that were popular several years ago in the global North. However, the quality of the material of used clothing — notwithstanding that many items are worn or soiled — is often greater than affordable new clothing, as the items were first produced for a more affluent class of consumers in Australia, Europe or North America. Used-clothing items are on average 35–40 per cent of the cost of new clothes sold in Maputo. Table 2 gives examples of the different prices of new and used clothes sold in Xipamanine based on a survey of 2,789 sales. Monthly household expenditure on clothing

TABLE 2   Average prices of second-hand and new clothes
sold in Xipamanine market

	Average price (MZN)	Average price (US$)
SECOND-HAND CLOTHES		
Men's shirts	104.7	3.61
Men's trousers, including jeans	128.1	4.42
Men's tracksuit bottoms	127.3	4.39
Men's tracksuit tops	207.0	7.14
Women's tops and blouses	53.0	1.83
Skirts	80.1	2.76
Women's night gowns	24.0	0.83
Women's shorts	83.4	2.88
Boys' and unisex T-shirts	66.0	2.28
Boys' shirts	60.3	2.08
Boys' trousers	72.4	2.50
Girls' dresses	53.4	1.84
Girls' tops and blouses	57.2	1.97
NEW CLOTHES		
Men's shirts	219.2	7.56
Men's T-shirts	179.7	6.20
Men's trousers	304.9	10.51
Men's shorts	286.4	9.88
Tracksuit trousers	250.0	8.62
Coats	770.0	26.55
Skirts	246.0	8.48
Women's tops and blouses	215.4	7.43
Women's trousers	217.0	7.48
Dresses	325.0	11.20

NOTE Reported sales prices recorded between July 2009 and June 2010.

in Mozambique averages 303 MZN ($10.50) in urban areas and 167 MZN ($5.80) in rural areas.[40] In Maputo a household would be able to afford only the equivalent of one average pair of men's new trousers each month. Consumption decisions are therefore crucial and people take care in deciding what to buy.

Despite the widespread poverty in Mozambique there is a degree of differentiation in consumption. Specialist traders search around the markets collecting the best items to sell in the centre of Maputo. Along the wide tree-lined avenues in the centre of town, high-quality second-hand shoes suitable for clerical workers are sold close to offices at Jardim dos Madjersumai, handbags are on sale outside boutique shops on Avenída 25 de Setembro, and rucksacks and satchels are hawked at the gates of schools such as Escola Josina Machel. Sometimes new items are sold alongside them and traders conceal the origins – both used sold as new and new sold as used. Intriguingly, some unscrupulous traders position cheap, poorly made shoes from China within supplies of used shoes, in order to trick customers, as second-hand items sell for more due to their higher quality. Second-hand clothes can also be physically transformed. Tailoring activities, though not common in Maputo, do occur; for instance, delicate bra straps are often repaired as they get damaged through processing and packing, and in the scurry of activity when potential customers rummage through a newly opened bale. Sometimes used clothes are tailored to meet local styles. Eduardo is one of the more entrepreneurial traders in the market. He records higher profits as he buys bales of long-sleeve ladies' tops, which sell at a relatively low price. He takes the tops to a tailor, who removes the sleeves. Short-sleeved tops are a local fashion among young women and are worth more. His stall is normally busy and he has a rapid stock turnover. Tailoring second-hand clothing is not common in Maputo, though. Elsewhere in Africa, there are examples of clothes being remade in Kenya and Zambia.[41]

People do things in Africa to *revalue* used clothing. Karen Tranberg Hansen argues that in Zambia this redefines used clothing as 'new' garments. A physical transformation or a change in the meaning and symbolic value facilitates, in her opinion, a second 'life'. Second-hand clothes can be altered to give them greater value, yet a new commodity is not truly being produced. Tailors and traders who modify and select used clothes are performing a similar role to the Igbo apprentices who select items in the UK and send clothes directly to colleagues in West Africa.[42] They are influencing the provision of certain types of clothes, yet not materially *creating* new commodities for a specific market. Rather, they are reacting to availability and using labour to add, enhance or select value. Second-hand clothing is not 'produced' as a commodity at any single moment; processes which enhance or diminish exchange-value (or price) continue up to the point of final sale. Throughout the system of provision all the activities are predicated on the past labour spent to initially produce new clothing goods for consumption in the global North, as detailed in the biography of jeans.

There is other evidence of used clothing being transformed in Africa. Oxfam reported that ladies' denim jeans are frequently retailored to fit male physiques, as African women tend not to wear jeans.[43] Such generalizations are problematic; this may be reported information Oxfam receives from West African clients, where body shapes and cultural values are different from those in Mozambique. In Maputo, it is common for men to purchase and wear ladies' trousers; however, tight-fitting jeans and trousers are also very popular among girls and women, especially in younger age groups. Field research in Mozambique showed that the availability of imported ladies' jeans stimulates demand. Furthermore, cultural diffusion affects their symbolic value. As discussed in the earlier biography of jeans, the international media, particularly film, television and online, present aspirational imagery, which is reinforced by return migration and diaspora connections as well as local advertising and domestic fashion icons. The provision of clothing is plagued by the *leakiness* of trends which spread through globalized society. Fashion tastes in the global South are influenced by the Northern-dominated new fashion systems of provision, which affects the symbolic value of second-hand clothing.

While culture is important, ultimately what is consumed is an adaptive response to the available goods. Placing an overemphasis on consumption as a purely symbolic activity – where people freely choose their own outfits – ignores the fact that decision-making is primarily framed by the affordability and material use-value of garments. The majority of Mozambicans cannot realistically aspire either to enjoy 'fast fashion' or to buy the clothes they really want. The first priority of the poor is to meet basic needs. Mozambicans and other Africans do respond to manipulated yearnings shaped by advertisers and media imagery, although postcolonial desires are aspirational, distant and overwhelmingly unachievable when measured against a Western model of (over) consumption. There is a rich and diverse history of African clothing culture and a continual development and flourishing of contemporary trends, but the global provision and distribution of clothing are dominated by a First World marketplace shaped by producers manipulating demand for (unnecessary) goods. Consumption in the global North is restricting the vibrancy of clothing culture in impoverished communities. Elsewhere, in societies which are not as poor as Mozambique, second-hand garments perform a different function. In the global North retro old clothes can be very desirable, and the used garment trade has diverse socio-economic impacts across different cultural groups. The next chapter explores some contrasting and vibrant examples of vintage fashion and used-clothing consumption from around the world.

CHAPTER 8

Old clothes and new looks

The M65 US military field jacket

Clothing helps narrate our identity. It tells us about people's role in society, presenting a visual story to read. Film-makers and other artists capitalize upon and amplify the cultural values associated with clothes. Hollywood contributes to shaping how we perceive different garments and what qualities we attribute to the people who wear them. In the 1976 movie *Taxi Driver*, Travis Bickle, played by Robert De Niro, wears an olive drab ex-military M65 field jacket. Square-cut and hip-length, made of functional hard-wearing cotton and nylon fabric, with four large pockets for ammunition, maps and snacks, and a zip hood in the collar, the M65 produced by Alpha industries was first developed for US servicemen in 1965 and became a design classic. Millions were produced in black, grey, khaki, navy, olive green and jungle camouflage, providing a Cold War uniform for all branches of the American military and seeing service from Vietnam to the Gulf War. Demobilized soldiers kept hold of their old M65s, which took on new and unforeseen meanings beyond the theatres of war. As disillusionment with the American war in Vietnam grew, M65s were worn by angry veterans and fellow protesters. Surplus

M65s became reappropriated symbols, part of an authentic visual message, along with beards, long hair, peace badges and floral prints; a subversive uniform which demonstrated opposition to military neocolonialism. Not all M65s represented this single narrative. In *Taxi Driver* Bickle's M65 is an essential part of the framing of his aggressive persona. Director Martin Scorsese paints a picture of De Niro's character as a flawed, violent drifter forced to the margins of society; his M65 represents violent prowess and his status as a former Marine. Subsequently the M65 field jacket became an iconic part of the uniform of Hollywood hard men and renegades. Another rogue veteran, John Rambo, played by Sylvester Stallone, wears one in *First Blood*, as does the maverick Sergeant Martin Riggs (Mel Gibson) in *Lethal Weapon*. Arnold Schwarzenegger has a redesigned one in *The Terminator*. M65s became popular across different social groups, including hippies, hunters, artists and photographers; and came to have resonance with diverse values – anti-establishment, heroism, masculinity – as well as being an essentially functional jacket with a high use value. Osama bin Laden even wore an M65 in his video addresses, perhaps a remnant of CIA supplies to mujahideen fighters in the 1980s, but surely also a careful choreographed part of his violent message.

The symbolic values and the different signs an M65 represents, along with the abundant used supply and the jacket's practicality, have made it a consistently popular second-hand buy in the USA, as well as being an item that has long been exported across the global North. An extensive system of provision has evolved, spawning many reproductions and influencing the design of other new militarized fashion apparel. In London, expensive boutique stores such as Rokit vintage clothing and the Vintage Store in Covent Garden specialize in mid-twentieth-century Americana, selling authentic examples which have been careful selected and repositioned to appeal to an affluent and savvy clientele. Neighbouring shops like H&M and Zara stock new fast-fashion styles, including some ever-evolving collections inspired by military uniform. M65 design cues and other army styles have crossed over to influence female blouses, blazers and trench coats. Cheaper M65s can be found in flea markets around Camden Lock in North London, although these also come with a high price tag, as the consumer is not so much buying an old army jacket as paying the price for the specialist and lucrative labour activities which have gone into sourcing, supplying and curating this commodity. Vintage clothing is *curated*, as, like an ancient museum artefact or an artwork on display, it has to be carefully situated and presented to the consumer so as to maximize its symbolic value. An M65 has come to fill a specific and sought-after market niche. Reproductions sell for around $50, whereas authentic vintage originals are likely to reach $100 on eBay. The M65 demonstrates how second-hand clothes form an important part of everyday cultural landscapes in the global North.

Old clothes influence new looks. This chapter explores further hidden sides to second-hand clothing systems of provision. A mosaic of different mini case studies shows how old and vintage clothing plays a role in communities around the world. Used clothes are not just exported from the global North to the South; the real economic geography is multilayered (see Table 3). Second-hand apparel passes between different groups both within the same societies and internationally.[1] The ways in which different values are attributed to 'vintage' second-hand clothes and how symbolism is shaped and enhanced merit critical attention. Vintage clothing is both praised as an environmental alternative to the excesses of fast fashion and celebrated as a way to produce distinctive looks.[2] The true story is somewhat different as retro garments also play an important role in inspiring new clothing collections and fuelling fast-fashion trends. The two sectors can, and do, operate in tandem.

TABLE 3   Examples of second-hand clothing export
and recipient countries

EXAMPLES DISCUSSED IN THIS BOOK

Australia to Mozambique, Papua New Guinea

Benin and Togo to Nigeria
(re-export of used clothing)

Canada to Mozambique, Zambia

Japan to the Philippines

India to UK (re-made fashions)

Mozambique to South Africa, Swaziland and Zimbabwe
(re-export of used clothing)

Mozambique to Germany (trade in designer fashions)

New Zealand to Papua New Guinea

Poland to Afghanistan, Uzbekistan
(re-export of used clothing)

Spain to Mozambique

UK to Benin, Ghana, India, Kenya, Lithuania, Malawi, Mozambique,
Pakistan, Poland, Senegal, Tanzania, Togo

US to Bolivia, Chile, Japan, Mozambique, Tanzania, UK, Zambia

OTHER NOTABLE EXAMPLES

Germany to Kurdistan (Northern Iraq)

Italy to Algeria

USA to Costa Rica, Hong Kong, Tonga

Senegal to France (trade in designer fashions)

NOTE The list provided in the table is not an exhaustive account but illustrates the
diverse geographies of the used clothing trade.

Vintage fashion is a much smaller sector than the global North–South trade, but attracts greater popular attention. This chapter begins to redress the balance: examples from around the world are discussed, complementing the patterns and trends identified in Africa. Poor people may have little agency in shaping used clothing systems of provision, but they can and do respond in creative and unanticipated ways to imports of used garments. Imports have diverse affects within different societies. Norms of dress are transmitted by the prevalence of Western clothing. Yet, rather than everyone being passive receivers of clothing culture, evidence shows how some individuals give textiles a new lease of life and re-create their own creolized trends. Table 3 gives examples of how second-hand clothing circulates around the world. There are even instances of used clothing being traded from the global South to the North, including 'upcycled' fashion. The final section of this chapter explores examples of the re-production of valuable new garments from used clothes.

Vintage fashion in cities

Wearing vintage or retro second-hand clothing emerged as a countercultural practice when people began to browse markets, charity shops and thrift stores out of curiosity rather than necessity. Affordable second-hand clothing could be used to produce individual and unique looks. Early research conducted by Jacqueline Wiseman from California in the 1970s found that 'women go because they can pick up items that would be too frivolous for them to consider buying retail, such as sequined blouses and gold-threaded leisure jump-suits'; other customers included 'Hippies hunting exotic clothes of by-gone eras'.[3] Cheap used clothing offered American and British urban youth the opportunity to produce affordable yet distinctive new looks and play with narrating their identity. Second-hand shopping was a social experience:

consumers were more likely to discuss purchases with one another and to participate in putting together outfits which differentiated them from the mainstream at a time when rigidly prescribed patterns of behaviour associated with modern Fordism were breaking down. Identities such as punk saw teenagers play creatively with the language of fashion, introducing a new grammar to the way in which outfits were constructed, and drawing upon and amending affordable used clothes to make powerful visual statements.

Second-hand clothes stores and markets are still searched for different types of authentic goods. Consumers attempt to attach themselves to the latest style or re-create a retro theme. Indeed the trend appears to be growing in popularity. Looks which have been *in* among young people in London include fads for American cowboy boots in small female sizes; 1930s' and 1940s' men's tailoring; and David Bowie-inspired costumes. Vintage fashion allows people to form an authentic style, but is not just about subscribing to a specific group identity. This is documented by Janna Michael, who interviewed Fred from Hamburg: 'Fred describes his passion for classic, English tweed looks and other specific traditional clothing. In these cases, where an expressive yet consistent style is chosen, the intention is not to indicate membership of a subculture, but rather a unique style that had to be found individually.'[4] Hipster sensibilities and uniqueness cannot persevere in isolation for long, hence interest in vintage clothing has crossed over and steadily become co-opted into the mainstream as retro trends are remade by fast-fashion brands. Clothing designers constantly borrow from fashion's past. This symbiotic relationship means that certain used-clothing articles become invested with enhanced symbolic value, as fads for flares or trends for 1920s' revival emerge. For instance, jeans designs from the 1950s influence Levi's new collections, and Nike has produced an M65 jacket from new synthetic materials which has the same shape and design features as the 1965 original. Distinctive vintage-inspired ideas are relayed through the fast-fashion system, leading to new cycles of production. The growing popularity of second-hand clothing has even made it to Italy, where there are now some 3,500 second-hand stores, an increase of 35 per cent between 2004 and 2008. Retro style is becoming a new way to form identity, in an increasingly post-industrial society, at the heart of Europe's fashion sector.[5]

The emergence of vintage boutiques has been part of gentrification in the North's global cities; examples include Castor & Pollux in New York's Meatpacking District, Razzo in Berlin's Prenzlauer Berg, and another branch of Rokit vintage clothing in Brick Lane in London's East End. All these shops are in cool areas, which progressed from being disadvantaged inner-city neighbourhoods to in-demand localities for retail and leisure. Gentrification alters the social mix of cities. Long-standing blue-collar communities are displaced and former areas of industry or light manufacturing transformed. Apartment blocks, factories and warehouses are remade in a seemingly beneficial process. According to urban geographer Tom Slater this is 'the popular, and increasingly scholarly, image of gentrification. The perception is no longer about rent increases, landlord harassment and working-class displacement, but rather street-level spectacles, trendy bars and cafés, i-Pods, social diversity and funky clothing outlets.'[6] Retro clothing shops fit within this broader landscape of renewal. Used clothes and industrial architecture are reappropriated by urbane trend-setters and are emblematic of many American and European cities' changing social relationship with their past histories as industrial centres. This type of cultural 'progress' should be considered critically, as urban change often results in displacements and uneven development, making large parts of cities unaffordable for the working classes.

Elsewhere in London, high-end stores specializing in vintage wedding-dress and retro couture in the West End compete on price with contemporary designer goods. On Oxford Street in one of Europe's most iconic retail locations, Topshop's flagship store has an internal vintage boutique. Topshop, a mass fast-fashion retail, has attached itself to the perceived authenticity and originality of second-hand clothing. Associations like this can have a halo effect, reflecting positively on the broader brand. Worn items like aged vintage Levi's 501s sold in Topshop's boutique or a Rokit retro store are a prized second-hand purchase. Aged denim encapsulates the symbolic values of authenticity and robustness, which new designers try to re-create through the 'lived-in' manufacturing processes.

It is not just 'any' pair of jeans that end up as an expensive vintage good. Before second-hand jeans become valuable a highly specific type of labour activity is required. Skilled buyers search for the right garments and recognize which jeans represent the cultural zeitgeist and can be positioned in a new marketplace for a high price. This type of work can create new value and wealth. Marx long ago observed that 'The *surplus labour of the mass* has ceased to be the condition for the development of general wealth…'[7] Physical work by labourers has become less important in forming value in goods in an economic system such as vintage fashion. Instead specialist skills concentrated in small groups of people produce surplus value or profit. Particular work processes go into internationally sourcing supplies, identifying and promoting trends, window-dressing and curating second-hand fashions.

Vintage fashions are sourced from sorting plants and local marketplaces. Choice garments are identified by expert pickers working on the conveyer belts at sorting plants, which can lead to great profits. For example, a pair of Christian Louboutin shoes were found at Oxfam Wastsaver and priced for second-hand sale at £340 ($566); and clothes such as 'vintage wedding dresses, cashmere and "Gatsby-style" items all sell well'.[8] These trendy clothes are diverted to a different system of provision to the ones that go to the global South and are purchased by vintage fashion retailers or directly sold by Oxfam's online store or eight specialist boutique shops. On a local scale buyers search through markets, thrift stores and charity shops seeking bargains and fashionable items which can be repositioned and expensively retailed in retro stores. Surplus is produced during these various specialized labour activities and the cost of vintage goods is inflated as the consumer is captivated by the fetish of market relations. Production is not some self-sufficient realm. Vintage clothing is not *made* at any single moment; it is continually co-produced as the symbolic value is enhanced when it is marketed in different social contexts. Consumers are not so much paying for the cost of a item, but supporting a system of provision. As rock star Steve Tyler of Aerosmith once sardonically observed: 'You have no idea how much it costs to look this cheap.'[9]

For some people pre-owned garments have romantic associations, and used clothes can even embody an imagined persona which is both nostalgic and individualistic.[10] The new owner may reflect upon their distinctive history – perhaps thinking about the last person who wore a pair of jeans. Nostalgia and heritage can be influential in shaping systems of provision. The promotion of heritage is a powerful cultural force. Museums and galleries, such as the Metropolitan Museum of Art in New York, Paris's Musée Galliera and the V&A in London, are devoted to the preservation and popularization of past clothing styles and thereby contribute to the commercialization of the provision of certain second-hand clothing styles. The cultural economy which surrounds consumption – exhibitions, blogs, themed parties, commercialized nostalgia – is all part of the social landscape that enables vintage clothing systems of provision.

The exchange of used clothing is as old as clothes themselves, but vintage fashion is relatively new, something which is distinctly postmodern, coming after the breakdown of Fordism and the flourishing of increasingly diverse clothing collections. Symbolism is the lifeblood of vintage fashion. In a Marxist sense, objects have a greater or lesser single use value, but from a social perspective use value can be broken down. Socially, clothes have two meanings: a first-order function, such as keeping you warm, which is their use value; and a second-order symbolic value, such as their fashionableness.[11] Vintage fashion systems depend upon bringing items with use value back to the market and amplifying their symbolic value. A systems-of-provision analysis accounts for how commodities have cultural or symbolic values produced through a concurrent chain or network of activities that includes their production, but also their circulation, distribution, marketing and consumption, as well as broader variegated arrangements such as class and gender relations, advertising, politics and media. For instance, film history and anti-war protests both affected the value of M65 jackets. The material culture which surrounds production and consumption can give rise to and erode different systems; this process has enabled the emergence of the vintage fashion sector. The following case study of the jeans sector in Japan provides a further example of how unique systems of provision can develop.

Japanese jeans

In Tokyo and Osaka some of the most exclusive and sought-after pairs of jeans in the world can be found. Specialist and artisanal producers such as Eternal, Fullcount, Strike Gold and Sugar Cane manufacture expensive and carefully detailed denim.[12] High-quality, expertly tailored jeans are made in Japan, although at first glance the styles look like they come straight from 1950s' America. Dark blue denims with tight and fine weaves are produced to exacting standards, and hand-finishing techniques are used for stitching jean patterns. Japan's denim industry provides a good example of how the new and used clothing trades influence one another. This system of provision was not spawned by market relations alone; it depended upon particular political and cultural events, which shaped production and consumption.

Following World War II, US forces occupied Japan. After the ravages of mass bombing campaigns, including the atomic devastation wrought on Hiroshima and Nagasaki, Japan was left broken. Large US Marine and Naval bases were established at Okinawa, Yokota and elsewhere. Both sides had suffered deeply. Among the Japanese, anti-American feelings were steadily replaced by a yearning for American culture; the US lifestyle became a model for the Japanese. Occupying Americans provided aspirational figures, and many servicemen wore denim jeans when off-duty. [13] Jeans were part of an American man's modern identity and were the trousers of choice for relaxed casual wear. The Japanese dubbed jeans 'G-pans' and the style crossed over and became popular among local youths, although getting hold of them was tough, as Rachel Snyder explains in her history of jeans: 'Because they were rare, jeans in Japan could cost upwards of half a month's salary in the immediate postwar period. Around Tokyo, secondhand markets for soldier's cast-off jeans thrived.' [14]

From the 1960s onwards a domestic denim manufacturing sector emerged. In Japan, jeans did not have a local history as workwear; the industry specialized in replicating the look of the post-war American blue jeans won by off-duty Marines, which became highly desirable leisure clothing. Meanwhile, the Japanese continued to source second-hand American jeans, which remained some of the most sought-after styles. A commercial trade developed, which extended to Japanese 'pickers' working in second-hand clothing sorting plants in the USA identifying classic styles, like Levi's 501s, which were popular back home. However, by the 1980s there was an insufficient second-hand supply of the 1950s' raw unwashed styles popular in Japan, as these had been phased out of the US market in the 1960s. Denim aficionado

Mikiharu Tsujita recalls how desirable styles were in short supply: 'At the time, many Japanese bought vintage jeans from the US ... It was becoming more and more difficult to find them, and they were becoming expensive. So Yamane and I suggested that we'd make vintage jeans ourselves.'[15] Despite the existence of a local denim industry, enthusiasts wanted a 'perfect' pair of jeans closer to the iconic US styles from the 1950s. In response Tsujita started his own brand, Fullcount. This was just one of several premium Japanese denim brands which emerged in the 1980s and 1990s as a fashion sector centred on Osaka grew up specializing in producing vintage style jeans. New techniques for treating, finishing and washing emerged, on account of which Japanese denim gradually established a reputation for innovation and quality.

Today, Japanese firms are some of the finest producers and their denims are exported to premium markets around the world, including North America. Japanese weaving mills have become expert in producing denim textile that encapsulates values associated with vintage wear. Technical processes give denim a lived-in aesthetic, but not the appearance of workwear. As a Canadian denim importer explains:

> Japanese fabrics are known to be some of the best in the world. The attention to detail, texture and colour makes the fabric stand out from the rest ... Over time, these indigo layers break away and you are left with an exposed white core, which will give your jeans a personalized, vintage look.[16]

Japanese jeans makers work hard on the detailing of their trousers, including features such as hidden rivets and chain-stitched hems, which are in demand among denim devotees. Manufacturing is often done using old machinery and specialist labour processes, approaches which are difficult to replicate and contribute to raising the cost.[17] Labour in Japan is also expensive, even compared to the EU countries and the USA. In Japan there is only a small immigrant population, which frequently fills repetitive production-line roles in the remaining fashion industries elsewhere in the global North. The Japanese workforce for blue-collar manual labour is shrinking and denim weaving is an ageing profession. These factors make for a sought-after and expensive product. Japanese jeans brands now sell for over $300 in North America. Simultaneously there also continues to be buoyant demand in Japan for authentic used items from the USA, which have great symbolic value, as Synder notes: 'they still covet the post-World War II-era vintage look; more than two thousand tons of vintage and contemporary American jeans are shipped annually to Japan.'[18]

The story of Japanese jeans shows how society and culture can shape the trade in new and used goods. US servicemen first provided an aspirational image in Japan and the post-World War II second-hand markets duly supplied jeans. Both the contemporary second-hand imported US jeans and the premium new Japanese manufactured denim trade are systems of provision which emerged because of the particular cultural values inscribed within jeans. As demand grew, a specialist domestic manufacturing sector inspired by mid-twentieth-century styles developed. However, this was not a piecemeal re-creation of American manufacturing. Jeans did not start out as *just* utilitarian wear in Japan, as they did in the USA; they were an expensive and indulgent fashion. And so a high-quality denim sector developed. The co-dependence and linkages with 'vintage' second-hand clothing persist and a parallel system of provision specializing in importing retro American jeans flourishes. This case study shows that it was not Levi Strauss, Lee or Wrangler that brought jeans to Japan; nor is there a mere imitation of vintage Americana, or a pattern which can be explained in narrow economic terms. Instead creolized patterns of production and consumption dependent on specific socio-historic circumstances are thriving.

Used clothing markets in the global South

Due south from Japan, across the Pacific Ocean, and as far away as can be in terms of economic development, Papua New Guinea's clothing systems of provision were shaped by isolation and poverty. Across the economy there are few indigenous Papua New Guinean businesses and no history of industrial clothing manufacturing. Australians, Filipinos and Indians run most companies, but Christian organizations including American evangelicals, Catholics and Lutherans are also powerful economic and political actors. Missionaries are active, trying to convert communities and translate tribal languages to enable the Bible to be written in every native tongue. Used clothes are brought to Papua New Guinea predominately by Christian organizations such as the Salvation Army. They are able to source clothing from their congregations and collection activities in the global North. Many of the clothes come from Melbourne and Sydney, a trading relationship that mirrors Papua New Guinea's broader dependency on Australia, which governed it as a colony until 1975. Through the strong role of churches, which can readily access supplies, and the absence of industrialization, second-hand clothing has become an entrenched system of provision. Used clothes make up the lion's share of the apparel market. Elsewhere in the Pacific used clothing is important in Tonga and Vanuatu as well.[19] The limited quantity of new garments sold in Papua New Guinea come from Asian producers and are sold in the stores run by Filipinos and Indians.[20]

In major towns like Madang, Mount Hagen and Port Moresby large warehouse-like stores have numerous rails of second-hand garments. Kalibobo Haus Colos (Kalibobo Clothing House) is one of the largest retailers in Madang; it claims to sell (an implausible) 10,000 items every day. Profits are rumoured to be high. Donations are regularly made to support local church activities.

Security guards patrol the entrance and often turn away customers who have already visited that day. Retail is carefully managed;
for instance coloured labels are stapled securely to shirts and
jeans to prevent customers tampering with prices, or picking
up garments and pretending they are their own. Nevertheless
crime is rife. Theft has long been a challenge for both second-
hand and new clothing retailers around the world. In the case of
Papua New Guinea, the problem is exacerbated by a traumatic
relationship with modernization and social change. Many Papua
New Guineans do not fully understand the connections between
production, retail and the market due to their late and partial
integration into the global capitalist economy. As manufacturing
is not understood, there is less social recognition of the work
and transactions that bring products to market, and thus less
obligation to exchange clothes for money.

During the Second World War many Papua New Guineans
were first exposed to Western manufactured goods such as canned
food, clothing, radios and vehicles, as well as money, but these
supplies disappeared after the foreign troops left. Cargo cults
materialized as an attempt to explain the origins and circulation
of these things, as communities had no experience of capitalism
and market relations. Some people believed that this 'cargo' was
coming from their ancestors 'but that Europeans have schemed
to hijack these shipments so that they fail to arrive'.[21] Prophets
prescribed ritualistic behaviour to entice new supplies and cults
emerged promising that new cargo would be delivered by Americans or other powerful outsiders. The term 'cargo cult' has grown
to become a powerful label for internal cultural dynamism and to
explain the enchantment with modernity, but it also signifies an
absence of understanding of modes of production. Some Papua
New Guineans may feel entitled to steal used clothing and other
imported goods, as they deem them to be their rightful inheritance
from ancestors. Although not confined to clothing, the prevalence

of cargo cults and other millennial thinking illustrates how used clothing can be a *thing* which has confusing origins that cannot easily be explained to local people. Second-hand clothes get used in unusual ways. In one Highlands village men took to wearing flowing ladies' floral dressing gowns, garments that became a way to show off; it was a statement associated with masculinity that was completely divorced from the gowns' previous symbolic values. Second-hand clothing dominates the garment sector; as with many developing nations, Papua New Guinea has grown to become dependent on used-clothing imports. In this society the opportunities for different models of production and consumption are further constrained by the absence of knowledge concerning industrial manufacturing processes.

Second-hand clothing markets are found throughout the global South. Contrasting examples from Bolivia, India, Pakistan and the Philippines show how systems of provision are shaped by interactions between culture and political economy. Clothing is highly politicized in Bolivia. Imports of second-hand clothing were made illegal in 2006, but continue to flourish. Research by feminist geographer Kate Maclean has explored the cultural and economic impacts. An estimated 8,000 tonnes of used clothing, worth more than $40,000,000, are imported each year from the USA via Chile.[22] The trade was banned after a contested government report estimated that the cost of imports was 'some $513,000,000 US in terms of jobs, tax and sales tax, on the assumption Bolivian production of clothing would have more of the market'.[23] Prohibition came about as President Evo Morales rejected neoliberalism and sought to protect national production. The ban led to protests, and then counter-protests. In the Bolivian cities of La Paz and nearby El Alto, however, markets dominated by female traders still sell *ropa american* (American clothes). Affluent urban women and poor rural migrants search for designer bargains; identities are re-created and negotiated as people find

styles from Gap to Gucci inside clothing bales. The politics of
the second-hand clothing trade are associated with the framing
of the nation and a reassertion of gender roles and traditional
identities. Informal second-hand clothing markets provide an
opportunity for female economic empowerment, but are in tension
with state-led policies which value the female citizen 'for her role
in the reproduction of population and culture'.[24]

In India a long-standing ban on the import of second-hand
clothing is much more successful at protecting domestic production, as it is a legacy of the opposition to imports of new British
clothing that formed part of the independence struggle. India has
partially resisted the hegemonic model of economic liberalization
promoted by the global North and has strategically integrated into
the world economy, although the country has many of its own
inequalities, including the presence of widespread poverty despite
rapid economic growth. In contrast, neighbouring Pakistan is
economically more open; as a consequence it is one of the largest
importers of used clothing from Europe. For instance, Choice
Textiles, the commercial partner of Help the Aged, sends a large
volume of white dress-shirts to Pakistan, where there is great
demand among lawyers, as this style is expected in the law courts,
yet another legacy of British colonialism.

India does not import second-hand clothing for local consumption and has resisted some of the impacts of economic and cultural
globalization, but facilities such as Canam's plant in Kandla take
advantage of India's strategic integration into the world economy
to sort and grade second-hand clothing supplies from North
America. In addition to re-exporting used clothes, India is also
a destination for recycling rags and clothing waste. This includes
the garments collected in the global North that are of too low a
quality to be re-worn. Western waste garments are imported and
deliberately torn, to prevent the possibility of them being illegally
resold. Sweaters and coats are remade into Indian blankets in

Panipat, Haryana, as Lucy Norris found: 'old woollens are sorted into colour families and stripped of their fastenings, linings and labels before being industrially shredded and pulped. Then the fibres are teased out, carded and spun into brightly colored new yarn, ready for reuse.'[25]

There is also a vibrant domestic trade in second-hand clothes that pass from the rich to the poor, which represents a microcosm of the global system. In a single wholesale market north-west of Delhi 2,000 dealers buy and sell used clothing, in a scene that is replicated across India.[26] Some clothes are obtained in a manner similar to that of the roving traders and rag-and-bone men that operated in America and Europe in the nineteenth and early twentieth centuries. Indian housewives and servants barter away unwanted clothes in exchange for new cooking pots and other hardware. Used garments provide a system of clothing provision for the poorest in society, but they are valued differently across India's diverse social and cultural landscape. For instance, in the south, in Kerala, where there is a high level of social development, people wear second-hand clothes, but it is not something they would openly talk about. Surplus supplies of used clothing are traded from Kerala to northern India, where there is less stigma attached.[27] Used Indian clothes are also recycled in various ways. Elaborate old saris which are too shabby to be worn again are burned to release and reclaim their gold thread. Saris and other patterned Indian fabrics are also transformed into new consumer products for foreign tourists. Out of piles of torn old clothing come new 'cushions, bedspreads and wall hangings ... halter-neck tops, skirts and trousers', which are produced as 'Western consumer goods'.[28] This is an example of the upcycling of old clothing, which is discussed further below.

Inequalities in global clothing systems of provision have a particularly acute expression in the Philippines. On the one hand there is a flourishing Filipino clothing industry which produces

for both the domestic market and the global North, but on the
other there is a burgeoning second-hand clothing trade. There
are two main routes for imports: clothing comes from North
America, Western Europe, Australia and Japan under the model
described in Chapter 3, and through a different pathway from
Hong Kong. In the 1970s rapid economic growth in Hong Kong
accompanied by increasing consumer participation in fashion,
with accelerated cycles of buying and discarding, provided a
ready supply of used clothing. At the same time, many working
couples in Hong Kong began to hire Filipino nannies, which
caused them to observe their clothing habits. Access to Hong
Kong provided the opportunity for used-clothing entrepreneurs
to link the supply to markets back in the Philippines. Clothes
from Hong Kong come in standard boxes priced according to
quality. Clothing from Hong Kong and Japan is preferred in the
Philippines, as the fit is better than with American jeans and
T-shirts, which are often too large. The problem of low-quality
stock is less than in the African cases studies. Indeed some entrepreneurial individuals have accumulated profits and made the
progression from market vendor to importer. Filipino business
people have access to capital and transnational connections and
the traders work in a well-developed market. In the street markets
of Baguio City competitive operators position branded goods
like Gap, Nike, Lacoste and Levi's to attract consumers, and
new stock arrivals are promoted. Some select stores specialize
in selling the highest quality and cherry-pick items from market
vendors, including hats and briefs. For Filipino consumers there
is a hierarchy of preferences and second-hand clothing may be of
higher quality than locally produced goods. As B. Lynne Milgram
observes, 'Baguio City shoppers explain, for example, that the
colour in my T-shirts will last longer because these garments
are "from your place", regardless of the fact that my T-shirt was
most likely produced outside Canada.'[29] Indeed Milgram's T-shirt

could even have been made in the Philippines. Nevertheless, the important elements of the system of provision found in Canada or elsewhere in the global North, including design, marketing and retail as well as affluent consumer demand, ensures the provision of high-quality goods in Canada. The second-hand clothing trade has affected the balance of trade, as imports have undermined sales of locally produced garments and market traders have shifted from selling *new local* to *used foreign* clothes, because these goods have higher profit margins.[30] This example shows some of the real inequalities of globalization. The Philippines 'closes the circle', making new and importing old garments. The same people who manufacture clothing for export may end up purchasing those same items years later as imported second-hand clothes. Filipino wage levels do not permit factory workers to wear the garments they make; they are the losers in a global division in consumption. The uneven development of the clothing sector plays a part in keeping locations of new clothing consumption rich and areas of production and second-hand consumption poor.

Upcycling

In Japan, Papua New Guinea, Bolivia, India, the Philippines and around the world, people use old clothes in new ways. Worn jeans, old ladies' dressing gowns and torn saris take on different lives in secondary markets. In some cases used clothes are physically transformed into new garments or other items. A vibrant 'upcycling' movement can be found in California, Paris, Stockholm and elsewhere. Upcycling uses old clothes as the basis for fresh fashions, reflecting both an environmental concern with the overconsumption of new clothing and a longing to invent unique garments that draw inspiration from past patterns of dress. Some people alter clothes themselves as an affordable way to amend their look, or just for fun, whereas other have built up boutique businesses. Tired fabric and energetic labour are combined to cut and tear away the old, and stitch and weave new life into dresses, skirts and shirts. Upcycling approaches replicate the handcraft practices of the pre-modern era. Energy and motivation are required for prospective upcyclers to sort through rails of used clothes in thrift stores and charity shops to find appealing items worthy of a second life. Old clothes take on new looks as dress hems are altered, blouses are adorned with buttons, and trouser pockets and zip fastenings are removed or refashioned to reflect new trends.

One Swedish upcycling designer is Amanda Ericsson, who has her own fashion brand dreamandawake and an accompanying arts project The Life of a Dress. The two currents represent both a successful small business and an artistic initiative. In the latter, dresses are presented together with powerful images to provide an abstract story of a woman and her dress's journey around the world to give audiences a hint as to how clothes travel, both as new garments and as second-hand goods.[31] Ericsson's projects have travelled to Mozambique and there provided the inspiration for Mima-te, a developing Mozambican upcycling fashion brand which takes dresses from Xipamanine market and remakes the garments into unique and original fashion pieces. Mima-te is run by sisters Nelly and Nelsa Guambe, who describe the business thus:

> Our intention is to upcycle and renew these textiles, bringing those forgotten clothes back to life and turn them into fashion-able, modern clothing ... Upcycling these clothes therefore be-comes an innovative way of creating a new image of Mozambican clothing and at the same time serves to harness environmental awareness, both in Mozambique and in the origin countries of these clothes. It also allows Mozambican people – from the seller to the sewer at the market – to be involved in creating something beautiful and new instead of just reselling things that were not wanted in rich countries anymore.[32]

The Guambes' creativity has attracted interest from international media and their redesigned second-hand clothes have even been exported to and sold in Germany. One of their aims has been to take the clothes back to their original markets as a way to forge a successful and profitable business, and to highlight both some of the ethical and environmental issues raised by the overconsumption of fast fashion and the large scale of the trade in second-hand clothing from the global North to Africa. Businesses such as dreamandawake and Mima-te use second-hand clothes as a starting point to produce new clothing fashions. These small-scale activities have complex relationships with the vintage and international used-clothing trades. They generate buzz and excitement around second-hand clothing, but also operate on the fuzzy boundaries between business, art and activism, and in so doing act as a critique of the new and used systems of provision.

In the global North, vintage fashion and upcycling systems of provision are much more visible than the export trade in second-hand clothing, but, as previous chapters have demonstrated, larger and hidden exports of second-hand clothes forge relationships of dependency between the global North and South. The patchwork of diverse case studies throughout this chapter show how second-hand and new clothes affect different societies; yet it is not actually the clothes themselves that are instrumental. Rather, it is the social relationships among people – such as those between film-makers and audiences, retro stores and hipsters, 1950s' American Marines and Japanese youths, American churches and Papua New Guineans, Bolivian women and state authority, vintage fashion designers and affluent consumers – that shape and produce different modes of clothing provision. The particular connections that are enabled by the circulation of second-hand clothing provide new opportunities for surplus extraction and capital accumulation. Vintage clothing systems in the rich cities of the global North enhance the symbolic value of old clothes and in parallel provide inspiration for new cycles of fast-fashion production and consumption, whereas the largely hidden activities in second-hand markets in Asia, Africa and Latin America provide a lens through which to view the uneven development of the global economy. Second-hand clothing is very important, but it is only an undercurrent to the main flow of the global clothing trade. To discuss critically some of the proposed solutions to the structural inequalities of clothing provision means we first have to explore the myths and realities behind new ethical approaches to production and consumption. This is the subject of the next chapter.

CHAPTER 9

Ethical clothing myths and realities

Toms shoes

A trend in footwear is steadily spreading across the USA. Throughout malls and college campuses it is easy to spot the distinctive slip-on espadrilles, flat unisex canvas shoes with a neat blue and white striped Toms flag sewn across the backstay of the heel. Toms shoes are popular, comfortable and different – fashionable and affordable whilst embodying distinctive values associated with care and compassion. The Toms success story is an important new chapter in the annals of so called responsible capitalism. From the brand's humble origins in 2006, this example of social entrepreneurship has become one of the most talked about instances of the contradictions of ethical consumption. The Toms model is simplicity itself: buy one, give one. For every purchase of Toms footwear a child in a developing country is given a pair of shoes. As the company's marketing material proclaims: 'When you buy a pair of Toms Shoes, you're also helping improve the health, education and well-being of a child.'[1]

Blake Mycoskie, the driving force behind the Toms project, is the epitome of a twenty-first-century socially responsible entrepreneur. Still in his thirties, with scruffy hair and a beard, Mycoskie

has met the Clintons and has featured in *Time* magazine's 'How
to Fix Capitalism' feature authored by Bill Gates.[2] He came up
with the 'one for one' business idea when travelling in Argentina,
where he found himself near Buenos Aires after Googling 'polo
lessons cheap'. Whilst hanging out with wealthy Argentines he
saw that they donated their unwanted shoes to local villages. This
provided him with the inspiration: 'It just hit me,' he says. 'Instead
of a charity with handouts why not create a company where
that's the whole purpose? I thought, you buy one pair of shoes
today so we can give one tomorrow. We'll call them Tomorrow
Shoes. No we'll call them Toms Shoes for Tomorrow.'[3] Blake's
business has been a runaway success, and especially effective at
encouraging young consumers not just to buy shoes, but to buy
into an idea. People like the shoes and the ethical benefits. The
simple 'classics' design that is the mainstay of Toms product lines
is modelled after the Argentine *alpargata* (aka espadrille) shoe,
a basic timeless shape which both signals personal authenticity
and has powerful social resonance. After going shopping and
slipping their bare feet into a pair of canvas Toms, wearers can
feel content with themselves, maybe even a little smug, as they
imagine their poorer counterpart also happily pushing their toes
inside a new pair of shoes.

What is special about Toms is that the brand has gone beyond
being an ethical business and has become a minor cultural movement, particularly in colleges and among teens. A sense of community is fostered through the online presence: toms.com is half
online fashion store, half social advocacy website. As well as
shoes, the marketplace features sunglasses, scarves, laptop sleeves
and clothes; and shoppers can choose to sort ethical products by
cause, region of impact or brand. In a biographical section Blake
Mycoskie is pictured tanned and smiling, fitting red and white
striped espadrilles on a young Latino girl. Stories and videos
from the global South look like materials from an up-market

Peace Corps campaign rather than corporate advertising. In a crowded market, these images help differentiate the brand and are particularly in tune with the cultural moment. Toms provides information and direction for young people, introducing devotees to development issues associated with education, health and well-being, just like an advocacy NGO. Foremost is the annual 'one day without shoes' event, which is when the Toms community goes barefoot to raise awareness for children around the world who do not have shoes. Images show groups of students walking around college campuses barefoot carrying large Toms flags as if supporting a political party or radical protest movement, rather than endorsing a shoe manufacturing company. The appealing and simple message has inspired other interventions, and indeed Mycoskie has carried the idea further. Toms are sold in Canada, France, Germany, the Netherlands and the UK. Mycoskie has written a bestselling book, *Start Something that Matters*, and has made many media appearances. Somewhat inevitably there has been a backlash involving important criticisms of the 'one for one' model. These require close analysis to separate the myths from the reality.[4]

The issue of the appropriateness of the donation is the first factor to consider. Do shoes actually satisfy a real need? Buying shoes in America leads to someone deserving getting shoes, but why shoes? Maybe something else, another item of clothing or cash, would be more useful. The poor are not consulted in the process and are cast as helpless, passive recipients of aid. Would it not be better to find target communities and identify what their greatest need is, such as access to clean water, or skills training, or debt relief, rather than arriving with a set 'solution' to a specific problem? A lack of footwear does not stand out as the most pressing development issue facing the poor in the global South.[5]

Next, the detail of the system of provision must be explored. Toms adult shoes sell for between $48 and $140 in the USA, far beyond the cost of manufacturing the *alpargata*-style shoes, which retail for around $5 in Argentina (which includes the local seller's profit). Without knowing the detail of private company accounts, there would appear to be plenty of opportunity for Blake Mycoskie to extract surplus from these sales, whilst maintaining the donation system. At best a $48 purchase of shoes represents a $5 donation. Additionally, the cost of distributing shoes in the global South is partly borne by the Toms 'community'. Espadrilles are handed out in recipient countries through 'shoe drops' by Toms' volunteers.[6] Toms shoe drops are very popular, oversubscribed volunteer experiences. The young people who take part pay their own air fares and when they return provide testimonials, becoming brand ambassadors. The cost of intercontinental flights would be more effective 'aid' if the ticket price were instead donated and directed towards employing local people to distribute the donations, but then that would not help foster the sense of community which has become such an essential part of the Toms brand. The whole system of provision is self-financing and provides more good news stories for the Toms website.

The Toms programme has given away more than 10 million pairs of shoes across sixty countries, a not insubstantial number.[7] The impact of this programme on global footwear production and markets is minimal, though, when we remember that there are billions of poor people in the world. Nevertheless, the potential economic relationships of the 'buy one, give one' approach are worth debating. As with the cheap imports of second-hand clothing, free shoe drops can displace existing footwear manufacturing in the target countries, reducing local markets and making it harder for industries which need protection to grow and compete.[8] Research carried out in El Salvador by economists working in cooperation with Toms found 'modest evidence' that donated shoes had negative impacts on local shoe markets, but results were inconclusive.[9] It is also important to consider scale:

should the small percentage of affluent people in the global North be freely choosing to consume (or not consume) goods which aid only a tiny fraction of the impoverished majority of the global population in the South? Would it not be better to ask deeper questions about the inequalities of the global economy? Rather than providing products, people should be empowered to escape poverty and not become structurally dependent on handouts.

Fostering solidarity between different groups can be a powerful force for social change. Good intentions are laudable, but often there are complex motivations for participating in seemingly virtuous interventions. The 'one day without shoes' initiative can be considered an example of 'slacktivism', the type of easy politically unengaged acts which have become a marker of the digital age.[10] In the global North people are able to access information about pressing social issues around the world, but we are not inclined to disrupt our own lifestyles to take direct action to alleviate poverty or environmental degradation. Concerned people just add their email address to an e-petitions, 'like' campaign posts on Facebook; buy charity music albums; or spend a day trying to walk around barefoot. Buying Toms is another *slack* attempt to change the world. Some consumers are motivated to buy ethical goods because they want to attach themselves to values of care and compassion. Young people especially compete to look cool; making distinctions is notably fuelled by particular brands which drive forward competitive consumption.[11] Toms are associated with charity and poverty alleviation; people want to link themselves to these ideals, rather than their purchases simply being a moment of pure altruism. One can envisage that most Toms shoppers already have several pairs of shoes, and so this type of consumerism is arguably as much about offsetting guilt as addressing poverty. In contrast, some Toms customers may just like the espadrilles and not even be aware of or interested in the charity aspect. Criticizing Toms for being shoes which make someone feel good about themselves may sound harsh, but this is normal, for actually all individual consumption – beyond that which is required to sustain life – satisfies a desire. Yet, it is deeply problematic that the sale of a pair of espadrilles should give someone the feeling that they are actually curing a problem or addressing a social issue when they are not. This is a particularly fetishistic characteristic of so-called ethical consumption.

Another issue that has been raised in the prominent critiques of Toms is the conditions of production. Would it not be better to think first about the shoe factory workers and make sure that there is an ethical supply chain? The 'trade not aid' argument has been one of the major lines of denunciation. To give Toms some credit, their founder has embraced this criticism: 'If you are really serious about poverty alleviation, our critics said, then you need to create jobs. At first I took that personally, but then I realized that they were right ... using our model to create jobs is the next level.'[12] Toms currently make most of their shoes in China, but have plans to produce one-third in countries where they make donations by the end of 2015, and to this end they are establishing factories in Ethiopia, Haiti and Kenya. Arguably, addressing the exploitative relationships which exist between labour and capital at source offers a more promising opportunity to mitigate some of the causes and consequences of uneven development.

The arguments against Toms have been raised by numerous commentators on social media as well as news outlets. A counter-reaction quickly follows, which paints critics of the brand as particularly callous individuals. Armchair detractors are labelled hateful figures by the Toms community, envious because they have never started a business, launched a brand or empowered a social movement.[13] Whether one believes Toms is 'a step in the right direction' or simply 'a cynical marketing ploy', the example opens up just one ethical dilemma associated with clothing consumption and production. The basic question boils down to this: should First World consumers of espadrilles be determining what footwear others in the global South access? Toms have harnessed a conventional fashion system of provision to a parallel supply system directed towards the deserving poor. This does not address the embedded inequalities of the linkages between clothing consumption and production and is not the solution to uneven development. Similar criticisms can be made of many other socially responsible brands. The further contradictions of ethical consumption are explored throughout this chapter.

Ethical consumption in theory and practice

Most Americans and Europeans love to consume. The great majority are largely uninterested in radical political change. Consumption means not just buying goods like clothes, but also eating out at restaurants, going on holiday, watching sports and movies, purchasing cars, carrying out home improvements and spoiling children with treats. Meanwhile, through the mass media and cultural globalization, people are more conscious than ever of global inequalities and of issues like climate change. Despite an increasing awareness of and a proclaimed concern for pressing developmental and environmental problems, widespread disenchantment with and indifference to conventional political processes are a hallmark of postmodern life. Capitalism, in partnership with liberal governments, has been effective at forestalling political dissent and inventive in bringing new forms of commodity to the market.[14] The political importance of shopping and its role in shaping life in the global North seem to be increasing to the point whereby citizens have become defined primarily as commodity-choosing consumers. In the USA a potential Democrat or Republican can be readily identified by the ways in which they spend their disposable income. Vacation destinations, transport decisions, what we eat and the clothes we wear are all potential markers of political persuasion as well as social standing.[15]

As consumption has grown and diversified, new politicized ways to exercise consumer choice have developed. Rather than engaging with formal political parties, progressive liberals are attracted to the fairly controllable and instantaneous consumption of new ethical products. Responsible capitalism has become a new means through which to promote environmental and social justice. Shopping for 'good' goods mediates our engagement with an ever-expanding range of economic, environmental and social topics. Wearing ethical clothes such as fair-trade cotton T-shirts, second-hand dresses from charity shops or organic woollen sweaters is a way to demonstrate solidarity with good causes. Buying commodities like recycled paper and fish fingers from sustainable maritime sources is shopping as a guilt-free and transformative exercise, marketed as a way to prevent deforestation, resolve overfishing or alleviate other global challenges.

Some clothing companies make ethics central to their businesses. Patagonia, an American outdoor appeal company, is a prime example. It promotes fair labour practices, provides mapping of the social and environmental footprints of its products, and uses fabrics like organic cottons and recycled polyester. Environmentalism is at the heart of the brand's appeal. Images of people fly fishing and mountaineering in pristine environments in the company's adverts help build associations with authenticity and the outdoor lifestyle. This extended to a unique ad campaign which featured the prominent strapline 'Don't Buy This Jacket', where the core message was that 'customers need to think twice before they buy'.[16] A self-serving connection is evident in the Patagonia system of provision. Buying ethically helps protect the environment; the consumer can enjoy both natural landscapes and the clothes when they go hiking and adventuring in nature. This type of consumption is distinguished by ethics, morality and the politics of responsibility, which motivate actions in a complex way. Whilst it is a growing sector, the power of ethical consumption should not be overstated. One of the most striking observations is that there is a large gap between intention and behaviour; people readily identify themselves as ethically minded consumers yet rarely purchase ethical products.[17]

A more radical approach to changing shopping habits is pursued by anti-consumption and boycott movements. Examples of anti-consumption protests in the clothing sector include the notorious PETA (People for the Ethical Treatment of Animals) 'I'd rather go naked than wear fur' photo shoots. Appearing in these anti-animal-cruelty adverts has become a near rite of passage for female celebrities, ranging from supermodels to reality TV stars. Such politicized acts are expressions of opposition to the consumption of specific types of unethical commodities resulting from 'unmet expectations', 'symbolic incongruity' or even 'ideological incompatibility'.[18] In contrast, consumer boycotts are a temporary suspension of consumption. What is interesting about a boycott is not the condemnation of market exchange per se but of a specific type of consumption. The boycott is an appealing option for commodity-choosing consumers to engage in discretionary politics and is a temporary measure, because explicit within a boycott is the principle that consumption will resume once conditions improve. Boycotts are thus in line with the mainstream idea of commodity-choosing citizen consumers opting to take individual responsibility for social and environmental issues.

Capitalist social relations are fundamentally ill-suited to resolving the problems of uneven development and environmental degradation fostered by the growth of free-market economies. Ethical consumption brings together morality and the market in what seems to be a contradiction in terms. To understand this let us first revisit the idea of commodity fetishism. One of the foundations of capitalism is that goods and services are purchased with money, a special type of commodity. Money always mediates relations between producers and consumers and in doing so creates a moral vacuum. Inequalities in exchange are concealed by apparently open and voluntary social relationships: one can choose to give Gap $50 and get a pair of new jeans; whereas if one 'chooses' to work sewing jeans in eastern China for eight or even ten hours a day one receives $1.80 a day.[19] As the case studies throughout this book have demonstrated, different parties in systems of provision are unaware of the networks of exploitation and the various ways in which surplus value is extracted in the clothing trade. Commodity fetishism transforms the abstract and subjective value of Gap jeans, vintage dresses, Toms shoes or any clothing item, turning them into objective things which people believe have intrinsic economic value. This is true of any commodity, including that other special type of commodity: human labour. Commodity fetishism makes it easy to assign variable wages to different types of work. Throughout clothing systems of provision different subjective values are assigned to various types of labour, which are exploited to a greater or lesser extent, be they Malian cotton growers, Cambodian garment workers or Walmart shop assistants.

Ethically produced goods are an attempt to de-fetishize the commodity. The most prominent example is Fairtrade. Food and beverages were the first Fairtrade products; premium bananas, chocolate and coffee have widespread appeal and are growing in popularity among middle-class consumers in the global North. Fairtrade has expanded and encompasses clothing products from babygrows to waterproof jackets. Buying Fairtrade may be intended by the consumer to be an individual progressive political act, but does little to disrupt the pre-existing relationships between capital, labour and nature. Liberal-minded citizens in the global North can indulge in their consumption habits without calling for the large-scale structural changes that could threaten their own privileged status in global society. Fairtrade aims to modify market relations by providing a *just price* for Third World labour, but does not even produce the appearance of equality. The value assigned to Fairtrade labour is a small premium above the market rate, but often covers only subsistence plus the basic cost of health care and education. Capitalist social relations are complicated; they include diverse cultural perceptions of value, but the salient point is that they are *modified* and not *transformed* by Fairtrade networks. [20]

Valuing Fairtrade clothes

Shopping for clothes in the global North is about much more than just choosing a 'thing'. It involves either passively or voluntarily subscribing to a system of provision and buying into a lifestyle. The material culture that surrounds the consumption of Fairtrade garments is an integral part of the system. Links between spaces of production and places of consumption in Fairtrade networks are exposed through adverts, documentaries and packaging, which lead to the reworking and creation of new spectacles for consumption. Marx first argued that shopping is stimulated by narratives and aesthetics: 'The need which consumption feels for the object is created by the perception of it. The object of art – like every other product – creates a public which is sensitive to art and enjoys beauty.'[21] So much of what determines the subjective symbolic value in clothing is the *spectacular* activities that lie beyond the narrow realm of physical production. Place can be influential in establishing value. With Fairtrade and other ethical goods, locations of production are often attractive parts of the global South, with which an enlightened and progressive consumer in the global North may be familiar, such as Himalayan blouses from the mountains of Nepal. Sometimes celebrity *artists* are able to play a key role in this performance and help modify the aesthetic narrative to make commodity-choosing consumers sensitive to different ethical issues. In adverts and documentaries they help create ideal images – such as visiting happy workers in stereotypical tropical landscapes – which are not an objective record of the conditions of production but, rather, a new fetish. As with other processes of image making in ethical consumption, this can serve to reinforce and perpetuate economic relationships that undermine other more radical efforts to address pressing social and environmental issues.

Yet political engagement has never been the only motivation for choosing 'good' clothes, as they also serve as means of making distinctions and class positioning. The premium pricing of most ethical garments excludes poorer consumers in the global North as well as the global South from choosing them. At worst they can be considered a petty-bourgeois indulgence. For capitalism ethical systems of provision are an elegant solution to the challenges and criticisms raised by the alliance of trade unions, NGOs, faith groups, celebrities and others. These sceptics and critics of globalization accept the limited progress and change that projects like Fairtrade represent and endorse such initiatives. Ethical trade offers a partial solution, whilst embedding the logic of inequality. Proponents argue that they are socially progressive, even though they also foreclose radical political possibilities. By absorbing some of the opposition to, and critiques of, capitalism – centred on the lack of care and compassion for labour in the global South and environments around the world – more radical alternatives are crowded out. This is not achieved by force or fierce competition, but by small-scale or 'molecular' social transformation as a tepid *revolution in shopping* without a revolution in society. Certain demands are addressed whilst at the same time international inequality between classes is encouraged.[22]

Fairtrade and other goods signify 'ethicalness'. The contradiction within Fairtrade is that, whilst partially acknowledging the inequity of market exchange and the reality of capitalist accumulation, this system of provision depends upon the persistence of the market and ordinary practices of commodity exchange. A voluntary premium is paid; yet, to maintain the price gap between conventional and Fairtrade products, consumption has to be further stimulated through the creation of symbolic use values. This results in the production of consumable adverts and producer vignettes which create a romantic and idealized vision of landscapes and livelihoods in the global South.[23]

Vivienne Westwood and political consumption

One example of the performance of ethicalness comes from Vivienne Westwood's 'Made with Love in Nairobi' fashion line, which is ethically manufactured in Kenya. Vivienne Westwood is an influential British fashion designer. In the 1970s she established her celebrity status and credibility by popularizing punk identity whilst highlighting the politics of social inequality in Margaret Thatcher's Britain. Later, she became a celebrated campaigner on gender, social and environmental issues and has been a critic of overconsumption. During the London Occupy protests she proclaimed, 'We were all trained up to be consumers ... throw away the past, the future will take care of itself, catch the latest thing and suck it up. We don't have any art today.'[24] Previously she had famously issued the rebellious statement 'don't buy clothes', but this was also an inauthentic message given that Westwood is the head of a very successful clothing label with a turnover in 2011 of £23.8 million ($39.6 million).[25] Through participating in countless seasonal fashion shows her brand helps inspire the fast-fashion system of provision, as Vivienne Westwood and other designer labels drive forward new clothing trends, which migrate rapidly from the catwalk to shopping malls. The conclusion to be drawn from Westwood's grandstanding is that her commodities are not just clothes or handbags, but are something above and beyond that. They are commodified art and have symbolic value among an affluent audience which is excited by her rebellious 'political' messages as well as the new fashionable designs.

Westwood's 'Made with Love in Nairobi' collection has been produced in collaboration with the International Trade Centre (ITC) since 2010. The ITC Ethical Production Model aims to reduce poverty by generating 'trade opportunities for marginalized communities and micro-producers in the developing world' and 'enables international fashion companies and distributors to source from African communities' by following 'a rigorous code of ethics and gender equality' designed to empower women and raise their incomes.[26] Like Fairtrade the model is 'not charity, just work'. ITC's 'Ethical Fashion Africa' initiative connects international fashion designers to African producers and organizes manufacturing activity, which 'enables some of the world's poorest people to enter fashion's value chain as producers, while also allowing designers, who want to source ethically, to do so'. In this scenario the emphasis is on liberal *choice* as individual designers have to 'want to source ethically'.[27]

In Kenya working conditions meet Fair Labour Association criteria, as a consequence of which craftswomen's incomes have increased from $3 to $6 dollars a day, enabling them to pay school fees and medical expenses. This evidence suggests that the value assigned to labour in the ITC programme is comparable to Fairtrade: wages include a small premium above the market rate, but do not enable much more than the physical reproduction of labour power. The women work on designs sent from London to Nairobi, which require 'community groups to be trained in the use of the specialised equipment needed to achieve them'.[28] Westwood says the Ethical Fashion Africa approach 'gives people control over their lives'. Yet control over the system of provision is constrained when they are unable to design and market the goods. Africans do not have access to distant international customers who have the power to pick and choose, and thus decide whether or not they support an ethical cause.

Through the ITC a new model of development is being promoted as a way to fuel African economic growth, but this is unlikely to lead to widespread poverty alleviation. There are three main problems with the economic geography of this type of intervention. First, rather than establishing 'modern' industrial patterns – as previously existed in Kenya and elsewhere in Africa – ITC advocates a fragmented approach to organizing production and 'essentially spread[s] out the different parts of a factory over entire regions'.[29] This promotes uneven development and amplifies spatial inequality by assisting only certain groups to enter the global capitalist economy on marginally better terms. Second, dispersed community-level production is also disadvantageous for labour as it reduces wage earners' bargaining power relative to international buying firms. Third, the ITC wants to develop large-scale production, but does not promote state intervention, preferential access to overseas markets, industrial development, or production for local consumers, and only responds to 'market demand'. The WTO sponsors ITC's Ethical Fashion Africa initiative. Yet it is important to note that the WTO's broad mission is to open up global trade, which is in line with the economic liberalization imposed upon Africa through the structural adjustment programmes that contributed to eroding industries and decreasing wage levels. Today's 'Made with Love in Nairobi' craftswomen are the daughters of a generation which had an established clothing industry that proved to be uncompetitive in a globalized free market. This type of niche production and small-scale employment cannot contribute to widespread poverty alleviation; rather than well-intentioned market 'solutions', more radical shifts in the mode of production are required. The re-establishment of an industrial working class will be necessary before poverty reduction can be achieved on a large scale.

Marketing 'Made with Love in Nairobi'

'Made with Love in Nairobi' has been promoted through magazine photo shoots, videos, Westwood's personal blog and numerous interviews. Vivienne Westwood has made a big 'media splash'.[30] The images and personal vignettes represent a controlled attempt to de-fetishize the commodity. Nairobian craftswomen have identities which add symbolic value to the commodities. In Fairtrade the romantic commodification of production has been used to a similar effect. Vivienne Westwood amplifies this by using her celebrity identity to draw greater attention to the production location and shape consumers' knowledge. A stylized vision of a de-fetishized relationship is offered, which is actually a caricature of reality. The creation of a new commodity fetish begins with the name of the products, 'Made with Love in Nairobi', which instantly draws attention to the conditions of production. The use of 'Love' cynically reworks the commodity fetish to capitalize on the notion of 'caring at distance'.[31] The acts of 'love' represent a two-way interaction: on the one hand, the bags are explicitly made 'with love' and carefully manufactured; on the other hand, the implicit subtext is that the consumer is performing a reciprocal *act of love* towards a deserving African woman by buying the bag. What could be a more effective way of obscuring the unequal relationship between consumer and producer? The name 'Made with Love in Nairobi' really says more about consumers' construction of their own identity than about the producers' situation. People are choosing a fashionable bag and aspiring to buy into a compassionate image.

The primary imagery used in 'Made with Love in Nairobi' projects a powerful message of lifting impoverished African female urban workers out of poverty. Photographs are shot in a 'slum' landscape of dusty and impoverished Nairobi streets, rubbish dumps and local workshops, showing where the goods are produced and who will benefit from their sale. In most of the photos local people are in the margins of the frames; Vivienne Westwood herself takes centre stage alongside established African supermodels. The promotional material presents a 'one-way' consumption of life.[32] A new text is created by Vivienne Westwood so that the consumer can 'know' what life in Nairobi looks like, but this is uni-directional as the producer does not 'know' the consumer. In some of the images Westwood re-creates a typical African scene after recognizing the commonplace practice of selling second-hand clothes and accessories in open-air markets;[33] 'We brought so many accessories with us to Africa that Juergen [the photographer] suggested we pretend we had a shop and were selling things like everybody else. I think you can see that I'm having fun selling.'[34] Westwood seems to mock the situation of the people around her. She places the $300 handbags among second-hand clothes consumed by the poor out of necessity rather than choice. The imagery in the adverts follows classical European representations of the continent, where Africans are reduced to the role of bystanders.[35] This marketing activity contrasts sharply with the livelihoods of African market traders, which are beset by risk, uncertainty and hardships.[36]

Some of the revenue from sales may help alleviate poverty in Kenya on a small scale, but meanwhile the promotional campaign creates new commodity fetishes that undermine the broader efforts to challenge the politics of global inequality. The Vivienne Westwood stylized and romantic vision of Kenya is obscuring the inequity between global North and South in a manner comparable to that of other celebrities' interventions in Africa, including Bono, Bob Geldof and Madonna.[37] In this case study a celebrity personality is attempting to allow individual consumers to make moral and economic connections to African producers in a flawed effort to de-fetishize commodity culture. Rather than eliminating the commodity fetish, the celebrity artist conjures up a new performance. The knowledge flows – newspaper and magazine features and interviews, blogs, and the ITC and Vivienne Westwood websites – formulate a new fetish and create another form of 'spectacle' for Northern consumers.

As with Fairtrade and the other ITC products, 'Made with Love in Nairobi' offers a limited acknowledgment of the inequities at the heart of capitalism, but still depends upon the market and ordinary practices of commodity exchange. A voluntary premium is paid to the Kenyan labour force, but to sustain the consumption of this product the commodity-choosing consumers have to be stimulated to buy the good through the creation of material and symbolic use values which grab their attention and so commend high prices. The proclaimed aim to move away from a charitable discourse is contradicted by the images of Kenyans which fall into the category of deserving poor rather than equal partners. Westwood wants the consumer to help poor Africans: 'It's quite incredible to think that we might be able to save the world through fashion.'[38] Instead of providing something different to charity, the result of 'Made with Love in Nairobi' is itself a contradiction which undermines efforts to give greater recognition to workers in the global South.

Ethical recycling and new cycles of consumption

Consumer ethics also play a role in how people in the global North dispose of clothes. Getting rid of old clothes and making rubbish are firmly entrenched as part of the broader practice of everyday consumption and use.[39] People are increasingly being directed towards ways to dispose of the masses of old, unwanted clothes that result from the global North's overconsumption, especially the same middle-class consumers who enjoy buying ethical products. This includes the growth in doorstep and clothing bank collections already discussed, but also new ethical commercial solutions are emerging. The link between shopping and disposal is something that retailers are beginning to exploit as they mix fast fashion and sustainability. Foremost is H&M, the world's second largest apparel retailer. H&M has initiated a garment collection scheme across thousands of stores worldwide: 'customers are encouraged to bring in unwanted garments of any brand and in any condition to H&M stores in all 53 markets to be given a new life.'[40] Cecilia Brannsten, project manager in the UK Sustainability Team, outlines H&M's aim: 'Basically, we want to change the mindset of the customer [so they] see their old clothes as a resource rather than throwing them into the garbage or letting them pile up at the back of their closet.'[41] When customers visit H&M they can hand over their old clothes, for which they get a voucher in return to encourage more shopping. In the USA, H&M offers a 15 per cent discount voucher for every bag of used clothing, with a limit of two vouchers a day. This is an incentive to bring in old clothes, but is not very generous when one considers that the company routinely posts a gross profit margin of around 60 per cent and a net profit margin of 15 per cent.[42] Clothes are sold on to I:CO, a Swiss headquartered textile recycler, which processes used clothing for second-hand markets in the global South, vintage retail in the global North, and recycling – just like the systems of provision which have already been discussed at length. The claim is that it is a non-profit making venture, with revenues covering H&M's running costs.[43] Donations are also made to charities: 'for each kilogram of clothes that H&M collects 0.02 Euro will be donated to a local charity organization chosen by H&M'.[44] This represents a small contribution when compared to the market price of used clothes.

Accepting donations of old clothes is not unique to H&M. Other retailers are establishing similar programmes, some of which involve closer integration with charities. In the UK 'JJB Sports has launched a new in-store trainer-recycling scheme to raise funds for [children's disability charity] Whizz-Kidz' with each donor receiving a £5 [$8] JJB voucher in exchange for every pair of trainers they donate.[45] The used shoes are sold by JJB: 'All profits that JJB makes from the sale of the unwanted shoes for re-use or recycling will support many more young disabled people.' A similar scheme has been operated between Oxfam and Marks & Spencer since 2008: 'Oxfam and M&S have teamed up to help shoppers support the world's poorest people. Just bring your old M&S clothes or soft furnishings to an Oxfam shop and we'll exchange them for a £5 [$8] voucher to use at M&S.'[46] Donations then go on to be sold in Oxfam shops or processed at Wastesaver.

Getting rid of clothes makes more room for new consumption. Commercial recycling by stores like H&M explicitly links discarding unwanted clothes to a new cycle of consumption, demonstrating a direct connection between the new and used clothing systems of provision. Clothing retailers want to provide a virtuous outlet for unwanted clothing in the global North, without interrupting the sale of fast fashion. They have begun to develop their own solution to the problem of clothing overconsumption. As with other collection schemes, the marketing materials downplay the broader social and economic impacts of the second-hand clothing system of provision in the global South. H&M and I:CO place a special emphasis on textile recycling, stating that it is possible to recycle up to 30 per cent of textiles and highlighting how these can be 'down-cycled' in to materials such as cushioning, flooring or packaging, or alternatively 'upcycled' into new clothes of equal or higher value.[47] Despite these narratives, profitability in clothing recycling is driven by the value of re-wearable garments rather than by remaking old clothes into new apparel or other goods. Closed loop recycling, where textile fibres could be reused and woven into new fabrics, is an appealing idea, but techniques and technologies are currently underdeveloped and not economically viable on a commercial scale. The complexity of the different combinations of materials used in new garments makes reusing modern mixed fibres very difficult.

Ethical recycling provides an appealing and intuitive solution to the issues of overconsumption, yet this does not address the myriad development and environmental problems that are formed through the interconnected new and second-hand clothing systems of provision. As has been shown in earlier chapters, second-hand clothing donations have diverse effects upon the economies and cultures of the global South. From an environmental perspective, the 'clothes miles' associated with the circulation of millions of tons of new and used textiles are a further issue that should be considered within any ethical audit of clothing systems of provision. Local rather than transnational commodity chains may offer Greener solutions. Furthermore, the environmental impacts of new clothing production need to be more extensively explored. Solutions are likely to require radical action. The challenges of making Green garments have become the preoccupation of a sustainable fashion movement.

Sustainable fashion

Sustainable, Green or eco fashion is a design philosophy and part of a wider trend towards sustainable forms of consumption. From origins among alternative and counter-culture groups, sustainable fashion has spread towards the mainstream, finding favour mainly among the middle classes in the global North. The language, if not always the reality, of sustainability has been leapt upon by the mainstream fashion press, most notably *Vogue*, and collections have found their way into malls and department stores. The overall concept of sustainability rests upon three pillars: society, economy and environment. Within fashion it is fair to say that the greatest attention has been drawn to the environmental pillar.

The politics of the environment are malleable and business can shape the eco agenda to dictate new ways of bringing profitable clothing goods to the market. In theory, through sustainable design, consideration is given to the lifespan of products, including the broad ecological footprint of clothes. However, there are many layers of engagement in Greening fashion. While the more committed proponents seek to dramatically rethink the relationships between design, consumption, use and reuse, and end of life, at the other limit of the spectrum some eco interventions resemble little more than token gestures, as business has capitalized upon the popularity of environmental movements to bathe their products in the appealing aura of Greenness.

Corporations have grown concerned about their brand image; in consequence, major fast fashion companies have made limited efforts to think progressively about material selection, resource flows and supply chain efficiencies.[48] Some of these interventions have the collateral benefit of making manufacturing and distribution more profitable, or enabling products to be attractively marketed. It can pay to consider the environment; however, reforms rarely extend to changes that will significantly disrupt the profitability of production. The crux of the matter is the inherent contradiction of sustainable fashion. Importantly, 'normal' or 'fast' fashion is driven by the logic of the market. Fashion in the broadest sense means the prevailing or conventional – that is, the socially acceptable – way of dressing. New clothes are framed as being *the latest fashion*, implying that there is change afoot and soon current fashions will become outmoded and obsolete. Fashions are the accelerating metronome for consumption, producing advancing beats, pulsing ever faster to draw more commodities through the circuits of global systems of provision. Zara's model of continually changing fashion lines and other strategies of ongoing replenishment compel the committed shopper to buy, and keep on buying, fast fashion. Ownership becomes transient as affordable garments are made of inferior materials and are constructed speedily in ways which mean they will fray, thin, unravel and fall apart.

Fashion is a practice that directly underpins the rapid despoiling of the earth's environmental systems. Under capitalism the necessity to continually increase profits brings more and more products to the market. Varied styles and makes of clothes all have different and baffling biographies that involve a near infinite array of ecological impacts. Difficulties in auditing and accounting for the directly attributable effects of consuming particular items of clothing stymie effective collective action, even though it is evident that clothes-making harms the natural world. On a global scale evidence abounds of the varied ways in which industrial capitalism is exceeding planetary boundaries; usage of fresh water, food and minerals has grown exponentially since the onset of the Industrial Revolution.[49] To go further back, ever since humans began to extract a permanent social surplus from the environment, they set in motion an irreversible destruction of what was natural. The size of the challenge is immense. How can consuming clothes be reconciled with preserving the environment through ecologically limited and careful practices that necessitate living within the boundaries of natural systems? How can fashion become sustainable? These are big questions. The focus of this book has been on humans and poverty, directing knowledge towards the social and economic (non)sustainability of systems of provision. The work of others, with a greater sensibility for design and knowledge of materials, is both advancing the understanding of the environmental impacts of clothing consumption and challenging how we think about the very idea of fashion. Foremost here is the work of Kate Fletcher, who recognizes the need for a holistic approach that looks across systems of provision. Viable alternatives must be located, studied and popularized to unlock creativity

and challenge contemporary relationships between people and
the garment sector:

> Ideas and expectations of fashion are 'locked in' to conventions,
> habits, social norms and industry structures that reflect a vision
> of our fashionable selves as individuals consuming new clothes,
> but ... other forms of fashion expression and provision exist and
> reflect resourceful, fulfilling and empowering engagement with
> garments. Tentatively, this points to a situation where ideas of
> progress are no longer tied to a societal narrative of economic
> growth through market transactions.[50]

Perspectives on ethical consumption

When debating the impacts of ethical consumption one of the fundamental issues to consider is whether the success of businesses
is consistent with social advancement and human development.
If capitalist progress is inherently good, then most enterprise will
have ethical benefits. The reality, however, indicates otherwise.
The global market economy has led to uneven development and
environmental degradation. Ethical consumption is both compat-
ible with and supportive of liberal free-market approaches to
governance of the global economy and environment. As such,
the ways in which ethical consumption is popularized dismantle
a sense of praxis. This means that more radical alliances and
voices of dissent can get crowded out as partial and deeply flawed
ethical solutions grab attention. Critical work which has been
undertaken on Fairtrade and similar products has illuminated
many of the problems of ethical consumption and exposed how
this type of activity sustains the smooth functioning of global
capitalism rather than being a brake on an exploitative mode of
production. To reiterate, ethical production systems alter rather
than eliminate the exploitation of labour and nature, especially in
the global South. 'Made with Love in Nairobi' provides a signal

case of particular interest as it uses advertising imagery which mimics African second-hand clothing markets, reinforcing the links between new and used clothes, but also embedding the logic of an uneven world in which different people have and do not have access to new clothes.

Ethical consumption satisfies a longing for 'action' on environmental and social issues by producing commodities with highly specific use values which meet peoples real (or imagined) needs. Yet, as the radical philosopher Slavoj Žižek argues, 'from the absolute standpoint of the system as a totality, the satisfaction of individuals' needs is just a necessary means to keep the machinery of capitalist (re)production going.'[51] Buying ethical clothes like Toms shoes is an individualized form of 'political' consumption which represents a limited force for social change that focuses attention only on convenient ethical topics. The maintenance of individual consumer sovereignty fits perfectly with extreme notions of liberalism whereby social relations are becoming 'purely atomic' and civic responsibility is rejected in favour of the 'apotheosis of the individual'.[52] This type of positional ethical consumption as class differentiation feeds into the reproduction of inequalities. Clothing is one of the most important types of consumer commodity, as it stands in for identity. People want to wear clothes that represent their personality, and so garments which are associated with values such as compassion and care are popular among certain consumers. 'Going Green' or supporting other topical issues can even be fashionable. From an environmental perspective the individually responsible decision is to choose to shop less often, wear clothes until they are worn out, and then repair or recycle them within the household or replace them with locally produced goods. Slowing the rate of clothing consumption by buying fewer higher-quality clothes is a far more environmentally friendly approach than continuing to buy fast fashion and donating excess clothes. However, these solutions are an 'opt in' approach to a massive problem and are unlikely to be taken up by more than a small section of society in the global North who have the opportunity to make the decision. Fundamentally, more radical social change is required, to which the capitalist mode of production does not provide the answer.

CHAPTER 10

Fast-fashion systems

London Fashion Week

For 500 years a palace has stood at the site of Somerset House on the north bank of the River Thames. The present design dates to the eighteenth century and is inspired by the columns and piazzas of Ancient Greece and Rome. Across the centuries this grand mansion in the heart of London has housed prestigious institutions and been a home to royalty, the Navy Board, the Inland Revenue, the Courtauld Institute of Art and King's College London. As a seat of empire and a centre for art and learning, the palace has a long history of hosting international political and cultural events. It is now a self-styled 'cultural beehive' that hosts creative and scholarly endeavour. Twice a year London Fashion Week comes to Somerset House. The calm of the English neoclassical palace is disturbed by a decadent celebration of clothing design and consumption. A catwalk is set up within a dark avant-garde prefabricated pavilion; pop music reverberates around the courtyard; and at night light shows project sponsors' logos onto the elegant stonework. Fashionistas spill out of Somerset House onto the Strand and into surrounding coffee shops, where they gossip and compare notes. And they wear the most outragous outfits – silver mackintoshes, orange playsuits, rubber trousers. Nothing seems over the top when the fashion community descends upon the palace. Meanwhile, design students hang around the arched stone gateways snapping photos of new looks, while promotional models hand out flyers to passing members of the clothing trade. Within the inner sanctums of Fashion Week, inside the jet-black pavilion, access is carefully controlled. Only the chosen few from the garment industry and their celebrity friends get a runway seat and see the new collections by Daks, Jasper Conran and Vivienne Westwood close up. Catwalk shows are pure theatre. The house lights dim, tension builds; then the runway is suddenly illuminated; at the same moment electronic music kicks in and models come down the catwalk in perfectly choreographed movements. Shows feature tall, elegant muses in couture designs. Many clothes are outrageous and will inspire future fashions rather than be worn in the real world. Other collections showcase new looks that will soon make it to clothing stores across the global North. Between shows, journalists, stylists, designers, fashion scouts and retail buyers mix at exclusive receptions, enjoying cocktails in bars on the Embankment terrace overlooking the river. At the end of the week the carnival departs, leaving hundreds of empty champagne bottles in its wake, at which point the mass clean-up operation commences to restore the palace grounds.[1]

In the days that follow, the designs showcased by runway models and the new trends worn by celebrities and the fashion community are reported in the printed press and relayed online around the world. Outfits are rated and debated. Fresh looks emerge and provide inspiration for new mass clothing production. Fashion shows in London, as well as in Milan, New York, Paris, Tokyo and elsewhere in the global North, herald much broader fast-fashion systems of provision. Clothing culture is influenced by wider processes and reflects social change. This makes fashion difficult to define. As Coco Chanel recognized, 'Fashion is not something that exists in dresses only. Fashion is in the sky, in the street. Fashion has to do with ideas, the way we live, what is happening.'[2] The types of couture collections that are exhibited at Somerset House, as well as the material culture that surrounds London Fashion Week and other fashion shows, feed into new clothing systems of provision, helping to generate retail demand and determine what is on sale in malls and department stores.

Consumers do also affect demand, but they have less autonomy than they imagine. Demand is stimulated. Only clothing which meets a consumer niche will sell; but these market niches are also shaped and manipulated by the fashion sector, as Alexandra Shulman, editor of British *Vogue*, notes: 'Fashion is smoke and mirrors. We create images, we create a world of stuff, yes, ultimately to make people want to have it.'[3] Image-making, led by fashion designers and retailers, and propelled by the media, creates new demands for clothing and simultaneously erodes the socially constructed value embedded in previous trends. Consumers are placed in a never-ending contest to purchase more. Changing meanings are attributed to clothing, deriving from the ways in which people think about colours, fabrics, the length of dresses or the design of logos. Broader behavioural norms and cultural values influence how fashions are perceived. Meanwhile the inherently expansionist elements of capitalist society work together to compel people to buy more clothes.[4]

The majority of consumers in the global North are not 'slaves to fashion'; the symbolic value of clothing is just part of their decision-making process when they go shopping.[5] Many people claim to have little or no interest in clothing, but everyone adheres to some culturally constructed norms of dress – business suits for office work, jeans for the weekend, cocktail dresses for Christmas parties and so forth – which continually change. Trends are never static, but rather are kept in motion, giving rise to fast-fashion

systems of provision. The collective growth in demand for consumer products is essential for capitalism to ensure the smooth
functioning of the world economy and diminish the opportunity
for crisis. The fact that good used clothing, which can be worn
again, is regularly disposed of in the global North demonstrates
that the market is very successful in stimulating the consumption
of new clothing principally for the sake of appearance and not for
practical use. People continually buy clothes they do not really
need because they are partial to the look of them, and get rid of
clothes they can still wear but which they no longer like.

Tying together strands of the argument developed earlier, this
final chapter will first explain how fast-fashion retail is linked to
the sale of second-hand clothing. Inequality is produced through
different patterns of commodity exchange. Across the clothing
sector radical alternatives are needed to deliver fundamental
social change. It is frustrating to come to terms with the reality
that there are no easy answers to reconciling the relationships
between the production of clothing and the persistence of poverty.
Sections on consumption and production assess the overall challenges in new clothing systems of provision and look towards
radical alternatives that would modify or temper capitalist social
relations. Such arguments may give hope; yet to affect change is
difficult when there is little progress towards substantive political
transformation on the horizon. A work like this can come to no
single conclusion. It finishes instead with a final discussion of
how the clothing trade has been part of the fabric of the uneven
worldwide development of capitalism.

Making markets for second-hand clothes

For the poor the availability of clothes is a welfare issue that ranks
just below access to education, health care, food, shelter and clean
water. There is nothing new about this situation. Good clothing

has long been difficult to obtain for marginalized members of society, especially prior to the growth in mass clothing manufacturing that emerged with the Industrial Revolution; and yet the global South of today should not be confused with the pre-industrial world. There is now a global division in consumption. The uneven development of capitalism has delivered great wealth to some through patterns of exploitation – including in cotton growing, textile manufacturing and garment production – and left much of the world impoverished. On a global scale the world is split between the affluent North and the poor South. Lives in the global South have been marginalized by virtue of capitalist class relations. In the poorer hemisphere hundreds of millions of people struggle to find employment and act as a surplus reserve of labour, who can be exploited when investment seeks out new territory to provide a spatial fix. However, there is a complicated geography to wealth and poverty. Patterns are changing: recent GDP (gross domestic product) growth in Africa and elsewhere, including the BRICS countries (Brazil, Russia, India, China and South Africa), has occurred alongside rising inequality.[6]

Within countries there are sharp divisions between rich and poor. In South Africa, one of the most unequal societies in the world, local elites shop for designer clothes in malls like the V&A Waterfront in Cape Town, which are just like their counterparts in the USA and Europe. The V&A mall is a modern-day cathedral to consumption, perfectly located in a World Heritage site along the historic and lavishly restored colonial harbour front, where for centuries goods were exported from Africa. Visitors can today buy the same global fashion brands – like Adidas, Diesel and Levi's – found worldwide. Outside such enclaves of privilege, the South African poor buy low-cost clothing in value retail stores like PEP and Shoprite in declining urban centres, and sometimes shop for illegally imported second-hand clothing sold by Nigerians in informal marketplaces in the deprived townships.[7]

From the colonial period onwards, declining terms of trade
and strategic approaches to market protection and liberalization
have made garments cheaper for rich consumers. New clothing sales are predicated on the exploitation of labour in places
such as Zambian cotton farms and Chinese clothing factories.
Capitalism is inherently expansionist; the need for new sales
drives excessive consumption of clothing in the global North.
Fast-fashion consumption in the North generates a surplus of unwanted used clothes, which are then exported back to the global
South, sometimes to the very same locations that manufacture
new clothes for export, such as Kenya, Tanzania, Pakistan and the
Philippines. The circulation of both new and used clothes locks
poor societies into relationships of dependency. Knowledge flows
and political agreements that connect the global North and South
also facilitate the used-clothing trade. Neoliberal policies and
SAPs have undermined local clothing production and promoted
imports, particularly in Africa and South America, helping to
create captive markets. Meanwhile trends in clothing that spread
northern styles of dress are forged, reinforced and disseminated
through the international circulation of garments and processes
of social and cultural globalization, such as the mass media and
returning migrants.[8]

Profitable design, marketing and retailing activities in the
global North help dictate the manufacture of high-quality items
for competitive, rich consumer markets. In the global South many
poor consumers are not served by systems of provision that bring
well-made or desirable clothing to market. Within Africa new
imported garments come primarily from China and compete
with second-hand clothing, but these new goods are very different to the Chinese-made products available in America and
Europe. As one Nigerian trader who works in Britain and West
Africa explains, 'I think China has flooded the whole African
market with cheap low-quality goods. At first the [second-hand]

trade in the UK was affected for two or three years ... When the Chinese first went in there was a slowdown ... but the stuff [used clothing] from the UK, you still get the quality.' This is because clothing made in China for the global North is much better. When Chinese factories produce for retailers like 'Marks & Spencer, they make [garments] to a strict specification', but the quality of goods exported to Africa is low.[9] In Mozambique, traders and consumers complain that the colours run and fabrics stretch when new garments are washed. New clothes are used carefully and only worn for special occasions like parties and weddings. Mozambicans and other poor Africans prefer to buy second-hand garments. In contrast, successful retailers in the global North know that they have to import good-quality apparel from China and elsewhere to meet consumer demand. The effort that went into the original production and marketing of clothes for retailers such as Marks & Spencer or fashion brands like Levi's is utilized again by businesses in the second-hand clothing sector. Used-clothing traders accumulate surplus value from past labour (the original work of manufacturing clothing), as well as from the new labour activities (collecting, sorting, grading) involved in bringing second-hand clothes to market.

When analysing how second-hand clothing is valued in Tanzania, the economist Petra Rivoli makes the bold claim that 'Africans are every bit as fashion-conscious as the Americans, and know whether lapels are wide or pants have cuffs this year, and make their demands accordingly.'[10] Research in African markets shows the opposite. Tastes are not met by the provision of second-hand clothes; nor are people able to *demand* particular styles.[11] Africans cannot follow the rapidly changing fashions of the global North because of the time-lag of several years between the emergence of new trends and the arrival of those used clothes in African markets. Desires and consumer demands are also different across Africa; in addition, local cultures influence how

garments are valued. Furthermore, Rivoli does not appreciate
the different ways people 'read' clothing. Africans, like any
other people, have diverse tastes, but to claim that they buy fast
fashion in the same way as affluent Americans and respond to
changing trends is wrong. What was repeatedly documented in
markets in Kenya, Mozambique and Zambia was that clothing
customers cared most about price and the physical quality of
clothing. Local or international styles influence purchases, but
are a secondary consideration. Poor people can also only afford
to buy clothes occasionally and own few garments, in contrast
to the overconsumption of clothing that is normal in America.
In Africa 'fashion-conscious' purchases are the exception rather
than the norm; yet this is also a generalization that obscures
differentiated patterns of consumption. There is a small middle
class of better-off people who cannot afford international prices
in the elite boutiques and shopping malls, but who can choose
to consume clothes primarily for their fashion value. Catering to
these clients is important for traders like Mario, whom we first met
in the Introduction. In cities like Maputo some people cultivate
sophisticated and cosmopolitan looks as they buy the *best* second-
hand clothes, browsing the markets or purchasing goods which
have been selected by street traders to sell at a premium price.[12]

In the medium term a realistic response to some of the problems identified with the second-hand clothing trade would be
to start with regulation of the collection and donation sectors
in the global North to address malpractice, such as the theft of
donations. Raising awareness among consumers of fast-fashion
clothing of the future trajectories of their donated second-hand
clothes is also important. In the global South import regulations
could control the market for second-hand clothes and, if parallel
protectionist measures and industrialization policies were implemented, could promote local clothing industries. This, though,
would have to be a carefully managed process rather than shock

treatment, as a sudden ban would disproportionately affect poor traders as well as impoverished consumers. Controls on imports would represent a reversal of economic liberalization programmes, a policy that is unlikely to be implemented in the current political climate. Equally, if clothing industries in Africa and elsewhere are to be protected, the type of businesses that should be fostered are those that pay living wages and not salaries like those at ZCMT, which barely sustain life. Furthermore, environmentally responsible agriculture and manufacturing should be encouraged. For such proposals to be successful and to transform markets and enable sustainable industries to emerge, the problems at the heart of production and consumption need to be addressed.

Post-consumption

Evidence throughout this book has shown that the capitalist development of the world economy spawned the exploitative fast-fashion system, and also gave rise to the international inequalities that have fuelled the boom in the second-hand clothing trade. The two sectors need to be considered in tandem. But can consumers do anything to rectify the problems linked to different clothing systems of provision? Under what we might think of as *late capitalism* – the present and crisis-ridden mode of production – individualism is promoted relentlessly. When affluent consumers venture into the market, the 'I consume, therefore I am' mentality is a pervasive force influencing behaviour.[13] Some people are interested in their personal social and environmental footprint; they want to make sure *they* do the right thing. But individual adjustments to behaviour, namely choosing to consume ethically, are not leading to widespread progressive change. Consumers across both the global North and South cannot be either expected, or trusted, to consistently make good decisions. That judgement may sound harsh, but it is justifiable on four interconnected levels.

First, it is unrealistic to expect consumers in the global North to be able to undertake an accurate ethical audit whenever they go to buy new clothes. Under capitalism the commodity fetish – how we value goods – obscures the relationship between labour, the owners of the means of production, and the consumer. Every time someone looks at a pair of jeans can they really be expected to 'get behind the veil, the fetishism of the market' and uncover the true story of the system of provision, given the incredible complexity of supply chains?[14] Likewise, when they want to get rid of a sweater should they stop, and, rather than throwing it away or donating it to charity, instead unpick the yarn and reuse the threads? Finding an ethical way to get rid of used clothing is just as problematic as trying to shop responsibly. Relying upon voluntary certification schemes, such as Fairtrade or charities like Oxfam, has not alleviated the problems at the heart of capitalist social relations either. Therefore depending upon people's good intentions would appear to offer a limited solution to solving fast-fashion consumption. And why stop at clothes? What of the ethical implications of, say, food shopping or transport choices or paper recycling? To consider everything would leave the consumer paralysed by indecision and inactivity. A handful of people may choose to follow sustainable lifestyles, but the majority in the global North do not want to be confronted by constant consumption dilemmas or really to transform their behaviour.

Second, shoppers cannot be trusted to shop less or consume differently. Impending ecological crisis means that the rate of consumption needs to be slowed down to mitigate the environmental impacts of fast fashion. The emerging sustainable fashion movement offers potential answers to ecological dilemmas, but new design approaches need to be coupled with a change in behaviour. Transforming behaviours and slowing consumption go against capitalist social relations, which depend upon the continual expansion of the market. The hegemony of the market means that people are bombarded by social pressure to consume, including adverts, marketing and media images, the expectations of friends and colleagues, and more broadly the socially accepted norms of what makes up everyday life. The obligation to consume and the fetish of the market pressurize even the most conscientious shopper into making the 'wrong' choice. It is just not possible to consistently rely on the consumer to do the right thing.[15]

Third, it is really difficult to do the right thing in the market, not just for individual people but also for other types of consumers who buy clothing, such as businesses and states. For instance, the US federal government has been found to routinely buy clothing from overseas suppliers that breaks local laws, thereby contravening their own well-intentioned yet neglected policies on responsible sourcing. If the state will not even follow ethical guidelines, what hope is there in persuading citizens to do so?[16]

Finally, although their individual buying power is weak, the vast majority of the world's consumers are poor people in the global South. This is an important fact often neglected in consumption research. Decisions regarding consumption can be a matter of life and death for households with limited resources, like the billions surviving on a dollar or two a day.[17] With regard to all low-income groups and not just the very poor, it is absurd to imagine them undertaking a social and environmental cost–benefit analysis when they buy clothes. The impoverished have immediate, pressing livelihood demands that override all other concerns. For example, a poor person in Kenya or Nigeria cannot realistically be expected to ignore affordable imported second-hand clothing and choose more expensive locally manufactured garments.

Consumption appears to offer a poor route to fixing the immense challenges at hand. Therefore we should look beyond consumption to a *post-consumption* approach to social relations.

The term 'post-consumption' is not intended to be taken literally; people can no more choose to stop consuming than they can elect to live without eating, drinking or finding shelter – essential life requirements presently subject to market exchange. Like postmodernism, which is not simply 'after modernism' but a departure from modern ways of perceiving society and culture, so post-consumption is an alternative way to think about the relationships between consumers and producers. There are two mutually reinforcing tenets to a post-consumption approach: defetishizing the market and political change.[18]

In the clothing sector, critical investigations by academics, journalists and others who seek to extend and elaborate defetishism research can do some of the work of getting behind the veil of market exchange, which it is unfeasible to expect the consumer to accomplish. New case studies can direct greater attention to the injustices within clothing systems of provision. This would involve rigorous exposés of labour exploitation (like the studies of Mulungushi Textiles and cotton farming in Mali) and robust and thoughtful discussion of so-called ethical initiatives (like Ragtex's used-clothing business and 'Made with Love in Nairobi'), as well as recognition for progressive enterprises (such as Mima-te and the improvements in Sri Lanka, discussed further in the next section). This is a departure from the ethical consumption agenda, which seeks to modify market relations. Instead of mild action within the current mode of production, work in a post-consumption school would promote radical advocacy and bring awareness of social justice to a popular audience. Evidence is only useful in a post-consumption approach if it informs 'spirited debate and animated conversation' that result in political action.[19] Social justice organizations, like Labour Behind the Label and the Institute for Global Labour and Human Rights, which have led the fight for improved workers' rights in the global South have some potential, but require much greater support from a concerned citizenry, which brings the interests of labour to the political centre stage.

De-fetishizing consumption also requires an understanding of the motivations behind the everyday compulsion to consume.[20] This means that the material culture which surrounds existing systems of clothing provision requires analysis along with the immediate structure of supply chains. Examples of how patterns of consumption are formed through diverse influences include the role of charities in creating the international second-hand clothing trade, the media's impact on changing perceptions of vintage fashion, and the influence of trade protection on garment manufacturing. Understanding the cultural and political context of trade can provide insights to enable action. Recognizing the reasons behind the uneven patterns of clothing consumption found across the world will offer a valuable case study to help to explain the wider totalizing nature of capitalism in shaping everyday life.

The prospects for the type of transformation of the political agenda required in a post-consumption approach seem at best remote at the present time. Global financial instability has led some to question capitalist social relations – the Occupy movement, protests, strikes – but not on a sustained and widespread scale. Clothing consumption is a sector that might provide potential for a collective sense of common responsibility to be forged on account of the shared intimacy associated with garments which are made, worn and re-worn around the world by diverse people. Further awareness of the hidden world of clothes provides an opportunity to ratchet up the debate about how people consume and open up the possibilities to shop less, shop differently and shop reflectively. This is more likely to come about by formal political action on local, national and international levels, as voluntary interventions are not working. Stricter regulation and legal protection are ultimately required to enforce the production of clothing in socially and environmentally responsible ways. In the clothing

sector a post-consumption agenda may seem incompatible with
the immense task at hand, but is a potentially important waypoint
towards a post-capitalist future.

Can production be fixed?

Within the existing structure of capitalist social relations, energy,
commitment and a will to fight are needed to disrupt the status quo
and provide a more equitable distribution of the fruits of clothing
production. Countless workers around the world are paid a few
dollars a day, sometimes less than a dollar, to make clothing. At
the same time vast profits are accumulated. The heads of clothing
empires are multi-billionaires. Amancio Ortega, former chairman
of Inditex, which owns the Zara brand, is the third richest person
in the world with a fortune of $57 billion; Christy Walton (and her
immediate family), part-owner of Walmart, is the eleventh richest,
with $35.4 billion; the twelfth richest is Stefan Persson, chairman
of H&M, with $28 billion.[21] These individuals all have personal
wealth which far exceeds the annual GDP of entire countries, such
as Mozambique ($14.2 billion) and Zambia ($20.7 billion).[22]

The problem is not so much that capitalism is making people
richer, but that there is an incredibly uneven distribution of
growth. One means to battle for increased wages for poor workers
is labour unionization. Current estimates suggest that globally
only 5–10 per cent of garment workers are members of independent unions.[23] For instance in China, Xiaomin Yu who carried
out research on the FS factory, which produces for Reebok,
found that 'independent trade unions are repressed ruthlessly and
strikes or other radical industrial actions are restricted strictly.'[24]
Unionization can help improve conditions, but is unlikely to be
a panacea, as the record of unions in the clothing sector is poor.
In Zambia, at Mulungushi Textiles the union was consistently
unable to bargain for improved conditions and wages. Only the

minority of permanent employees were able to join unions, and the destitution of these workers made it difficult for them to challenge management's decisions. Impoverishment meant that when unionized permanent employees, and indeed casual labourers, took action in the form of strikes, the weakened bonds between workers meant that they could not unite effectively to oppose oppressive management regimes.

In addition to poverty, there are further factors that weaken the power of workers in the global South. The deskilling of labour in the textile and clothing industries and the use of advanced technologies have served to concentrate power in the hands of management. Meanwhile, the degradation of work and alienation of the predominately female workers, the surplus supply of labour at a global level, and local political conditions make it impossible to bargain effectively for substantial improvements. Crisis-ridden factories just close and reopen elsewhere. The mobile and footloose nature of fast-fashion factories means that production can easily relocate to new lower-wage locations when the cost of labour increases, be that in response to union demands, competition for employees or other social pressures. Crises develop when capital encounters a barrier such as a labour dispute and business takes advantage of the spatial fix. An example of capital switching the location of production is the movement of manufacturing from Europe and Taiwan to mainland China.

Rather than pitching different wage earners against one another in a race to the bottom regarding labour standards, the unity of labour across different scales – factories, regions, nations and worldwide – is ultimately required. The potential for unionized labour to bargain for a reduction in exploitation on a global scale is distant, but this should not be misread as an argument against action. Instead this is a realistic appraisal. Union power can help highlight local injustice and is one of the few tools available to leverage potential political change and stall the relentless push by capital to suppress wages, but the fact is that fundamental transformation is required.

A different approach could be to return to the compromise between labour and capital of Fordist-era America and Europe. This scenario is, yet again, utopian, but it merits exploring. Reform along Fordist lines on a global scale would involve regulating the market and raising minimum wages in the global South to close the gap with those in the global North. Comparing the different costs of garment manufacturing in the developed and developing worlds can demonstrate how this would affect retail prices. Calculating accurately the cost of producing clothes in different locations is difficult; however, one estimate from the Institute for Global Labour and Human Rights is indicative. The total manufacturing costs of making a denim shirt in the USA were calculated at $13.22 (labour $7.47, materials $5.00, industrial laundry $0.75), compared to $3.72 in Bangladesh (labour $0.22, materials $3.30, industrial laundry $0.20).[25] What is amazing here is the difference in wages: rather than the American worker earning twice, or five times, or even ten times what the Bangladeshi receives, they are paid approximately thirty-four times the latter's rate. Improving wages in countries like Bangladesh would help human development. The comparative cost difference for a denim shirt would be an increase of $7.25 (the difference in wage level between the USA and Bangladesh), which would be passed on to the consumer. Wage increases would also reverse the erosion of industrial bases in the global North, as there would be fewer incentives for manufacturers to relocate and seek out a spatial fix.

Unfortunately this strictly hypothetical scenario is another politically unrealistic proposal. The suggestion runs counter to the direction of global policymaking. Instead, increasing trade liberalization is promoted by powerful organizations such as the WTO, which favours market-based 'solutions' like the 'Made with Love in Nairobi' project. Transforming capitalism is far beyond a remote prospect. The crisis-prone nature of capitalism means it would likely be plunged into deep recession by radical attempts to modify the degree of surplus value extracted form labour in a sector such as clothing. The apparel trade is by no means unique in this respect. It is simply representative of the established pattern of inequality present under unbridled economic globalization.

Radical transformation in terms of the wages paid to labour in low-income countries is unlikely ever to occur under capitalism. Although there may be little cause for hope when the system is viewed as a whole, nevertheless phased improvements are taking place in some emerging economies. Sri Lanka stands out as an example where wages are increasing and working standards improving' furthermore the country prides itself on being the 'World's #1 Ethically Sourced Destination'. In-depth ethnographic research by Kanchana N. Ruwanpure has illuminated the progress that has been made. Working conditions in Sri Lankan apparel factories are very good, especially at the high end. The state has been an important factor in the improvement of industrial standards; the workforce is highly educated and has access to good health care, and is 'by and large ... content with factory conditions'. Eco-friendly production approaches are also employed, although there is still room for improvement.[26]

We must continue to be vigilant regarding individual success stories. Li & Fung Group, one of China's leading producers of fast fashion, has developed new monitoring technologies in its factories. In a meeting with a manager – who contacted me as the company was considering expanding into Africa – we discussed my grave misgivings about the general treatment of labour, both in China and from my experiences in Zambia. To address this concern, she explained a recent change in manufacturing. Some of the Group's production lines now have digital read-outs linked to specific machines which show how many garments individual workers have completed. This was drawn to my attention as an example of a positive development. Workers were able to request a bonus when they were productive, using evidence from the digital displays. Nevertheless, I was left thinking that this system also represented a potential management tool. Imagine that the time comes when the rate of profit falls for Li & Fung – perhaps because Chinese producers are outcompeted by Burmese or Vietnamese factories – this technology will then offer a ready-made solution. Management could monitor individual rates of work and set new higher targets, forcing employees to work ever harder for their wages in an attempt to maintain profitability. So, rather than welcoming the digital displays that now enable them to bargain for bonuses, the workers may end up cursing the read-outs, which leave them sweating more than ever.

Since the Industrial Revolution textile and clothing production has always depended on labour exploitation. By and large the people who weave fabric and stitch garments have remained poor, while surplus value has been extracted by the owners of factories. Unions may help by negotiating a reduction in the rate of extraction of surplus value, and Fordist compromises and new technologies could improve conditions, but exploitation will persist. For, as long as capitalism continues, the only way to begin to address the unequal relationships of exchange is for clothing workers to own their own means of production. Mutual and cooperative business models, which have been used successfully in others sectors, could offer an answer. However, a means whereby garment workers can achieve the collective ownership of factories needs to be found, either within or beyond capitalism.

Conclusion

The book opens by asking how used jeans ended up in a Mozambican market. In answering that question it has unveiled some of the world's hidden clothing systems of provision. On a global scale there is a connection between the rapid rate at which people in the North buy fast fashion and the lack of opportunities for clothing consumption on the part of many of the world's poor. Fast-fashion production has been effective in driving down the price of clothing goods. Rich consumers around the world enjoy a great range of clothes, but sadly are complicit in a process that locks many of the world's poor in Africa, Asia and Latin America into a partial dependency on second-hand clothing imports. The systems-of-provision approach taken in this book has illustrated that patterns of clothing consumption both respond to and influence the process of uneven economic development. The continual and collective maintenance of consumer demand is essential to sustaining economic growth. As the quotation from Shulman earlier in the chapter suggests, clothing systems of provision are shaped by producers, who in turn stimulate consumer demand. Overconsumption of clothing in the global North has widespread negative environmental and social impacts, although these are difficult to map. One of the effects is the circulation of used clothing. The trade in second-hand clothing to impoverished countries only exists because there is something deeply wrong at the heart of capitalism. The market, despite its ability to push forward the development of technologically impressive production systems, like Zara's approach to fast fashion, is still failing to meet the basic needs of a vast proportion of society. Spatial inequality is a fundamental principle of economic globalization.

In the final analysis of David Harvey's ground-breaking work *The Limits to Capital* the crisis-prone nature of capitalism leads to insanely destructive warfare as the ultimate means of devaluation and resolution of absolute crisis.[27] It is a deeply depressing conclusion. Violence does not have to occur on the apocalyptic scale that Harvey envisions. Capitalism continually adjusts and moulds environments, whilst gradually strangling and choking societies. We live in violent times now. The everyday violence of life in the global South is readily apparent if we think of the lived experiences of poverty that are a reality for over a billion people. Violence here means the types of aggressive and extreme exploitation faced by the employees of Mulungushi Textiles, or the struggles to provide for families all too familiar to West African cotton farmers. The latter are likely to experience ever greater challenges as problems are intensified by the ecological crisis that is emerging as an outcome of human-induced global environmental change.

Among those who enjoy wealth and the opportunity to consume new clothing fashions in the global North there is no real political appetite for transformation that could disrupt everyday life. As long as society is governed by the political rule of capital, change will not happen. In every decade in living memory statesmen from America and Europe have declared they will 'make poverty history' or pledged their efforts to help the poor help themselves. Efforts to bury the spectre of poverty are invariably fruitless. Under capitalism impoverishment and inequality will not die; they will merely learn new ways of expressing themselves. A system that is based upon the accumulation of profit from the surplus labour of others will always amplify social difference and lead to a wider gap between rich and poor, meaning that some will have greater wealth than others, enjoy better food and possess more clothes. Exploitation will shift and spread around the globe as the hunt for a spatial fix for capital drags different territories into crisis. What we are left with is the reality that answers to the problems posed by economic globalization are distant, near to the point of vanishing. Hope lies only with the building of momentum through action, activism and critical research, the forces able to bring that horizon closer.

Notes

INTRODUCTION

1. See Chapter 3 n7 for a discussion of United Nations Comtrade data on the volume and value of second-hand clothes traded around the world.

CHAPTER 1

1. Ben Fine, *The World of Consumption: The Material and Cultural Revisited*, Routledge, London, 2002, p. 79.
2. Robert Ross, *Clothing: A Global History*, Polity Press, Cambridge, 2008.
3. James Sullivan, *Jeans: A Cultural History of an American Icon*, Gotham, New York, 2006.
4. David Harvey, *The Limits to Capital*, Verso, London, 2006, p. 7.
5. Daniel Miller, 'Anthropology in Blue Jeans', *American Ethnologist*, vol. 37, no. 3, 2010, pp. 415–28, p. 422.
6. Levi Strauss & Co., 'Our Team', 2013, www.levistrauss.com/careers/our-team.
7. Mylene Mizrahi, '"Brazilian Jeans"': Materiality, Body and Seduction at a Rio de Janeiro Funk Ball', in Daniel Miller and Sophie Woodward, eds, *Global Denim*, Berg, Oxford, 2011, p. 103.
8. Daniel Miller and Sophie Woodward, 'Manifesto for a Study of Denim', *Social Anthropology*, vol. 15, no. 3, 2007, pp. 335–51, p. 339.
9. WWF, 'Cotton Farming', 2013, http://wwf.panda.org/about_our_earth/about_freshwater/freshwater_problems/thirsty_crops/cotton.

10. Francesca Mancini et al., 'Acute Pesticide Poisoning among Female and Male Cotton Growers in India', *International Journal of Occupational and Environmental Health*, vol. 11, no. 3, 2005, pp. 221–32.

11. Tony Allen, *Virtual Water: Tacking the Threat to Our Planet's Most Precious Resource*, I.B. Tauris, London, 2011, pp. 348–9.

12. A.K. Chapagain et al., 'The Water Footprint of Cotton Consumption: An Assessment of the Impact of Worldwide Consumption of Cotton Products on the Water Resources in the Cotton Producing Countries, *Ecological Economics*, vol. 60, no. 1, 2006, pp. 186–203.

13. Cotton Campaign, 'Stop Forced and Child Labour in Cotton Industry of Uzbekistan', 2013, www.cottoncampaign.org.

14. Oxfam International, 'The Effect of the Free Trade Agreement with the US on Cotton Farmers in Peru: Cotton is No Longer 'White Gold', 2007, www.oxfam.org/en/programs/development/samerica/peru_cotton.

15. All figures are in US dollars unless otherwise stated. Humphrey Hawksley, 'India's Exploited Child Cotton Workers', *BBC News Asia*, 19 January 2012, www.bbc.co.uk/news/world-asia-16639391.

16. Author's interview with cotton growers in Zambia.

17. Rachel Louise Synder, *Fugitive Denim: A Moving Story of People and Pants in the Borderless World of Global Trade*, W.W. Norton, New York and London, 2008, pp. 46, 117.

18. Shelia MacVicar, 'Jean Factory Toxic Waste Plagues Lesotho', CBS Evening News, 8 January 2010, www.cbsnews.com/8301-18563_162-5205416.html.

19. Synder, *Fugitive Denim*, p. 148.

20. Ibid., p. 95.

21. Kanchana N. Ruwanpura, 'Metal Free Factories: Straddling Worker Rights and Consumer Safety?', *Geoforum*, vol. 51, no. 1, 2014, pp. 224–32.

22. Jennifer Bair and Garry Gereffi, 'Local Clusters in Global Chains: The Causes and Consequences of Export Dynamism in Torreon's Blue Jeans Industry', *World Development*, vol. 29, no. 11, 2001, pp. 1885–1903.

23. Julie McCarthy, 'Bangladesh Collapse: The Garment Workers Who Survived', National Public Radio, 10 July 2013, www.npr.org/blogs/parallels/2013/07/10/200644781/Bangladesh-Collapse-The-Garment-Workers-Who-Survived.

24. Cotton Incorporated, 'Historical Denim Ownership among U.S. Consumers', 2013, http://lifestylemonitor.cottoninc.com/historical-denim-ownership-among-u-s-consumers.

25. Miller and Woodward, 'Manifesto for a Study of Denim', p. 336.

26. Synder, *Fugitive Denim*, p. 161.
27. Ellen R. Shell, *Cheap: The High Cost of Discount Culture*, Penguin, Harmondsworth, 2009.
28. Ben Fine, *Marx's Capital,* Macmillan, London, 1976.
29. David Harvey, *The Condition of Postmodernity: An Enquiry into the Origins of Cultural Change*, Blackwell, Oxford and Cambridge MA, 1990, p. 422.

CHAPTER 2

1. Ha-Joon Chang, *Bad Samaritans: The Myth of Free Trade and the Secret History of Capitalism*, Bloomsbury, London, 2007.
2. WTO, 'Chronological List of Dispute Cases', 2014, www.wto.org/english/tratop_e/dispu_e/dispu_status_e.htm.
3. 'A Temporary Truce on Textiles', *The Economist*, 7 September 2005.
4. Michael White and David Gow, 'EU and China in "Bra Wars" Deal', *Guardian,* 6 September 2005.
5. A trend documented by the classical economist David Ricardo as well as Karl Marx.
6. David Harvey, *The Urbanization of Capital*, Blackwell, Oxford, 1985, p. 128.
7. David Harvey, *The Enigma of Capital and the Crises of Capitalism*, Profile Books, London, 2010, p. 117.
8. David Harvey, *The Limits to Capital,* Verso, London, 2006, p. 440.
9. European Commission, 'Fashion Competiveness', 2014, http://ec.europa.eu/enterprise/sectors/fashion/competitiveness/index_en.htm.
10. Linda: The Bra Lady, 'How Long Do Bras Really Last?' 2012, http://blog.lindasonline.com/2012/01/09/how-long-do-bras-really-last.
11. Noel Castree, *Nature*, Taylor & Francis, London, 2005.
12. Neil Smith, *Uneven Development*, Blackwell, Oxford, 1985.
13. Jared Diamond, *Guns, Germs and Steel: A Short History of Everybody for the Last 13,000 Years*, Vintage, London, 1998.
14. James M. Blaut, 'Diffusionism: A Uniformitarian Critique', *Annals of the Association of American Geographers*, vol. 77, no. 1, 1987, pp. 30–47.
15. Eric R. Wolf, *Europe and the People without History*, University of California Press, Berkeley, 1982.
16. Lucinda Blackwell, Francesco d'Errico and Lyn Wadley, 'Middle Stone Age Bone Tools from the Howiesons Poort Layers, Sibudu Cave, South Africa', *Journal of Archaeological Science,* vol. 35, no. 6, 2008, pp. 1566–80.
17. Olga Soffer, 'Recovering Perishable Technologies through Use Wear on Tools: Preliminary Evidence for Upper Paleolithic Weaving and

Net Making', *Current Anthropology*, vol. 45, no. 3, 2004, pp. 407–13.

18. Katka Krosnar, 'Now You Can Walk in Footsteps of 5,000-year-old Iceman – Wearing His Boots', *Daily Telegraph*, 17 July 2005.

19. Proverbs 31:10–24.

20. Marianne Vedeler and Lise Bender Jørgensen, 'Out of the Norwegian Glaciers: Lendbreen – a Tunic from the Early First Millennium AD', *Antiquity*, vol. 87, no. 337, 2013, pp. 788–801.

21. Worshipful Company of Weavers, 'History', 2014, www.weavers.org. uk/history.

22. Robert Ross, *Clothing a Global History*, Polity Press, Cambridge, 2008.

23. Frederick Engels, *The Condition of the Working Class in England*, trans. Florence Kelly Wischnewetzky, George Allen & Unwin, London, 1942 (1844), p. 7.

24. Ben Fine, *Marx's Capital*, Macmillan, London, 1976.

25. See Chapter 5 for a detailed case study of labour exploitation in a contemporary factory.

26. J. Smith, *Memoirs of Wool*, vol. II, 1747, p. 308; quoted by E.P. Thompson, *The Making of the English Working Class*, Vintage Books, London, 1966.

27. Eric Hobsbawm, *The Age of Revolution*, Abacus, London, 1962, p. 48.

28. Engels, *The Condition of The Working Class in England*, p. 7.

29. Karl Marx, *Capital: A New Abridgment*, Oxford University Press, Oxford, 1995, p. 274.

30. Ross, *Clothing*.

31. Jeremy Seabrook, 'Song of the Shirt', *Economic and Political Weekly*, vol. 49, no. 21, 24 May 2014.

32. Gregory Clark and Robert C. Feenstra, 'Technology in the Great Divergence', in Michael D. Bordo, Alan M. Taylor and Jeffery G. Williamson, eds, *Globalization in Historical Perspective*, University of Chicago Press, Chicago, 2003.

33. Ross, *Clothing*.

34. Antonio Gramsci, *Selections from the Prison Notebooks*, Lawrence & Wishart, London, 1971.

35. Kate Fletcher, 'Other Fashion Systems', in Kate Fletcher and Mathilda Tham, eds, *The Routledge Handbook of Sustainability and Fashion*, Routledge, London, 2015, p. 18.

36. Peter Dicken, *Global Shift: Mapping the Changing Contours of the World Economy*, Sage, London, 2011, p. 305.

37. Ibid., p. 320.

CHAPTER 3

1. Based on the author's own observations when living and working in Papua New Guinea in 2006.

2. Beverley Lemire, 'Shifting Currency: The Culture and Economy of the Secondhand Trade in England, c. 1600–1850, in Alexandra Palmer and Hazel Clark, eds, *Old Clothes, New Looks: Second Hand Fashion*, Berg, Oxford, 2005.

3. Ann Matchette, 'Women, Objects and Exchange in Early Modern Florence', *Early Modern Women: An Interdisciplinary Journal 3*, 2008, pp. 245–51.

4. Terry Satuki Milhaupt, 'Second Hand Kimono Migrating across Borders', in Palmer and Clark, eds, *Old Clothes, New Looks*.

5. Adam Smith, *An Inquiry into the Nature and Causes of the Wealth of Nations*, vol. 1, Methuen, London, 1904, p. 27.

6. Kellow Chesney, *The Victorian Underworld*, Pelican, London, 1970, p. 230.

7. Charles Dickens, *Oliver Twist or The Parish Boy's Progress*, Baudry's European Library, Paris, 1839, p. 161.

8. Karl Marx, *Capital: A New Abridgment*, Oxford University Press, Oxford, 1995, pp. 279–80.

9. Susan Strasser, *Waste and Want: A Social History of Trash*, Metropolitan Books, New York, 1999, p. 49.

10. Aldous Huxley, *Brave New World*, Flamingo, London, 1994, p. 49.

11. Quoted in 'Fashion: Brave New Look', *Time*, 3 July 1950.

12. Strasser, *Waste and Want*.

13. Oliver Balch, 'H&M: Can Fast Fashion and Sustainability Ever Really Mix?', *Guardian, 3* May 2013.

14. Kate Fletcher, 'Other Fashion Systems', in Kate Fletcher and Mathilda Tham, eds, *The Routledge Handbook of Sustainability and Fashion*, Routledge, London, 2015, p. 18.

15. Interview with Paul Ozanne, National Recycling Coordinator, Salvation Army Trading Company Limited, 21 November 2008.

16. Research by Juliet B. Schor and Kristen Heim, cited by Juliet B. Schor, 'Prices and Quantities: Unsustainable Consumption and the Global Economy, *Ecological Economics*, vol. 55, no. 3, 2005, pp. 309–20, p. 314.

17. Oxfam, *Inside Oxfam*, Summer 2008, p. 17; Oxfam, 'How and What to Donate to our Shops', 2011, www.oxfam.org.uk/donate/shops/index.html.

18. Andrew Brooks, 'Riches from Rags or Persistent Poverty? Inequality in the Transnational Second-hand Clothing Trade in Mozambique,

Ph.D. thesis, Royal Holloway, University of London, 2012.

19. North West Leicestershire District Council, 'Door to Door Charity Bag Collectors Fined', 2011, www.nwleics.gov.uk/news/2011/01/31/door_to_door_charity_bag_collectors_fined.

20. Richmondshire District Council, 'Bogus Charity Collections on Rise', 2012, www.richmondshire.gov.uk/news-and-publications/press-releases/boguscharitycollections.aspx?theme=textonly.

21. Jennifer Shea and Patrick Brennan, *Addressing Commercial Threats to Charity Shop Collections*, nfpSynergy (unpublished report), London, 2008, p. 29.

22. 'Clothing Donation Bins Spark Turf War in Ontario', *CBC News*, 30 January 2012, www.cbc.ca/news/canada/story/2012/01/26/charity-clothing-bins-millions.html.

23. Sharon Bernstein, 'Battle Erupts in California over Clothes Donation Bins', Reuters, 6 April 2013, www.reuters.com/article/2013/04/06/usa-charity-fight-idUSL2N0CR1OT20130406; Meghan Hoyer and Jayne O'Donnell, 'Clothing Bin Donations Don't Always Reach Needy', *USA Today*, 30 December 2012.

24. Nick J. Morley, Caroline Bartlett and Ian McGill, *Maximising Reuse and Recycling of UK Clothing and Textiles: A Report to the Department for Environment, Food and Rural Affairs*, Oakdene Hollins, London, 2009, p. 14.

25. Interview with Brian Lincoln, Regional Team Leader, YMCA, 10 March 2009.

26. 'Clothing Donation Bins Spark Turf War in Ontario', *CBC News*.

27. Interview with Paul Ozanne, 21 November 2008.

28. Interview with Steve Wooldridge, Head of Property and Stock Operations, Help the Aged, 3 December 2008.

29. Hoyer and O'Donnell, 'Clothing Bin Donations Don't Always Reach Needy'. Controversies surrounding Planet Aid are discussed further in Chapter 7.

30. Interview with Steve Wooldridge, 3 December 2008.

31. British Heart Foundation, 'Charitable Public Misled by Commercial Collection Companies', 2011, www.bhf.org.uk/media/news-from-the-bhf/charitable-public-misled.aspx.

32. Interview with Brian Lincoln, 10 March 2009.

33. 'Clothing Donation Bins Spark Turf War in Ontario', *CBC News*.

34. Strasser, *Waste and Want*, p. 225.

35. Shea and Brennan, 'Addressing Commercial Threats to Charity Shop Collections', p. 13.

36. Interview with Paul Ozanne, 21 November 2008.

37. United Nations Comtrade, *UN Comtrade Database*, 2014, http://

comtrade.un.org/db/default.aspx. The calculations are based on an average weight for a pair of jeans of 523 grams and a T-shirt of 123 grams.

38. Pietra Rivoli, *The Travels of a T-shirt in the Global Economy: An Economist Examines the Markets, Power, and Politics of World Trade*, Wiley, London, 2009, p. 219.

39. United Nations Comtrade, *UN Comtrade Database*, 2014, http:// comtrade.un.org/db/default.aspx. All UN Comtrade statistics quoted in this book are SITC code 26701 (Rev. 1) 'Old Clothing & Other Textile Waste Imported'. In 2013, 113 nations reported exporting old clothing and the total value was $4.3 billion and weight was 3.9 billion kg. The equivalent weight calculations are based on an average weight for a pair of jeans of 523 grams and a T-shirt of 123 grams.

40. Karen Tranberg Hansen, *Salaula: The World of Secondhand Clothing and Zambia*, Chicago University Press, Chicago, 2000, p. 110.

41. Interview with Tony Clark, Oxfam Wastesaver, 13 March 2009.

42. 'Wonder Where Your Donations Go? Oxfam Has Got It Sorted', *Guardian*, 15 February 2014.

43. Interview with Tony Clark, 13 March 2009.

44. 'Wonder Where Your Donations Go?', *Guardian*.

45. Ben Fine, *The World of Consumption: The Material and Cultural Revisited*, Routledge, London, 2002, p. 26.

CHAPTER 4

1. Christopher Wrigley, 'Speculations on the Economic Prehistory of Africa', *Journal of African History*, vol. 1, no. 2, 1960, pp. 189–203.

2. Roland Oliver and John D. Fage, *A Short History of Africa*, Penguin, London, 1962.

3. Linda Newson, 'The Slave-trading Accounts of Manoel Batista Peres, 1613–1619: Double-entry Bookkeeping in Cloth Money', *Accounting History*, vol. 18, no. 3, 2013, pp. 343–65, pp. 356–7.

4. Walter Rodney, 'African Slavery and Other Forms of Social Oppression on the Upper Guinea Coast in the Context of the Atlantic Slave Trade', *Journal of African History*, vol. 7, no. 3, 1966, pp. 431–43, p. 434.

5. Basil Davidson, *Africa in History*, Paladin, London, 1984.

6. Newson, 'The Slave-trading Accounts of Manoel Batista Peres, 1613–1619', p. 360.

7. Linda Newson, Africans and Luso-Africans in the Portuguese Slave Trade on the Upper Guinea Coast in the Early Seventeenth Century', *Journal of African History*, vol. 53, no. 1, 2012, pp. 1–24, pp. 22–3.

8. Karl Marx, *The Eighteenth Brumaire of Louis Bonaparte*, Wildside Press, 2008, p. 15.

9. Kathleen E. Sheldon, *Pounders of Grain: A History of Women, Work, and Politics in Mozambique*, Heinemann Educational Books, Portsmouth NH, 2002.

10. Quoted in Eduardo Mondlane, *The Struggle for Mozambique*, Penguin, London, 1969, p. 79.

11. Sayaka Funada-Classen, *The Origins of War in Mozambique: A History of Unity and Division,* African Books Collective, Oxford, 2013.

12. Quoted in Mondlane, *The Struggle for Mozambique*, p. 87.

13. Ibid., p. 83.

14. Joseph Hanlon, *Mozambique: The Revolution under Fire,* Zed Books, London, 1984; Allen Isaacman, *Cotton is the Mother of Poverty: Peasants, Work, and Rural Struggle in Colonial Mozambique, 1938–1961,* Heinemann, Portsmouth NH, 1995.

15. Jean-Claude Berthelemy and François Bourguignon, *Growth and Crisis in Côte d'Ivoire*, World Bank, Washington DC, 1996.

16. John Rapley, *Ivoirian Capitalism: African Entrepreneurs in Côte d'Ivoire,* Lynne Rienner, Boulder CO and London, 1993.

17. Kate Meagher, 'A Back Door to Globalisation? Structural Adjustment, Globalisation and Transborder Trade in West Africa', *Review of African Political Economy*, vol. 30, no. 95, 2003, pp. 57–75.

18. Kate Manzo, 'Modern Slavery, Global Capitalism and Deproletarianisation in West Africa', *Review of African Political Economy*, vol. 32, no. 106, 2005, pp. 521–34.

19. Rapley, *Ivoirian Capitalism*.

20. Manzo, 'Modern Slavery, Global Capitalism and Deproletarianisation in West Africa'.

21. Oxfam, *Pricing Farmers Out of Cotton*, Oxfam Briefing Paper, March 2007, www.oxfam.org.uk/resources/policy/debt_aid/downloads/bp99 _cotton.pdf, p. 2.

22. Andrea R. Woodward, 'The Impact of U.S. Subsidies on West African Cotton Production', in Per Pinstrup-Andersen and Fuzhi Cheng, eds, *Food Policy for Developing Countries: Case Studies*, Cornell University Press, Ithaca NY, 2007, p. 12.

23. International Centre for Trade and Sustainable Development, *Cotton: Trends in Global Production, Trade and Policy*, 2013, www.ictsd.org/ downloads/2013/06/cotton-trends-in-global-production-trade-and-policy.pdf, p. 4.

CHAPTER 5

1. Franz Wild, 'China Swaps Gusto for Rigor as it Learns from Africa', Bloomberg, 3 June 2014, www.bloomberg.com/news/2014-06-02/ china-swaps-gusto-for-rigor-in-africa-as-it-learns-from-mistakes.html.

2. Giovanni Arrighi, *Adam Smith in Beijing: Lineages of the Twenty-first Century*, Verso, London, 2007, p. 361.

3. Pun Ngai, 'Global Production, Company Codes of Conduct, and Labor Conditions in China: A Case Study of Two Factories', *China Journal* 54, 2005, pp. 101–13.

4. Xiaomin Yu, 'Impacts of Corporate Code of Conduct on Labor Standards: A Case Study of Reebok's Athletic Footwear Supplier Factory in China', *Journal of Business Ethics* 81, 2007, pp. 513–29.

5. Robert B. Potter, Tony Binns, Jennifer A. Elliot and David Smith, *Geographies of Development: An Introduction to Development Studies*, Pearson, Harlow, 2008, p. 360.

6. Yongzheng Yang and Chuanshui Zhong, 'China's Textile and Clothing Exports in A Changing World Economy', *The Developing Economies*, vol. 36, 1998, no. 1, pp. 3–23, p. 4.

7. Pun Ngai, 'Global Production, Company Codes of Conduct, and Labor Conditions in China', p. 109.

8. Xiaomin Yu, 'Impacts of Corporate Code of Conduct on Labor Standards'.

9. Ha-Joon Chang, *Bad Samaritans: The Myth of Free Trade and the Secret History of Capitalism*, Bloomsbury, London, 2007, p. 9.

10. Rudolf Traub-Merz, 'The African Textile and Clothing Industry: From Import Substitution to Export Orientation', in Herbert Jauch and Rudolf Traub-Merz, eds,*The Future of the Textile and Clothing Industry in Sub-Saharan Africa*, Friedrich-Ebert-Stiftung, Bonn, 2006.

11. TAZARA provided a route to the Indian Ocean that avoided apartheid South Africa. It is reflected upon fondly as a symbol of Sino-African solidarity by both parties.

12. Deborah Brautigam, *The Dragon's Gift: The Real Story of China in Africa*, Oxford University Press, Oxford, 2009, p. 216.

13. Alastair Fraser and John Lungu, 'For Whom the Wind Falls? Winners and Losers in the Privatisation of Zambia's Copper Mines', Mine Watch Zambia, 2007, p. 8.

14. James Ferguson, *Expectations of Modernity: Myths and Meanings of Urban Life on the Zambian Copperbelt*, University of California Press, Berkeley, 1999.

15. Antonio Gramsci, *Selections from the Prison Notebooks*, Lawrence & Wishart, London, 1971.

16. Miles Larmer, 'Reaction and Resistance to Neo-liberalism in Zambia', *Review of African Political Economy*, vol. 32, no. 103, 2005, pp. 29–45.

17. Peter Gibbon and Stefano Ponte, *Africa, Value Chains and the Global Economy*, Temple University Press, Philadelphia PA, 2005.

18. Dorothy McCormick, Mary Njeri Kinyanjui and Grace Ongile, 'Growth and Barriers to Growth among Nairobi's Small and Medium-sized Garment Producers', *World Development*, vol. 25, no. 7, 1997, pp. 1095–110.

19. Traub-Merz, 'The African Textile and Clothing Industry', p. 17.

20. Raphael Kaplinsky, 'What Does the Rise of China Do for Industriali-sation in Sub-Saharan Africa?', *Review of African Political Economy*, vol. 35, no. 115, 2008, pp. 7–22.

21. Ndubisi Obiorah, 'Who's Afraid of China in Africa? Towards an African Civil Society Perspective on China–Africa Relations', in Firoze Manji and Stephen Marks, eds, *African Perspectives on China in Africa*, Fahamu, Oxford, 2007, p. 39.

22. Stephen Breslin and Ian Taylor, 'Explaining the Rise of "Human Rights", in Analyses of Sino-African Relations', *Review of African Political Economy*, vol. 35, no. 115, 2008, pp. 59–71.

23. Fraser and Lungu, 'For Whom the Wind Falls?', p. 8.

24. Brautigam, *The Dragon's Gift*.

25. Henning Melber, 'The (Not So) New Kid on The Block: China and The Scramble for Africa's Resources – An Introductory Review', in Henning Melber, ed., *China in Africa*, Current African Issues No. 33, Nordiska Afrikainstitutet, Uppsala, 2007.

26. Brautigam, *The Dragon's Gift*, p. 218.

27. 'New Form of Chinese Aid Revives Zambia's Largest Textile Com-pany', *People's Daily*, 27 November 2003.

28. Quoted in Laurie Goering, 'China's Investment and Growing Clout in Africa Cause Concern', *Chicago Tribune*, 19 February 2006.

29. Interviews with ex-employees were carried out in Kabwe, 12–24 May 2008. All interviewees have been anonymized. Extended discussion is provided in an earlier article by Andrew Brooks: 'Spinning and Weaving Discontent: Labour Relations and the Production of Meaning at Zambia–China Mulungushi Textiles', *Journal of Southern African Studies*, vol. 36, no. 1, 2010, pp. 113–32. Unless otherwise stated, quotations from former workers throughout this chapter are taken from this article.

30. Duncan Gallie, *In Search of the New Working Class: Automation and Social Integration within the Capitalist Enterprise*, Cambridge University Press, Cambridge, 1978.

31. Melissa W. Wright, 'Factory Daughters and Chinese Modernity: A

Case from Dongguan', *Geoforum* 34, 2003, pp. 291–301.

32. Ministry of Defence, Zambia, *Report of Inter-Ministerial Technical Committee for Labour Reduction at Zambia-China Mulungushi Textiles (JV) Ltd (ZCMT)*, Lusaka, 2007, p. 1.

33. David Harvey, *Limits to Capital,* Verso, London, 2006.

34. Gramsci, *Selections from the Prison Notebooks.*

35. Harvey, *The Limits to Capital.*

36. Yongzheng Yang and Chuanshui Zhong, 'China's Textile and Clothing Exports in a Changing World Economy'.

37. Ching Kwan Lee, 'Raw Encounters: Chinese Managers, African Workers and the Politics of Casualization in Africa's Chinese Enclaves, *The China Quarterly*, vol. 199, no. 1, 2009, pp. 647–66, p. 8.

38. Gallie, *In Search of the New Working Class.*

39. Gillian Hart, *Disabling Globalization: Places of Power in Post-apartheid South Africa*, University of California Press, Berkeley, 2002.

40. Ching Kwan Lee, 'Raw Encounters', p. 7.

41. Hart, *Disabling Globalization.*

42. Government of Zambia, *The Minimum Wages and Conditions of Employment Act*, Statutory Instrument No. 56 of 2006, Laws, vol. 15, cap. 276.

43. Kaplinsky, 'What Does the Rise of China Do for Industrialisation in Sub-Saharan Africa?'

44. 'Chinese Textile Firm in Zambia Having Cash Flow Problems', *Africa Business*, 3 January 2007, http://africabusiness.wordpress.com/2007/01/03/chinese-textile-firm-in-zambia-having-cash-flow-problems.

45. Jacob Goldstein, 'Global Poverty and the Cost of a Pair of Jeans', NPR, 3 March 2010, www.npr.org/blogs/money/2010/03/how_much_does_a_pair_of_jeans.html.

46. Peter Gibbon, 'AGOA, Lesotho's "Clothing Miracle" and the Politics of Sweatshops', *Review of African Political Economy*, vol. 30, no. 96, 2003, pp. 315–50, p. 320.

CHAPTER 6

1. NFL, 'Super Bowl XLVIII Most-watched TV Program in U.S. History', 3 February 2014, www.nfl.com/superbowl/story/0ap2000000323430/article/super-bowl-xlviii-mostwatched-tv-program-in-us-history.

2. World Vision, *World Vision News*, vol. 11, no. 1, 2007, http://media.worldvision.org/docs/WV.WinterNews07.pdf. The true worth of these goods is debatable given that gifts in kind are often valued at US retail prices, which are completely disproportionate to their true economic worth in developing countries.

3. Scott Bixby, 'The Super Bowl Loser 49ers Still Win in, Sa, Chad', *Bloomberg Businessweek*, 4 February 2013, www.businessweek.com/articles/2013-02-04/the-super-bowl-loser-49ers-still-win-in-say-chad; Cathleen Falsani, 'The NFLs Donation to World Vision: Charity or Closet Cleaning?', *Huffington Post*, 20 February 2011, www.huffington-post.com/cathleen-falsani/nfl-steelers-world-vision_b_824864.html; Tim Rogers, 'Where New England Won the Super Bowl', *Time*, 15 February 2008, http://content.time.com/time/world/article/0,8599,1713846, 00.html; Darren Rovell, 'Merchandise Donated to Charity', ESPN, 5 February 2013, http://espn.go.com/nfl/playoffs/2012/story/_/id/8918957/2013-super-bowl-san-francisco-49ers-championship-mer-chandise-donated-charity?src=mobile; CNN, 'Helping Clothe Countries in Need', 4 February 2011, http://edition.cnn.com/video/?/video/sports/2011/02/04/mckay.world.vision.cnn.

4. Uganda Manufacturers' Association, quoted by Carter Dougherty, 'Trade Theory vs. Used Clothes in Africa', *New York Times*, 3 June 2004.

5. Author's own observations; Karen Tranberg Hansen, *Salaula: The World of Secondhand Clothing and Zambia*, Chicago University Press, Chicago, 2000.

6. Myriam Velia, Imraan Valodia and Baruti Amisi, *Trade Dynamics in Used Clothing: The Case of Durban, South Africa*, SDS Research Report 71, School of Development Studies, University of Kwazulu-Natal, Durban, 2006.

7. Interview with Steve Wooldridge, head of Property and Stock Operations, Help the Aged, 3 December 2008.

8. Hansen, *Salaula*, p. 116.

9. Quoted by Simone Field, 'The Internationalisation of the Second-hand Clothing Trade: The Zimbabwe Experience', Ph.D. thesis, Coventry University, 2000, p. 161.

10. Interviews, 27 May 2008. This confusion may be because used clothes have transited via Germany.

11. Hansen, *Salaula*, p. 182.

12. Maureen Chigbo, 'High Cost of an Imported Used Spiderman T-Shirt', *Electronic Journal of Governance and Innovation*, Southern African Institute of International Affairs, 25 April 2008, www.saiia. org.za/archive-eafrica/high-cost-of-an-imported-used-spiderman-t-shirt.html.

13. Hansen, *Salaula*, p. 118.

14. Field, 'The Internationalisation of the Second-hand Clothing Trade', p. 3.

15. Ragtex UK, 'About Ragtex UK', 2011, www.ragtexuk.com/about.htm;

clothing is also exported by Ragtex to elsewhere in southern Africa and Pakistan.

16. See Chapter 3.

17. Michael Durham, 'The Clothes Line', *Guardian,* 25 February 2004.

18. Interview with Tony Clark, General Manager, Oxfam Wastesaver, 13 March 2009.

19. Field, 'The Internationalisation of the Second-hand Clothing Trade', p. 159.

20. Ibid., p. 160.

21. Olumide Abimbola, 'The International Trade in Secondhand Clothing: Managing Information Asymmetry between West African and British Traders', *Textile: The Journal of Cloth and Culture*, vol. 10, no. 2, 2012, pp. 184–99, p. 192.

22. METL, 'Mohammed Enterprise Trading Limited: Company Profile', 2011, www.metl.net/about/company-profile.

23. Pietra Rivoli, *The Travels of a T-shirt in the Global Economy: An Economist Examines the Markets, Power, and Politics of World Trade,* Wiley, London, 2009.

24. See Chapter 3.

25. Author's observations, August 2003.

26. Cyril Obi and Siri Aas Rustad, 'Introduction: Petro-violence in the Niger Delta – the Complex Politics of an Insurgency', in Cyril Obi and Siri Aas Rustad, eds, *Oil and Insurgency in The Niger Delta,* Zed Books, London, 2011.

27. Cyril Obi, 'Oil as a "Curse" of Conflict in Africa: Peering through the Smoke and Mirrors', *Review of African Political Economy*, vol. 37, no. 126, 2010, pp. 483–95.

28. Michael Watts, Petro-insurgency or Criminal Syndicate? Conflict and Violence in the Niger Delta, *Review of African Political Economy*, vol. 34, no. 114, 2007, pp. 637–60.

29. Ademola Oyejide, Olawale Ogunkola and Abiodun Bankole, 'Import Prohibition as a Trade Policy Instrument: The Nigerian Experience', in Peter Gallagher, Patrick Low and Andrew L. Stoler, eds, *Managing the Challenges of WTO Participation – 45 Case Studies*, Cambridge University Press, Cambridge, 2005, p. 440.

30. Reported used-clothing exports from global North calculated using OECD country data, 1981-2000, in United Nations Comtrade, *UN Comtrade Database*, 2014, http://comtrade.un.org/db/default.aspx.

31. Interview with Aloysius Ihezie, director, Choice Textiles Division, 19 March 2009.

32. J. Joost Beuving, 'Nigerien Second-hand Car Traders in Cotonou: A Sociocultural Analysis of Economic Decision-making, *African*

Affairs, vol. 105, no. 420, 2006, pp. 353–73.

33. Gunilla Andræ and Björn Beckman, *Union Power in the Nigerian Textile Industry*, Nordiska Afrikainstitutet, Uppsala, 1998; Economist Intelligence Unit, *Country Reports: Nigeria*, London, November 2007.

34. *Guardian*, January 2004, cited by Oyejide et al., 'Import Prohibition as a Trade Policy Instrument', p. 440.

35. Author's observations, May–July 2010.

36. 'Smuggling, Used-Clothing Sales, Hurt Kenya Textile Industry', *Voice of America*, 14 September 2010, www.voanews.com/english/ news/africa/Smuggling-Used-Clothing-Sales-Hurt-Kenya-Textile-Industry-102953119.html.

37. Andrew Brooks, Networks of Power and Corruption: The Trade of Japanese Used Cars to Mozambique, *Geographical Journal*, vol. 178, no. 1, 2012, pp. 80–92.

38. Tonia Kandiero, 'Malawi in the Multilateral Trading System', in Gallagher, Low and Stoler, eds, *Managing the Challenges of WTO Participation*, p. 335.

39. See Andrew Brooks and David Simon, 'Unraveling the Relationships between Used-clothing Imports and the Decline of African Clothing Industries', *Development and Change*, vol. 43, no. 6, 2012, pp. 1265–90.

CHAPTER 7

1. 'In Mozambique, Annan Sees Model of Progress for Africa and the World', UN News Centre, 2002, www.un.org/apps/news/story.asp? NewsID=4592&Cr=mozambique&Cr1.

2. 'UN Chief Promotes Education, Gender Empowerment during Final Day of Mozambique Visit', UN News Centre, 21 May 2013, www. un.org/apps/news/story.asp?NewsID=44955#.U5gXlPldXms.

3. Joseph Hanlon and Teresa Smart, *Do Bicycles Equal Development in Mozambique?* James Currey, Woodbridge, 2008.

4. African Development Bank, *Mozambique Economic Outlook*, 2014, www.afdb.org/en/countries/southern-africa/mozambique/ mozambique-economic-outlook.

5. World Bank, *Mozambique*, 2014, http://data.worldbank.org/country/ mozambique?display=default; UNDP, *Human Development Index*, 2014, https://data.undp.org/dataset/Table-1-Human-Development-Index-and-its-components/wxub-qc5k; USAID, *Mozambique*, 2014, www.usaid.gov/mozambique.

6. Anne Pitcher, *Transforming Mozambique: The Politics of Privatization, 1975–2000*, Cambridge University Press, Cambridge, 2002, p. 195.

7. Kathleen E. Sheldon, *Pounders of Grain: A History of Women, Work, and Politics in Mozambique*, Heinemann, Portsmouth NH, 2002.

8. Peter Coughlin, Musa Rubin and L. Amedée Darga, 'The SADC Textile and Garment Industries: Towards a Global Vision?', in Dorothy McCormick and Christian Rogerson, eds, *Clothing and Footwear in African Industrialisation*, Africa Institute of South Africa, Pretoria, 2004, p. 20.

9. Peter Minor, *Strategies for Mozambique's Textile and Apparel Sector*, technical report by Nathan Associates for USAID, Washington DC, 2005, p. 2.

10. World Bank, *Mozambique – CEM – Industry Section – Apparel Sector, Draft*, 7 May 2008, http://siteresources.worldbank.org/intdebtdept/Resources/468980-1218567884549/5289593-1259608803444/MozambiqueCEMapparel20090508.pdf, p. 1.

11. 'Mozambique: Moztex Exporting Clothes to South Africa', *AllAfrica*, 16 December 2010, http://allafrica.com/stories/201012170661.html; 'Mozambique: Two Textiles Factories Expected to Re-launch Production This Year in Mozambique', *Maccauhub*, 5 September 2008, www.macauhub.com.mo/en/2008/09/05/5703.

12. Christopher M. Rogerson, 'Sunrise or Sunset Industries? South Africa's Clothing and Footwear Sectors', in Dorothy McCormick and Christian Rogerson, eds, *Clothing and Footwear in African Industrialisation*, Africa Institute of South Africa, Pretoria, 2004.

13. Caroline Skinner and Imraan Valodia, 'Labour Market Policy, Flexibility, and the Future of Labour Relations: The Case of KwaZulu-Natal Clothing Industry', *Transformations: Critical Perspectives on Southern Africa* 50, 2002, pp. 56–76, p. 56.

14. Andrew Brooks, 'Networks of Power and Corruption: The Trade of Japanese Used Cars to Mozambique', *Geographical Journal,* vol. 178, no. 1, 2012, pp. 80–92; Jason Sumich, 'The Party and the State: Frelimo and Social Stratification in Post-socialist Mozambique', *Development and Change,* vol. 41, no. 4, 2010, pp. 679–98.

15. Pitcher, *Transforming Mozambique*, p. 173.

16. Research findings, including the various quotations and figures, are based on thirteen months of ethnographic fieldwork in Maputo (July 2009–July 2010) carried out by the author.

17. Interview, 4 April 2010. He was asked to confirm if he was certain it was Nigeria; his answer remained unchanged.

18. Lucy Norris, personal communication, 5 February 2010.

19. Interview with Steve Wooldridge, Head of Property and Stock Operations, Help the Aged, 3 December 2008.

20. United Nations Comtrade, *UN Comtrade Database*, 2013, http://

comtrade.un.org/db/default.aspx; for a full discussion, see Andrew Brooks and David Simon, 'Unraveling the Relationships between Used-Clothing Imports and the Decline of African Clothing Industries', *Development and Change*, vol. 43, no. 6, 2012, pp. 1265–90.

21. Andrew Brooks, 'Stretching Global Production Networks: The International Second-hand Clothing Trade', *Geoforum* 44, 2013, pp. 10–22.

22. These reflections were recorded in a diary in Portuguese kept by Maria between 1 March and 11 April 2010; they have been translated by the author. Mary was one of nine traders who recorded all their daily business transactions in a research diary for a six-week period. For further discussion, see Andrew Brooks, 'Riches from Rags or Persistent Poverty? The Working Lives of Secondhand Clothing Vendors in Maputo, Mozambique', *Textile: The Journal of Cloth and Culture*, vol. 10, no. 2, 2 2012, pp. 22–237.

23. 'Ghana Bans Second-hand Knickers', *BBC News Online*, 26 November 2010, www.bbc.co.uk/news/world-africa-11845851.

24. For sale in Vlinakulo Market, 25 March 2010.

25. The most extensive work has been done by Karen Tranberg Hansen, who undertook a detailed ethnographic investigation in Zambia: *Salaula: The World of Secondhand Clothing and Zambia*, Chicago University Press, Chicago, 2000.

26. Textile Recycling Association, *'Textile Recycling Association Welcomes Research Papers about the Impact of Second Hand Clothing Industry on Sub-Saharan Africa*, 12 December 2005, www.textile-recycling.org.uk/press121205.htm.

27. Figures quoted by Francis N. Wegulo, 'Shoes for All: Second-hand Shoe Traders in Nakuru Town, Kenya', in Dorothy McCormick and Christian Rogerson, eds, *Clothing and Footwear in African Industrialisation,* Africa Institute of South Africa, Pretoria, 2004, p. 580.

28. Salvation Army, 'Salvation Army Trading Company Limited', www.satradingco.org 2009.

29. Total employment figures for the second-hand clothing trade in Mozambique are not available.

30. As there is great variance in second-hand clothing vendors' earnings, this figure in isolation is of limited utility, because it is based on a small sample size.

31. Andrew Brooks, 'Riches from Rags or Persistent Poverty? Inequality in the Transnational Second-hand Clothing Trade in Mozambique', Ph.D. thesis, Royal Holloway, University of London, 2012.

32. Wegulo, Shoes for All, pp. 578, 580.

33. ADPP, 'ADPP Mozambique', 2011, http://adpp-mozambique.org/index.php/about-us.html.

34. TRAID, 'TRAID History', 2011, www.traid.org.uk/history.html.
35. Michael Durham, 'Enigma of the Leader', *Guardian*, 9 June 2003.
36. Monica Eng, 'Clothing Operations Linked to Controversial Danish Group Continue to Thrive', *Chicago Tribune*, 14 May 2011
37. 'DAPP in "secret money swindling"', *Nyasa Times*, 1 March 2011.
38. See http://tvindalert.com.
39. 'Mexican Police Tracking Down Cult School Leader', *Copenhagen Post*, 6 January 2014.
40. INE, *Inquérito sobre orçamento familiar 2008/09*, Instituto Nacional de Estatística, Maputo, 2010, cited in Margarida Paulo, Carmeliza Rosário and Inge Tvedten, '"Xiculungo" Revisited: Assessing the Implications of PARPA II in Maputo 2007–2010', Chr. Michelsen Institute, 2011, www.cmi.no/publications/publication/?4000=xiculungo-revisited-assessing-the-implications-of, p. 7.
41. Based on the author's observations in Kenya and Zambia. The Upcycling of vintage clothes is discussed in the next chapter.
42. See Chapter 6.
43. Interview with Tony Clark, General Manager, Oxfam Wastesaver, 13 March 2009.

CHAPTER 8

1. Hazel Clark, 'Second Hand Fashion, Culture and Identity in Hong Kong', in Alexander Palmer and Hazel Clark, eds, *Old Clothes, New Looks: Second Hand Fashion*, Berg, Oxford, 2005.
2. Lucy Norris, 'Trade and Transformation of Secondhand Clothing: Introduction', *Textile*, vol. 10, no. 2, 2012, pp. 128–143.
3. Jacqueline P. Wiseman, 'Close Encounters of the Quasi-primary Kind: Sociability in Urban Second-hand Clothing Stores, *Journal of Contemporary Ethnography*, vol. 8, no. 1, 1979, pp. 23–51, pp. 30–31.
4. Janna Michael, 'It's Really Not Hip to be a Hipster: Negotiating Trends and Authenticity in the Cultural Field', *Journal of Consumer Culture*, 2013, pp. 8–9.
5. Fabio Marzella, 'Second-hand Goods Use in the Italian Post-industrial Society: A First Theoretical View', n.d., http://univr.academia.edu/FabioMarzella, p. 1.
6. Tom Slater, 'The Eviction of Critical Perspectives from Gentrification Research', *International Journal of Urban and Regional Research*, vol. 30, no. 4, 2006, pp. 737–57, p. 738.
7. Karl Marx, *Grundrisse: Foundations of the Critique of Political Economy*, Vintage, London, 1973, p. 705.
8. 'Wonder Where Your Donations Go? Oxfam Has Got It Sorted', *Guardian*, 15 February 2014.

9. Steven Tyler was quoted as saying this in Season 10 of *American Idol*, 2011; Carlos Ramirez, 'Our 20 Favorite, Most Outrageous Steven Tyler One-Liners', *Noise Creep*, 25 May 2011, http://noisecreep.com/most-outrageous-steven-tyler-one-liners.

10. Michael, 'It's Really Not Hip to Be a Hipster'.

11. Elaine R. Hartwick, 'Geographies of Consumption: A Commodity-chain Approach', *Environment and Planning D*, vol. 16, no. 4, 1998, pp. 423–37.

12. Cold Summer, 'Why Are Japanese Jeans So Expensive?' RAWR Denim, 31 July 2013, www.rawrdenim.com/2013/07/why-are-japanese-jeans-so-expensive.

13. Shunya Yoshimi and David Buist, 'America as Desire and Violence: Americanization in Postwar Japan and Asia during the Cold War', *Inter-Asia Cultural Studies*, vol. 4, no. 3, 2003, pp. 433–50.

14. Rachel Louis Snyder, *Fugitive Denim: A Moving Story of People and Pants in The Borderless World of Global Trade*, W.W. Norton, New York, 2009, p. 142.

15. Kjeld Duits, 'The Quest for Perfect Jeans', Japanese Streets, 4 January 2012, www.japanesestreets.com/reports/1313/the-quest-for-perfect-jeans.

16. Jordan Caronm, 'Second Narrow: Perfect Jeans, Made in Japan, Water Resistant', Kickstarter, 2013, www.kickstarter.com/projects/864140473/second-narrow-perfect-jeans-made-in-japan-water-re5.

17. Cold Summer, 'Why are Japanese Jeans so Expensive?'

18. Snyder, *Fugitive Denim*, p. 143.

19. Niko Besnier, 'Consumption and Cosmopolitanism: Practicing Modernity at the Second-hand Marketplace in Nuku'alofa, Tonga', *Anthropological Quarterly*, vol. 77, no. 1, 2004, pp. 7–45.

20. Examples in this section are based on the author's own fieldwork in Papua New Guinea in 2006.

21. Lamont Lindstrom, 'Cargo Cult', in *Encyclopedia of Social and Cultural Anthropology*, ed. Alan Barnard and Jonathan Spencer, Routledge, London and New York, 2002, p. 129.

22. Kate Maclean, 'Evo's Jumper: Identity and the Used Clothes Trade in "Post-neoliberal" and "Pluri-cultural" Bolivia', *Gender, Place and Culture*, vol. 21, no. 8, 2014, p. 964.

23. Ibid., p. 970.

24. Ibid., p. 968.

25. Lucy Norris, *Recycling Indian Clothing: Global Contexts of Reuse and Value,* Indiana University Press, Bloomington and Indianapolis, 2010, p. 181.

26. Lucy Norris, Recycling and Reincarnation: The Journeys of Indian

Saris, *Mobilities*, vol. 3, no. 3, 2008, pp. 415–36, p. 415.

27. Authors own research in Kerala, South India, 2013.

28. Lucy Norris, 'Creative Entrepreneurs: The Recycling of Second Hand Indian Clothing', in Palmer and Clark, eds, *Old Clothes, New Looks*, p. 119.

29. B. Lynne Milgram, 'Reconfiguring Margins: Secondhand Clothing and Street Vending in the Philippines, *Textile,* vol. 10, no. 2, 2012, pp. 200–221, p. 206.

30. B. Lynne Milgram, '*Ukay-Ukay* Chic: Tales of Second Hand Clothing in the Philippine Cordillera', in Palmer and Clark, eds, *Old Clothes, New Looks*.

31. Amanda Ericsson and Andrew Brooks, 'African Second-hand Clothes: Mima-te and the Development of Sustainable Fashion', in Kate Fletcher and Mathilda Tham, eds, *The Routledge Handbook of Sustainability and Fashion*, Routledge, London, 2015.

32. Nelly and Nelsa Guambe, 'The Story behind Mima-te', 2013, www. mimate-maputo.com/?page_id=51.

CHAPTER 9

1. Toms, 'Our Movement', 2014, www.toms.com/our-movement/l# why-give-shoes.

2. Toms, 'Blake Mycoskie', 2014, www.toms.com/blakes-bio/l.

3. Christina Binkley, Charity Gives Shoe Brand Extra Shine, *Wall Street Journal,* 1 April 2011.

4. Toms, 'Our Movement'; Toms, 'Blake Mycoskie'.

5. From the author's own observation, lack of access to shoes is not a common development impasse in sub-Saharan Africa.

6. There have also been rumours that some distributions have been selective, with priority going to Christian groups when shoe drops are run with faith-based organizations.

7. Toms, 'Giving Report', 2013, www.toms.com/media/TOMS_Giving _Report_2013.pdf.

8. Andrew Brooks and David Simon, Unraveling the Relationships between Used-Clothing Imports and the Decline of African Clothing Industries, *Development and Change*, vol. 43, no. 6, 2012, pp. 1265–90.

9. Bruce Wydick, Elizabeth Katz and Brendan Janet, 'Do In-kind Transfers Damage Local Markets? The Case of TOMS Shoe Donations in El Salvador', *Journal of Development Effectiveness*, vol. 6, no. 3, 2014, pp. 249–67.

10. Henrik Serup Christensen, 'Political Activities on the Internet: Slacktivism or Political Participation by Other Means?' *First Monday*, vol. 16, no. 2, 2011.

11. Celia Lury, *Brands: The Logos of the Global Cultural Economy*, Routledge, London, 2004.

12. Blake Mycoskie quoted by Kevin Short, 'Toms CEO Blake Mycoskie Offers Surprising Answer to His Critics', *Huffington Post*, 14 November 2013, www.huffingtonpost.com/2013/11/14/toms-ceo-critics_n_4274637.html.

13. James Poulos, 'Toms Shoes: A Doomed Vanity Project?', *Forbes*, 11 April 2011, www.forbes.com/sites/jamespoulos/2012/04/11/toms-shoes-a-doomed-vanity-project.

14. Fredric Jameson, *Postmodernism, or, the Cultural Logic of Late Capitalism*, Duke University Press, Durham NC, 1990.

15. Deirdre Shaw, Terry Newholm and Roger Dickinson, 'Consumption as Voting: An Exploration of Consumer Empowerment', *European Journal of Marketing*, vol. 40, no. 9/10, 2006, pp. 1049–67.

16. Patagonia, 'Don't Buy This Jacket, Black Friday and the New York Times', *The Cleanest Line*, 2011, www.thecleanestline.com/2011/11/dont-buy-this-jacket-black-friday-and-the-new-york-times.html.

17. Michal J. Carrington, Benjamin A. Neville and Gregory J. Whitwell, 'Why Ethical Consumers Don't Walk Their Talk: Towards a Framework for Understanding the Gap between the Ethical Purchase Intentions and Actual Buying Behaviour of Ethically Minded Consumers', *Journal of Business Ethics*, vol. 97, no. 1, 2010, pp. 139–58.

18. Michael Lee, Judith Moron and Denise Conroy, 'Anti-consumption and Brand Avoidance', *Journal of Business Research* 62, 2008, pp. 169–80, p. 178.

19. Robert B. Potter, Tony Binns, Jennifer A. Elliot and David Smith, *Geographies of Development: An Introduction to Development Studies*, Pearson, Harlow, 2008, p. 360.

20. Matthias Zick Varul, 'Consuming the Campesino: Fair Trade Marketing between Recognition and Romantic Commodification', *Cultural Studies*, vol. 22, no. 5, 2008, pp. 654–79, p. 662.

21. Karl Marx, *Grundrisse: Foundations of the Critique of Political Economy*, Vintage, London, 1973, p. 92.

22. Antonio Gramsci, *Selections from the Prison Notebooks*, Lawrence & Wishart, London, 1971.

23. Caroline Wright, 'Consuming Lives, Consuming Landscapes: Interpreting Advertisements for Cafédirect Coffees', *Journal of International Development*, vol. 16, no. 5, 2004, pp. 665–80.

24. 'Designer Vivienne Westwood Addresses at St Paul's Camp', *BBC News Online*, 19 November 2011, www.bbc.co.uk/news/uk-england-london-15806945.

25. Richard Tyler, 'Vivienne Westwood Undervalues Itself', *Telegraph*, 28 August 2011.

26. ITC, 'Ethical Fashion: Not Charity, Just Work', International Trade Centre, 2012, www.intracen.org/trade-support/ethical-fashion.

27. Simome Cipriani, Jeremy Brown and Chloe Mukai, *The Ethical Fashion Programme. Not Charity, Just Work: 2011 Aid for Trade Global Review: Case Study*, International Trade Centre, Geneva, 2011.

28. ITC, 'Vivienne Westwood: Fashion Icon', International Trade Centre, 2012, www.intracen.org/trade-support/ethical-fashion/vivienne-westwood.

29. Cipriani, Brown and Mukai, *The Ethical Fashion Programme. Not Charity, Just Work*.

30. Clar Ni Chonghaile, 'From King's Road to Kenya: Westwood's New Fashion Journey', *Guardian*, 24 November 2011.

31. Michael K. Goodman, 'Reading Fair Trade: Political Ecological Imaginary and the Moral Economy of Fair Trade Foods', *Political Geography*, vol. 23, no. 7, 2004, pp. 891–915.

32. Wright, 'Consuming Lives, Consuming Landscapes', p. 671.

33. These have been observed by the author in both Nairobi and rural Kenya.

34. Vivienne Westwood, 'Made with Love in Nairobi', 2011, www.viviennewestwood.co.uk/multimedia/made-with-love-in-nairobi.

35. Edward Said, *Orientalism*, Vintage Books, New York, 1979.

36. Author's interviews in Pokot, Kenya, 2010.

37. Stefano Ponte, Lisa Ann Richey and Mike Baab, 'Bono's Product (RED) Initiative: Corporate Social Responsibility that Solves the Problems of "Distant Others"', *Third World Quarterly*, vol. 30, no. 2, 2009, pp. 301–17; Jemima Repo and Riina Yrjölä, 'The Gender Politics of Celebrity Humanitarianism in Africa', *International Feminist Journal of Politics*, vol. 13, no. 1, 2011, pp. 42–62.

38. Quoted by Olivia Bergin, 'Vivienne Westwood's Mission to Save the World, One Handbag at a Time', *Telegraph*, 9 August 2011.

39. Nicky Gregson and Louise Crewe, *Second-hand Cultures*, Berg, London, 2003.

40. H&M, 'Garment Collecting', 2014, http://about.hm.com/en/About/Sustainability/Commitments/Reduce-Reuse-Recycle/Garment-Collecting.html.

41. Olivier Balch, 'H&M: Can Fast Fashion and Sustainability Ever Really Mix?' *Guardian*, 3 May 2013.

42. Kyle Stock, 'The Brilliant Business Model Behind H&M's Clothes Recycling Plan', *Bloomberg Businessweek*, 24 June 2013, www.businessweek.com/articles/2013-06-24/the-brilliant-business-model-be-

hind-h-and-ms-clothes-recycling-plan#rshare=email_article.
43. Balch, 'H&M'.
44. H&M, 'Charity Star', 2014, www.hm.charitystar.com/en/home.
45. Whizz-Kidz, 'Matthew Pinsent Helps JJB Launch National Trainer Recycling Scheme for Whizz-Kidz', 2011, www.whizz-kidz.org.uk/news/2011/03/matthew-pinsent-helps-jjb-launch-national-trainer-re-cycling-scheme-for-whizz-kidz.
46. Oxfam, 'The M&S and Oxfam Clothes Exchange', 2011, www.oxfam.org.uk/shop/content/secondhandstore/fashion/ms_clothes_exchange.html?ito=2841&itc=0.
47. I:CO, 'How Does I:CO Work?', 2014, www.ico-spirit.com/en/about-ico.
48. Kate Fletcher, *Sustainable Fashion and Textiles: Design Journeys*, 2nd edn, Routledge, London, 2014.
49. Royal Society, *People and the Planet*, Royal Society Science and Policy Centre Report 01/12, London, 2012.
50. Kate Fletcher, 'Other Fashion Systems', in Kate Fletcher and Mathilda Tham, eds, *The Routledge Handbook of Sustainability and Fashion*, Routledge, London, 2015, p. 23.
51. Slavoj Žižek, *The Year of Dreaming Dangerously*, Verso, London, 2012, pp. 100–101.
52. Don Mitchell, 'The S.U.V. Model of Citizenship: Floating Bubbles, Buffer Zones, and the Rise of the"Purely Atomic" Individual', *Political Geography*, vol. 24, no. 1, 2005, pp. 77–100.

CHAPTER 10

1. Based on the author's own observations at Somerset House, February 2014, and Graduate Fashion Week, May 2014.
2. Coco Chanel, quoted in Jessica Wolfendale and Jeanette Kennett, *Fashion – Philosophy for Everyone: Thinking with Style,* John Wiley & Sons, London, 2011, p. xiv.
3. Quoted by Deborah Orr in 'Life in Vogue: The Fashionable World of Alexandra Shulman', *Independent Magazine*, 31 January 2009.
4. Ben Fine, *The World of Consumption: The Material and Cultural Revisited*, Routledge, London, 2002.
5. Conrad Lodziak, 'On Explaining Consumption', *Capital and Class* 72, 2000, pp. 111–33.
6. David Harvey, *The Enigma of Capital and the Crises of Capitalism*, Profile Books, London, 2010, p. 72.
7. Sally Peberdy, 'Monitoring Small Scale Cross Border Trade in Southern Africa: Contributions, Costs and Opportunities', paper presented at Urban Informality and Migrant Entrepreneurship in Southern

African Cities workshop, University of Cape Town, 10-11 February 2014.

8. Andrew Brooks and David Simon, 'Unraveling the Relationships between Used-Clothing Imports and the Decline of African Clothing Industries', *Development and Change*, vol. 43, no. 6, 2012, pp. 1265-90.

9. Interview Aloysius Ihezie, director, Choice Textiles Division, 19 March 2009.

10. Petra Rivoli, *The Travels of a T-shirt in the Global Economy: An Economist Examines the Markets, Power, and Politics of World Trade*, Wiley, London, 2009, p. 224.

11. Based on the author's fieldwork in Kenya, Malawi, Mozambique and Zambia between 2010 and 2014.

12. Karen Tranberg Hansen, *Salaula: The World of Secondhand Clothing and Zambia*, Chicago University Press, Chicago, 2000.

13. Andrew Brooks and Raymond Bryant, 'Consumption', in Carl Death, ed., *Critical Environmental Politics*, Routledge, London, 2013.

14. David Harvey, Between Space and Time: Reflections on the Geographical Imagination, *Annals of the Association of American Geographers*, vol. 80, no. 3, 1990, pp. 418-34, p. 422.

15. Michal J. Carrington, Benjamin A. Neville and Gregory J. Whitwell, 'Why Ethical Consumers Don't Walk Their Talk: Towards a Framework for Understanding the Gap between the Ethical Purchase Intentions and Actual Buying Behaviour of Ethically Minded Consumers', *Journal of Business Ethics*, vol. 97, no. 1, 2010, pp. 139-58.

16. Ian Urbina, 'U.S. Flouts Its Own Advice in Procuring Overseas Clothing, *New York Times*, 22 December 2013.

17. Daryl Collins, Jonathan Morduch, Stuart Rutherford and Orlanda Ruthven, *Portfolios of the Poor: How the World's Poor Live on $2 a Day*. Princeton University Press, Princeton NJ, 2009.

18. Kate Soper, 'Other Pleasures: The Attractions of Post-consumerism', *Socialist Register 36*, 2000, pp. 116-32.

19. Michael F. Maniates, 'Individualization: Plant a Tree, Buy a Bike, Save the World? *Global Environmental Politics* 1, 2001, pp. 31-52, p. 50.

20. Jon Goss, 'Geography of Consumption I', *Progress in Human Geography* 28, 2004, pp. 369-80.

21. Forbes, 'The World's Billionaires', 2014, www.forbes.com/billionaires/list.

22. World Bank, *Mozambique*, 2014, http://data.worldbank.org/country/mozambique; World Bank, 2014, *Zambia*, http://data.worldbank.org/country/zambia.

23. Liz Parker, 'Fashion Brands and Workers' Rights', in *The Routledge Handbook of Sustainability and Fashion*, ed. Kate Fletcher and Mathilda Tham, Routledge, London, 2015, p. 212.

24. Xiaomin Yu, 'Impacts of Corporate Code of Conduct on Labour Standards: A Case Study of Reebok's Athletic Footwear Supplier Factory in China', *Journal of Business Ethics* 81, 2007, pp. 513–29, p. 523.

25. Institute for Global Labour and Human Rights, 'Bangladesh vs. the U.S.: How Much Does It Cost to Make a Denim Shirt?, 2 May 2013, www.globallabourrights.org/press/bangladesh-vs-the-u-s-how-much-does-it-cost-to-make-a-denim-shirt.

26. Kanchana N. Ruwanpura, 'Metal Free Factories: Straddling Worker Rights and Consumer Safety?', *Geoforum*, vol. 51, no. 1, 2014, pp. 224–32, pp. 225–6.

27. David Harvey, *The Limits to Capital*, Verso, London, 2006.

Further reading

Brautigam, Deborah, *The Dragon's Gift: The Real Story of China in Africa*, Oxford University Press, Oxford, 2009.

Chang, Ha-Joon, *Bad Samaritans: The Myth of Free Trade and the Secret History of Capitalism*, Bloomsbury, London, 2007.

Engels, Frederick, *The Condition of The Working-Class in England*, trans. Florence Kelly Wischnewetzky, George Allen & Unwin, London, 1943 (1844).

Ferguson, James, *Expectations of Modernity: Myths and Meanings of Urban Life on the Zambian Copperbelt*, University of California Press, Berkeley, 1999.

Fine, Ben, *Marx's Capital*, Macmillan, London, 1976.

Fine, Ben, *The World of Consumption: The Material and Cultural Revisited*, Routledge, London, 2002.

Fletcher, Kate, *Sustainable Fashion and Textiles: Design Journeys*, 2nd edn, Routledge, London, 2014.

Fletcher, Kate, and Mathilda Tham, eds, *The Routledge Handbook of Sustainability and Fashion*, Routledge, London, 2015.

Gregson, Nicky, and Louise Crewe, *Second-hand Cultures*, Berg, London, 2003.

Hanlon, Joseph, and Teresa Smart, *Do Bicycles Equal Development in Mozambique?*, James Currey, Woodbridge, 2008.

Hansen, Karen Tranberg, *Salaula: The World of Secondhand Clothing and Zambia*, Chicago University Press, Chicago, 2000.

Hart, Gillian, *Disabling Globalization: Places of Power in Post-apartheid South Africa*, University of California Press, Berkeley, 2002.

Harvey, David, *The Limits to Capital*, Verso, London, 2006.

Harvey, David, *The Enigma of Capital and the Crises of Capitalism*, Profile Books, London, 2010.

Marx, Karl, *Grundrisse: Foundations of the Critique of Political Economy*, Vintage, New York, 1973.

Marx, Karl, *Capital: A New Abridgment*, Oxford University Press, Oxford, 1995.

Norris, Lucy, *Recycling Indian Clothing: Global Contexts of Reuse and Value*, Indiana University Press, Bloomington and Indianapolis, 2010.

Palmer, Alexandra, and Hazel Clark, eds, *Old Clothes, New Looks: Second Hand Fashion*, Berg, Oxford, 2005.

Ross, Robert, *Clothing: A Global History*, Polity Press, Cambridge, 2008.

Smith, Neil, *Uneven Development*, Basil Blackwell, Oxford and New York, 1985.

Strasser, Susan, *Waste and Want: A Social History of Trash*, Metropolitan Books, New York, 1999.

Synder, Rachel Louise, *Fugitive Denim: A Moving Story of People and Pants in the Borderless World of Global Trade*, W.W. Norton, New York and London, 2008.

Wolf, Eric R., *Europe and the People without History*, California University Press, Berkeley, 1982.

Index

V&A Museum, London, 192
V&A Waterfront, Cape Town, 237
value retail stores, 237; Value Village, 80, 171
value(s): ecological, 82; exchange, 49; surplus, 57; symbolic, 17, 35, 182, 205; use, 13, 35, 47
value enhancement, used clothes tailoring, 181
Vasco da Gama, 107
Victoria Beckham jeans, 18
Victorian England, used clothing markets, 77
vintage clothing/fashion, 81-2, 205; curated, 186; Italy, 190; origins, 188; price rises, 91; specialist skills need, 15, 191-2; symbolic values, 193
Vogue: British, 235
Von Bismarck, Otto, 105

wages: differentials USA-Bangladesh, 248; downward pressure on, 58, 134; Sri Lanka increases, 249
Wall Street Crash 1929, 44
Walmart, 18, 28, 83, 246
Walton, Christy, wealth of, 246
Wastesaver (Oxfam), 226; conveyor belts, 94; Huddersfield plant, 93
water: cotton consumption, 19-20; pollution, 24
wealth and poverty, geography of, 237
weaving: Bengali weavers, 63; Flemish emigrés, 53; origins of, 50; power looms, 56
Wegulo, Francis, 176
West Africa, 182; British colonial legacy, 152; colonial balance of trade shift, 104; cotton, 101; early cloth production, 52; Portuguese traders, 103; pre-European textiles, 102
West Indies, cotton slavery, 59
Western dress style, export of, 62
Westwood, Vivienne, 7, 219, 220, 222-4, 234

Wilson, Russell, 142
Wiseman, Jacqueline, 188
Woodward, Sophie, 30
wool, 50; English export ban, 53
Wooldridge, Steve, 89
work ethic, African 'backward' perception, 137
World Bank, 111, 113-14, 121, 163
World Heritage, 237
World Trade Organization, 115, 158, 221, 248; Brazil lobbying, 115; laissez-faire ideology, 40
World Vision, 143; /NFL provision system, 144
Wrangler, 17

Xipamanine market, Maputo, 1-2, 147, 167, 170, 173, 175, 204; average income, 176

YMCA, 80, 86; shops, 84, 87
Yorubaland, 102

Zambia, 5, 131, 149, 158-9, 166, 177, 181, 240; American football jerseys, 143; Chinese clothing factory, 6; cotton, 101, 238; economic liberalization, 128; GDP, 246; labour casualization, 129; state-owned corporations Fordist model, 127, 135; used clothing scale, 145
Zambia China Mulungushi Textiles factory (ZCMT), 22, 24, 137, 140, 241, 246; casual workers, 139; derelict, 118-19, 126; extreme exploitation, 252; first closure, 129; 'Fordist' jobs, 127; labour causalization, 134-5; racial division, 138; resurrection of, 131; second closure, 132; workforce, 133
Zara, 8, 30, 186, 228, 246; fast fashion, 251; short batch orders, 70
Zimbabwe, 100-101, 157, 166; used clothing scale, 145
Žižek, Slavoj, 231